MODERN JOURNAL OF NOTARIAL EVENTS

INTRODUCTION

Thank you for choosing the *Modern Journal of Notarial Events*. This journal should be used to chronicle your official acts as a notary public. Also referred to as log books, record books and registers, notary journals are an essential tool in the prevention and prosecution of fraud. Maintaining a thorough and accurate historical account of your actions may help protect you and other parties in the event of future legal proceedings. It is also required by law in many states. The *Modern Journal* is based on feedback and observations of experienced notaries public and has been carefully crafted to provide the ultimate in usability. Journal features are detailed below and complete instructions are provided on pages iv and v, with concluding instructions on the final page.

JOURNAL FEATURES
Quality Construction and Superior Usability

Featuring heavy-weight pages, a tamper-proof binding, and durable cover material, *The Modern Journal* is capable of recording nearly 500 entries. Each entry has the capacity to store a single notarial event or multiple notarizations, with the capability of documenting thousands of individual acts. Checkboxes are provided for rapid selection of common document types, including various affidavits, deeds, trusts and wills. Several signer identification methods are also provided as checkbox choices: driver's license, passport, personally known and identification by credible witness(es).

Additional usability features include right-side thumbprint spaces, sequentially numbered pages with eight numbered rows per page, a shaded **Sign Here** label, and an area in each row to record additional information and comments. Further, each journal entry spans two pages. Context and fee information is recorded on the left-hand side of the left page while the right-hand side of the right page is reserved for signer identification.

Important Notice: Every attempt has been made to ensure this journal conforms to all state requirements. Nonetheless, it is your responsibility as a notary public to familiarize yourself with the notary public laws in your state. You are ultimately responsible for following proper notarial procedures and for the proper use of this journal.

Manufactured in the United States of America

This Journal Belongs To ▼

Name:

Address:

Phone 1:

Phone 2:

E-Mail:

Emergency Contacts ▼

Contact 1:

Contact 2:

Notes ▼

Notarial Information ▼

This journal is a record of notarial events in which the owner has participated.

Date of First Event:

Date of Last Event:

Commission #1

State:

Comm. #:

Comm. Exp.:

Other Info:

Official Signature:

Commission #2

State:

Comm. #:

Comm. Exp.:

Other Info:

Official Signature:

If this journal is found, please notify the notary listed above to arrange for its return. If he or she cannot be reached, please notify the emergency contacts listed above if present. If you are unable to contact anyone, visit www.notaryrotary.com for further instructions or contact the branch of your state government responsible for notary public commissions.

Entry 1

Notarization Date and Time: **4/1/03 7:00pm** [A]

Date on Document(s): **4/1/03** [B] Reference #: **153968** [C]

Fees: **$ 125** [D] Paid? ✓ **4/27/03**

Documents:
- [F] ☑ Compliance Agmt. A J E & O A Proof of ID Aff. A J Adv. Health. Dir. A J SDB Verification
- ☐ Correction Agmt. / Occ. Aff. (Sig.)/Name Aff. A J Trust - Irr. / Living A J Vehicle - O+VIN / TT
- / DOT (Mortgage) A J Own. Aff. Survey Aff. A J Will - LWT / Living A J
- A J Deed - G / QC / W / POA - (L) / D A J A J A J C ☐ Other ▼

[G]

Additional Information [H]:

AmericasBestClosers.com - E-Docs
Notary Rotary Document #200304378
HUD was faxed by title co due to last minute change

Odometer: 57,635 - 57,652 - 57,670 = 35 mi.

Entry 2

Notarization Date and Time: **4/2/03 8:30am**

Date on Document(s): **4/2/03** Reference #:

Fees: **$ 0** Paid? ☐ [E]

Documents:
- A J Compliance Agmt. A J E & O A J Proof of ID Aff. A J Adv. Health. Dir. A J SDB Verification
- A J Correction Agmt. A J Occ. Aff. A J Sig./Name Aff. A J Trust - Irr. / Living A J Vehicle - O+VIN / TT
- A J DOT / Mortgage A J Own. Aff. A J Survey Aff. / Will - (LWT) / Living A J
- A J Deed - G / QC / W A J POA - L / D A J A J A J C ☐ Other ▼

Additional Information:

Notarized as a favor to Carissa

INSTRUCTIONS

[A] Enter the date and time of the event.

[B] Enter the date printed on the document(s) being notarized, if applicable.

[C] Enter any reference number associated with the document(s) or proceeding. This field and can be used to record work order numbers, invoice numbers, loan numbers, etc.

[D] Enter your fees for the event. Where maximum notarial fees are prescribed by law, you might consider making a distinction between the fees collected for the acts of notarization and the fees collected for other services.

[E] If the fees have been paid, check the box and, optionally, record the date of payment.

[F] This section lists over twenty of the most common document types encountered by notaries. Each document type is preceded by a series of checkboxes representing the type of notarial act being performed. Place a check or line through the appropriate box to indicate the type of act: [A]cknowledgment, [J]urat or [C]opy Certification. The empty box in front of "Other" should be used to indicate other notarial acts, such as protests. In these cases, check the empty box and describe the type of notarization along with the document(s) or proceeding in Box G. Note: a Jurat represents your certification of the proper administration of an oath or affirmation. Selecting [J] indicates that you have successfully administered either an oath or affirmation and have completed an affidavit/jurat in support of it. Box G can be used to record additional details of the event.

Next, notice how the forward slash (/) is used to separate similar document types within a single entry. The line that reads "Will - LWT / Living," for example, can be used to indicate either a Last Will and Testament (LWT) or a Living Will. When using these entries, you should circle the type of document you are notarizing. For an explanation of the abbreviations used above, please see the following section.

[G] Enter any additional description for the document(s) or proceeding you have notarized. If you checked the blank box in front of Other, describe the type of notarization.

[H] Use this area for notes, additional observations, the recording of mileage or anything else you deem important.

ABBREVIATIONS

Abbreviation	Document Description
Compliance Agmt.	Compliance Agreement
Correction Agmt.	Correction Agreement
DOT / Mortgage	Deed of Trust or Mortgage
Deed - G / QC / W	Deed - Grant Deed / Quitclaim Deed / Warranty Deed
E & O	Errors & Omissions
Occ. Aff.	Occupancy Affidavit
Own. Aff.	Owner's Affidavit
POA - L / D	Power of Attorney - Limited / Durable
Proof of ID Aff.	Proof of Identification Affidavit
Sig./Name Aff.	Signature/Name Affidavit
Survey Aff.	Survey Affidavit
Adv. Health. Dir.	Advanced Healthcare Directive
Trust - Irr. / Living	Trust - Irrevocable / Living
Will - LWT / Living	Will - Last Will & Testament / Living Will
SDB Verification	Safety Deposit Box Verification
Vehicle - O+VIN / TT	Vehicle - Odometer+VIN Verification / Transfer of Title

Abbreviation	Description

User-Defined Abbreviations

The *Description of Document(s) or Proceeding* section of the journal, labeled as Item F above, contains room for three "write-in" abbreviations, located in columns three, four and five of the documents section.

Please provide abbreviations and descriptions at left for other documents you routinely notarize and/or types of notarial acts. You may then use these abbreviations in the write-in spaces explained above or when providing additional details in Box G.

I | Samuel J. Smith
42 John Galt Way
Des Moines, IA 50312

J
- ☑ Driver's License
- ☑ Passport
- ☐ Other ID #1 - describe
- ☐ Other ID #2 - describe
- ☐ Personally Known
- ☐ Credible Witness(es)

Ref. #1
IA DL # 531XX5720
Exp. 10/16/2007 DOB 11/28/62 **K**

Ref. #2
US Passport # 400622051
Exp. 2/6/2012

L x _Samuel J. Smith_

Right Thumbprint **M**

1

Carissa M. Adams
316 Roark St
Des Moines, IA 50311

- ☐ Driver's License
- ☐ Passport
- ☐ Other ID #1 - describe
- ☐ Other ID #2 - describe
- ☑ Personally Known
- ☐ Credible Witness(es)

Ref. #1

Ref. #2

x _Carissa M. Adams_

Right Thumbprint

2

Row 1 details a loan signing that occurred on 4/1/2003 beginning at 7:00pm. The notary was contracted by AmericasBestClosers.com to notarize the signing of loan papers for a fee of $125 (which was received by the notary on 4/27/2003). According to the entry, the loan package was sent to the notary electronically and the following documents were notarized during the signing: Compliance Agreement, Mortgage, Occupancy Affidavit, Limited Power of Attorney, Signature Affidavit and Survey Affidavit. The order was assigned and tracked using the Notary Rotary website as document # 200304378. The signer's identity was verified using an Iowa driver's license and a United States Passport. The notary recorded their mileage in the form of three odometer readings: one at their home, the next at the borrower's home - where the signing occurred - and the final reading back at the starting point.

Row 2 details the notarization of a Last Will and Testament that occurred on 4/2/2003 beginning at 8:30am. The notary was contacted by Carissa Adams, a long-time family friend, serving in the National Guard. Carissa was recently called to active duty and wanted to make sure her affairs were in good order before leaving the country. The notarization was provided at no charge.

E X P L A N A T I O N S

1	Dates and Fees	Description of Document(s) or Proceeding	Additional Information

Entry 1

Notarization Date and Time

Date on Document(s) — Reference #

Fees $ — Paid? ☐

- A J Compliance Agmt. — A J E & O — A J Proof of ID Aff. — A J Adv. Health. Dir. — A J SDB Verification
- A J Correction Agmt. — A J Occ. Aff. — A J Sig./Name Aff. — A J Trust - Irr. / Living — A J Vehicle - O+VIN / TT
- A J DOT / Mortgage — A J Own. Aff. — A J Survey Aff. — A J Will - LWT / Living — A J
- A J Deed - G / QC / W — A J POA - L / D — A J — A J — A J C ☐ Other ▼

Entry 2

Notarization Date and Time

Date on Document(s) — Reference #

Fees $ — Paid? ☐

- A J Compliance Agmt. — A J E & O — A J Proof of ID Aff. — A J Adv. Health. Dir. — A J SDB Verification
- A J Correction Agmt. — A J Occ. Aff. — A J Sig./Name Aff. — A J Trust - Irr. / Living — A J Vehicle - O+VIN / TT
- A J DOT / Mortgage — A J Own. Aff. — A J Survey Aff. — A J Will - LWT / Living — A J
- A J Deed - G / QC / W — A J POA - L / D — A J — A J — A J C ☐ Other ▼

Entry 3

Notarization Date and Time

Date on Document(s) — Reference #

Fees $ — Paid? ☐

- A J Compliance Agmt. — A J E & O — A J Proof of ID Aff. — A J Adv. Health. Dir. — A J SDB Verification
- A J Correction Agmt. — A J Occ. Aff. — A J Sig./Name Aff. — A J Trust - Irr. / Living — A J Vehicle - O+VIN / TT
- A J DOT / Mortgage — A J Own. Aff. — A J Survey Aff. — A J Will - LWT / Living — A J
- A J Deed - G / QC / W — A J POA - L / D — A J — A J — A J C ☐ Other ▼

Entry 4

Notarization Date and Time

Date on Document(s) — Reference #

Fees $ — Paid? ☐

- A J Compliance Agmt. — A J E & O — A J Proof of ID Aff. — A J Adv. Health. Dir. — A J SDB Verification
- A J Correction Agmt. — A J Occ. Aff. — A J Sig./Name Aff. — A J Trust - Irr. / Living — A J Vehicle - O+VIN / TT
- A J DOT / Mortgage — A J Own. Aff. — A J Survey Aff. — A J Will - LWT / Living — A J
- A J Deed - G / QC / W — A J POA - L / D — A J — A J — A J C ☐ Other ▼

Entry 5

Notarization Date and Time

Date on Document(s) — Reference #

Fees $ — Paid? ☐

- A J Compliance Agmt. — A J E & O — A J Proof of ID Aff. — A J Adv. Health. Dir. — A J SDB Verification
- A J Correction Agmt. — A J Occ. Aff. — A J Sig./Name Aff. — A J Trust - Irr. / Living — A J Vehicle - O+VIN / TT
- A J DOT / Mortgage — A J Own. Aff. — A J Survey Aff. — A J Will - LWT / Living — A J
- A J Deed - G / QC / W — A J POA - L / D — A J — A J — A J C ☐ Other ▼

Entry 6

Notarization Date and Time

Date on Document(s) — Reference #

Fees $ — Paid? ☐

- A J Compliance Agmt. — A J E & O — A J Proof of ID Aff. — A J Adv. Health. Dir. — A J SDB Verification
- A J Correction Agmt. — A J Occ. Aff. — A J Sig./Name Aff. — A J Trust - Irr. / Living — A J Vehicle - O+VIN / TT
- A J DOT / Mortgage — A J Own. Aff. — A J Survey Aff. — A J Will - LWT / Living — A J
- A J Deed - G / QC / W — A J POA - L / D — A J — A J — A J C ☐ Other ▼

Entry 7

Notarization Date and Time

Date on Document(s) — Reference #

Fees $ — Paid? ☐

- A J Compliance Agmt. — A J E & O — A J Proof of ID Aff. — A J Adv. Health. Dir. — A J SDB Verification
- A J Correction Agmt. — A J Occ. Aff. — A J Sig./Name Aff. — A J Trust - Irr. / Living — A J Vehicle - O+VIN / TT
- A J DOT / Mortgage — A J Own. Aff. — A J Survey Aff. — A J Will - LWT / Living — A J
- A J Deed - G / QC / W — A J POA - L / D — A J — A J — A J C ☐ Other ▼

Entry 8

Notarization Date and Time

Date on Document(s) — Reference #

Fees $ — Paid? ☐

- A J Compliance Agmt. — A J E & O — A J Proof of ID Aff. — A J Adv. Health. Dir. — A J SDB Verification
- A J Correction Agmt. — A J Occ. Aff. — A J Sig./Name Aff. — A J Trust - Irr. / Living — A J Vehicle - O+VIN / TT
- A J DOT / Mortgage — A J Own. Aff. — A J Survey Aff. — A J Will - LWT / Living — A J
- A J Deed - G / QC / W — A J POA - L / D — A J — A J — A J C ☐ Other ▼

Signer Name and Address	Method of Identification	Signature and Thumbprint	

Signer Name and Address — **Method of Identification** — **Signature and Thumbprint**

☐ Driver's License ☐ Other ID #1 - describe ☐ Personally Known
☐ Passport ☐ Other ID #2 - describe ☐ Credible Witness(es)

Ref. #1

Ref. #2

x SIGN HERE

Right Thumbprint

1

☐ Driver's License ☐ Other ID #1 - describe ☐ Personally Known
☐ Passport ☐ Other ID #2 - describe ☐ Credible Witness(es)

Ref. #1

Ref. #2

x SIGN HERE

Right Thumbprint

2

☐ Driver's License ☐ Other ID #1 - describe ☐ Personally Known
☐ Passport ☐ Other ID #2 - describe ☐ Credible Witness(es)

Ref. #1

Ref. #2

x SIGN HERE

Right Thumbprint

3

☐ Driver's License ☐ Other ID #1 - describe ☐ Personally Known
☐ Passport ☐ Other ID #2 - describe ☐ Credible Witness(es)

Ref. #1

Ref. #2

x SIGN HERE

Right Thumbprint

4

☐ Driver's License ☐ Other ID #1 - describe ☐ Personally Known
☐ Passport ☐ Other ID #2 - describe ☐ Credible Witness(es)

Ref. #1

Ref. #2

x SIGN HERE

Right Thumbprint

5

☐ Driver's License ☐ Other ID #1 - describe ☐ Personally Known
☐ Passport ☐ Other ID #2 - describe ☐ Credible Witness(es)

Ref. #1

Ref. #2

x SIGN HERE

Right Thumbprint

6

☐ Driver's License ☐ Other ID #1 - describe ☐ Personally Known
☐ Passport ☐ Other ID #2 - describe ☐ Credible Witness(es)

Ref. #1

Ref. #2

x SIGN HERE

Right Thumbprint

7

☐ Driver's License ☐ Other ID #1 - describe ☐ Personally Known
☐ Passport ☐ Other ID #2 - describe ☐ Credible Witness(es)

Ref. #1

Ref. #2

x SIGN HERE

Right Thumbprint

8

3 | Dates and Fees   Description of Document(s) or Proceeding   Additional Information

1

Notarization Date and Time

Date on Document(s) Reference #

Fees $ Paid? ☐

A J Compliance Agmt.	A J E & O	A J Proof of ID Aff.	A J Adv. Health. Dir.	A J SDB Verification
A J Correction Agmt.	A J Occ. Aff.	A J Sig./Name Aff.	A J Trust - Irr. / Living	A J Vehicle - O+VIN / TT
A J DOT / Mortgage	A J Own. Aff.	A J Survey Aff.	A J Will - LWT / Living	A J
A J Deed - G / QC / W	A J POA - L / D	A J	A J	A J C ☐ Other ▼

2

Notarization Date and Time

Date on Document(s) Reference #

Fees $ Paid? ☐

A J Compliance Agmt.	A J E & O	A J Proof of ID Aff.	A J Adv. Health. Dir.	A J SDB Verification
A J Correction Agmt.	A J Occ. Aff.	A J Sig./Name Aff.	A J Trust - Irr. / Living	A J Vehicle - O+VIN / TT
A J DOT / Mortgage	A J Own. Aff.	A J Survey Aff.	A J Will - LWT / Living	A J
A J Deed - G / QC / W	A J POA - L / D	A J	A J	A J C ☐ Other ▼

3

Notarization Date and Time

Date on Document(s) Reference #

Fees $ Paid? ☐

A J Compliance Agmt.	A J E & O	A J Proof of ID Aff.	A J Adv. Health. Dir.	A J SDB Verification
A J Correction Agmt.	A J Occ. Aff.	A J Sig./Name Aff.	A J Trust - Irr. / Living	A J Vehicle - O+VIN / TT
A J DOT / Mortgage	A J Own. Aff.	A J Survey Aff.	A J Will - LWT / Living	A J
A J Deed - G / QC / W	A J POA - L / D	A J	A J	A J C ☐ Other ▼

4

Notarization Date and Time

Date on Document(s) Reference #

Fees $ Paid? ☐

A J Compliance Agmt.	A J E & O	A J Proof of ID Aff.	A J Adv. Health. Dir.	A J SDB Verification
A J Correction Agmt.	A J Occ. Aff.	A J Sig./Name Aff.	A J Trust - Irr. / Living	A J Vehicle - O+VIN / TT
A J DOT / Mortgage	A J Own. Aff.	A J Survey Aff.	A J Will - LWT / Living	A J
A J Deed - G / QC / W	A J POA - L / D	A J	A J	A J C ☐ Other ▼

5

Notarization Date and Time

Date on Document(s) Reference #

Fees $ Paid? ☐

A J Compliance Agmt.	A J E & O	A J Proof of ID Aff.	A J Adv. Health. Dir.	A J SDB Verification
A J Correction Agmt.	A J Occ. Aff.	A J Sig./Name Aff.	A J Trust - Irr. / Living	A J Vehicle - O+VIN / TT
A J DOT / Mortgage	A J Own. Aff.	A J Survey Aff.	A J Will - LWT / Living	A J
A J Deed - G / QC / W	A J POA - L / D	A J	A J	A J C ☐ Other ▼

6

Notarization Date and Time

Date on Document(s) Reference #

Fees $ Paid? ☐

A J Compliance Agmt.	A J E & O	A J Proof of ID Aff.	A J Adv. Health. Dir.	A J SDB Verification
A J Correction Agmt.	A J Occ. Aff.	A J Sig./Name Aff.	A J Trust - Irr. / Living	A J Vehicle - O+VIN / TT
A J DOT / Mortgage	A J Own. Aff.	A J Survey Aff.	A J Will - LWT / Living	A J
A J Deed - G / QC / W	A J POA - L / D	A J	A J	A J C ☐ Other ▼

7

Notarization Date and Time

Date on Document(s) Reference #

Fees $ Paid? ☐

A J Compliance Agmt.	A J E & O	A J Proof of ID Aff.	A J Adv. Health. Dir.	A J SDB Verification
A J Correction Agmt.	A J Occ. Aff.	A J Sig./Name Aff.	A J Trust - Irr. / Living	A J Vehicle - O+VIN / TT
A J DOT / Mortgage	A J Own. Aff.	A J Survey Aff.	A J Will - LWT / Living	A J
A J Deed - G / QC / W	A J POA - L / D	A J	A J	A J C ☐ Other ▼

8

Notarization Date and Time

Date on Document(s) Reference #

Fees $ Paid? ☐

A J Compliance Agmt.	A J E & O	A J Proof of ID Aff.	A J Adv. Health. Dir.	A J SDB Verification
A J Correction Agmt.	A J Occ. Aff.	A J Sig./Name Aff.	A J Trust - Irr. / Living	A J Vehicle - O+VIN / TT
A J DOT / Mortgage	A J Own. Aff.	A J Survey Aff.	A J Will - LWT / Living	A J
A J Deed - G / QC / W	A J POA - L / D	A J	A J	A J C ☐ Other ▼

Signer Name and Address	Method of Identification	Signature and Thumbprint	4

1
- ☐ Driver's License ☐ Other ID #1 - describe ☐ Personally Known
- ☐ Passport ☐ Other ID #2 - describe ☐ Credible Witness(es)
- Ref. #1
- Ref. #2
- X _SIGN HERE_
- Right Thumbprint

2
- ☐ Driver's License ☐ Other ID #1 - describe ☐ Personally Known
- ☐ Passport ☐ Other ID #2 - describe ☐ Credible Witness(es)
- Ref. #1
- Ref. #2
- X _SIGN HERE_
- Right Thumbprint

3
- ☐ Driver's License ☐ Other ID #1 - describe ☐ Personally Known
- ☐ Passport ☐ Other ID #2 - describe ☐ Credible Witness(es)
- Ref. #1
- Ref. #2
- X _SIGN HERE_
- Right Thumbprint

4
- ☐ Driver's License ☐ Other ID #1 - describe ☐ Personally Known
- ☐ Passport ☐ Other ID #2 - describe ☐ Credible Witness(es)
- Ref. #1
- Ref. #2
- X _SIGN HERE_
- Right Thumbprint

5
- ☐ Driver's License ☐ Other ID #1 - describe ☐ Personally Known
- ☐ Passport ☐ Other ID #2 - describe ☐ Credible Witness(es)
- Ref. #1
- Ref. #2
- X _SIGN HERE_
- Right Thumbprint

6
- ☐ Driver's License ☐ Other ID #1 - describe ☐ Personally Known
- ☐ Passport ☐ Other ID #2 - describe ☐ Credible Witness(es)
- Ref. #1
- Ref. #2
- X _SIGN HERE_
- Right Thumbprint

7
- ☐ Driver's License ☐ Other ID #1 - describe ☐ Personally Known
- ☐ Passport ☐ Other ID #2 - describe ☐ Credible Witness(es)
- Ref. #1
- Ref. #2
- X _SIGN HERE_
- Right Thumbprint

8
- ☐ Driver's License ☐ Other ID #1 - describe ☐ Personally Known
- ☐ Passport ☐ Other ID #2 - describe ☐ Credible Witness(es)
- Ref. #1
- Ref. #2
- X _SIGN HERE_
- Right Thumbprint

5 Dates and Fees Description of Document(s) or Proceeding Additional Information

1

Notarization Date and Time

Date on Document(s) Reference #

Fees Paid?
$

- [A] [J] Compliance Agmt.
- [A] [J] Correction Agmt.
- [A] [J] DOT / Mortgage
- [A] [J] Deed - G / QC / W
- [A] [J] E & O
- [A] [J] Occ. Aff.
- [A] [J] Own. Aff.
- [A] [J] POA - L / D
- [A] [J] Proof of ID Aff.
- [A] [J] Sig./Name Aff.
- [A] [J] Survey Aff.
- [A] [J]
- [A] [J] Adv. Health. Dir.
- [A] [J] Trust - Irr. / Living
- [A] [J] Will - LWT / Living
- [A] [J]
- [A] [J] SDB Verification
- [A] [J] Vehicle - O+VIN / TT
- [A] [J]
- [A] [J] [C] Other ▼

2

Notarization Date and Time

Date on Document(s) Reference #

Fees Paid?
$

- [A] [J] Compliance Agmt.
- [A] [J] Correction Agmt.
- [A] [J] DOT / Mortgage
- [A] [J] Deed - G / QC / W
- [A] [J] E & O
- [A] [J] Occ. Aff.
- [A] [J] Own. Aff.
- [A] [J] POA - L / D
- [A] [J] Proof of ID Aff.
- [A] [J] Sig./Name Aff.
- [A] [J] Survey Aff.
- [A] [J]
- [A] [J] Adv. Health. Dir.
- [A] [J] Trust - Irr. / Living
- [A] [J] Will - LWT / Living
- [A] [J]
- [A] [J] SDB Verification
- [A] [J] Vehicle - O+VIN / TT
- [A] [J]
- [A] [J] [C] Other ▼

3

Notarization Date and Time

Date on Document(s) Reference #

Fees Paid?
$

- [A] [J] Compliance Agmt.
- [A] [J] Correction Agmt.
- [A] [J] DOT / Mortgage
- [A] [J] Deed - G / QC / W
- [A] [J] E & O
- [A] [J] Occ. Aff.
- [A] [J] Own. Aff.
- [A] [J] POA - L / D
- [A] [J] Proof of ID Aff.
- [A] [J] Sig./Name Aff.
- [A] [J] Survey Aff.
- [A] [J]
- [A] [J] Adv. Health. Dir.
- [A] [J] Trust - Irr. / Living
- [A] [J] Will - LWT / Living
- [A] [J]
- [A] [J] SDB Verification
- [A] [J] Vehicle - O+VIN / TT
- [A] [J]
- [A] [J] [C] Other ▼

4

Notarization Date and Time

Date on Document(s) Reference #

Fees Paid?
$

- [A] [J] Compliance Agmt.
- [A] [J] Correction Agmt.
- [A] [J] DOT / Mortgage
- [A] [J] Deed - G / QC / W
- [A] [J] E & O
- [A] [J] Occ. Aff.
- [A] [J] Own. Aff.
- [A] [J] POA - L / D
- [A] [J] Proof of ID Aff.
- [A] [J] Sig./Name Aff.
- [A] [J] Survey Aff.
- [A] [J]
- [A] [J] Adv. Health. Dir.
- [A] [J] Trust - Irr. / Living
- [A] [J] Will - LWT / Living
- [A] [J]
- [A] [J] SDB Verification
- [A] [J] Vehicle - O+VIN / TT
- [A] [J]
- [A] [J] [C] Other ▼

5

Notarization Date and Time

Date on Document(s) Reference #

Fees Paid?
$

- [A] [J] Compliance Agmt.
- [A] [J] Correction Agmt.
- [A] [J] DOT / Mortgage
- [A] [J] Deed - G / QC / W
- [A] [J] E & O
- [A] [J] Occ. Aff.
- [A] [J] Own. Aff.
- [A] [J] POA - L / D
- [A] [J] Proof of ID Aff.
- [A] [J] Sig./Name Aff.
- [A] [J] Survey Aff.
- [A] [J]
- [A] [J] Adv. Health. Dir.
- [A] [J] Trust - Irr. / Living
- [A] [J] Will - LWT / Living
- [A] [J]
- [A] [J] SDB Verification
- [A] [J] Vehicle - O+VIN / TT
- [A] [J]
- [A] [J] [C] Other ▼

6

Notarization Date and Time

Date on Document(s) Reference #

Fees Paid?
$

- [A] [J] Compliance Agmt.
- [A] [J] Correction Agmt.
- [A] [J] DOT / Mortgage
- [A] [J] Deed - G / QC / W
- [A] [J] E & O
- [A] [J] Occ. Aff.
- [A] [J] Own. Aff.
- [A] [J] POA - L / D
- [A] [J] Proof of ID Aff.
- [A] [J] Sig./Name Aff.
- [A] [J] Survey Aff.
- [A] [J]
- [A] [J] Adv. Health. Dir.
- [A] [J] Trust - Irr. / Living
- [A] [J] Will - LWT / Living
- [A] [J]
- [A] [J] SDB Verification
- [A] [J] Vehicle - O+VIN / TT
- [A] [J]
- [A] [J] [C] Other ▼

7

Notarization Date and Time

Date on Document(s) Reference #

Fees Paid?
$

- [A] [J] Compliance Agmt.
- [A] [J] Correction Agmt.
- [A] [J] DOT / Mortgage
- [A] [J] Deed - G / QC / W
- [A] [J] E & O
- [A] [J] Occ. Aff.
- [A] [J] Own. Aff.
- [A] [J] POA - L / D
- [A] [J] Proof of ID Aff.
- [A] [J] Sig./Name Aff.
- [A] [J] Survey Aff.
- [A] [J]
- [A] [J] Adv. Health. Dir.
- [A] [J] Trust - Irr. / Living
- [A] [J] Will - LWT / Living
- [A] [J]
- [A] [J] SDB Verification
- [A] [J] Vehicle - O+VIN / TT
- [A] [J]
- [A] [J] [C] Other ▼

8

Notarization Date and Time

Date on Document(s) Reference #

Fees Paid?
$

- [A] [J] Compliance Agmt.
- [A] [J] Correction Agmt.
- [A] [J] DOT / Mortgage
- [A] [J] Deed - G / QC / W
- [A] [J] E & O
- [A] [J] Occ. Aff.
- [A] [J] Own. Aff.
- [A] [J] POA - L / D
- [A] [J] Proof of ID Aff.
- [A] [J] Sig./Name Aff.
- [A] [J] Survey Aff.
- [A] [J]
- [A] [J] Adv. Health. Dir.
- [A] [J] Trust - Irr. / Living
- [A] [J] Will - LWT / Living
- [A] [J]
- [A] [J] SDB Verification
- [A] [J] Vehicle - O+VIN / TT
- [A] [J]
- [A] [J] [C] Other ▼

Signer Name and Address	Method of Identification	Signature and Thumbprint	6

1
- ☐ Driver's License ☐ Other ID #1 - describe ☐ Personally Known
- ☐ Passport ☐ Other ID #2 - describe ☐ Credible Witness(es)
- Ref. #1
- Ref. #2
- X SIGN HERE
- Right Thumbprint

2
- ☐ Driver's License ☐ Other ID #1 - describe ☐ Personally Known
- ☐ Passport ☐ Other ID #2 - describe ☐ Credible Witness(es)
- Ref. #1
- Ref. #2
- X SIGN HERE
- Right Thumbprint

3
- ☐ Driver's License ☐ Other ID #1 - describe ☐ Personally Known
- ☐ Passport ☐ Other ID #2 - describe ☐ Credible Witness(es)
- Ref. #1
- Ref. #2
- X SIGN HERE
- Right Thumbprint

4
- ☐ Driver's License ☐ Other ID #1 - describe ☐ Personally Known
- ☐ Passport ☐ Other ID #2 - describe ☐ Credible Witness(es)
- Ref. #1
- Ref. #2
- X SIGN HERE
- Right Thumbprint

5
- ☐ Driver's License ☐ Other ID #1 - describe ☐ Personally Known
- ☐ Passport ☐ Other ID #2 - describe ☐ Credible Witness(es)
- Ref. #1
- Ref. #2
- X SIGN HERE
- Right Thumbprint

6
- ☐ Driver's License ☐ Other ID #1 - describe ☐ Personally Known
- ☐ Passport ☐ Other ID #2 - describe ☐ Credible Witness(es)
- Ref. #1
- Ref. #2
- X SIGN HERE
- Right Thumbprint

7
- ☐ Driver's License ☐ Other ID #1 - describe ☐ Personally Known
- ☐ Passport ☐ Other ID #2 - describe ☐ Credible Witness(es)
- Ref. #1
- Ref. #2
- X SIGN HERE
- Right Thumbprint

8
- ☐ Driver's License ☐ Other ID #1 - describe ☐ Personally Known
- ☐ Passport ☐ Other ID #2 - describe ☐ Credible Witness(es)
- Ref. #1
- Ref. #2
- X SIGN HERE
- Right Thumbprint

1

Notarization Date and Time

Date on Document(s)   Reference #

Fees   Paid?
$

A	J	Compliance Agmt.	A	J	E & O	A	J	Proof of ID Aff.	A	J	Adv. Health. Dir.	A	J	SDB Verification
A	J	Correction Agmt.	A	J	Occ. Aff.	A	J	Sig./Name Aff.	A	J	Trust - Irr. / Living	A	J	Vehicle - O+VIN / TT
A	J	DOT / Mortgage	A	J	Own. Aff.	A	J	Survey Aff.	A	J	Will - LWT / Living	A	J	
A	J	Deed - G / QC / W	A	J	POA - L / D	A	J		A	J		A	J	C	Other ▼

2

Notarization Date and Time

Date on Document(s)   Reference #

Fees   Paid?
$

A	J	Compliance Agmt.	A	J	E & O	A	J	Proof of ID Aff.	A	J	Adv. Health. Dir.	A	J	SDB Verification
A	J	Correction Agmt.	A	J	Occ. Aff.	A	J	Sig./Name Aff.	A	J	Trust - Irr. / Living	A	J	Vehicle - O+VIN / TT
A	J	DOT / Mortgage	A	J	Own. Aff.	A	J	Survey Aff.	A	J	Will - LWT / Living	A	J	
A	J	Deed - G / QC / W	A	J	POA - L / D	A	J		A	J		A	J	C	Other ▼

3

Notarization Date and Time

Date on Document(s)   Reference #

Fees   Paid?
$

A	J	Compliance Agmt.	A	J	E & O	A	J	Proof of ID Aff.	A	J	Adv. Health. Dir.	A	J	SDB Verification
A	J	Correction Agmt.	A	J	Occ. Aff.	A	J	Sig./Name Aff.	A	J	Trust - Irr. / Living	A	J	Vehicle - O+VIN / TT
A	J	DOT / Mortgage	A	J	Own. Aff.	A	J	Survey Aff.	A	J	Will - LWT / Living	A	J	
A	J	Deed - G / QC / W	A	J	POA - L / D	A	J		A	J		A	J	C	Other ▼

4

Notarization Date and Time

Date on Document(s)   Reference #

Fees   Paid?
$

A	J	Compliance Agmt.	A	J	E & O	A	J	Proof of ID Aff.	A	J	Adv. Health. Dir.	A	J	SDB Verification
A	J	Correction Agmt.	A	J	Occ. Aff.	A	J	Sig./Name Aff.	A	J	Trust - Irr. / Living	A	J	Vehicle - O+VIN / TT
A	J	DOT / Mortgage	A	J	Own. Aff.	A	J	Survey Aff.	A	J	Will - LWT / Living	A	J	
A	J	Deed - G / QC / W	A	J	POA - L / D	A	J		A	J		A	J	C	Other ▼

5

Notarization Date and Time

Date on Document(s)   Reference #

Fees   Paid?
$

A	J	Compliance Agmt.	A	J	E & O	A	J	Proof of ID Aff.	A	J	Adv. Health. Dir.	A	J	SDB Verification
A	J	Correction Agmt.	A	J	Occ. Aff.	A	J	Sig./Name Aff.	A	J	Trust - Irr. / Living	A	J	Vehicle - O+VIN / TT
A	J	DOT / Mortgage	A	J	Own. Aff.	A	J	Survey Aff.	A	J	Will - LWT / Living	A	J	
A	J	Deed - G / QC / W	A	J	POA - L / D	A	J		A	J		A	J	C	Other ▼

6

Notarization Date and Time

Date on Document(s)   Reference #

Fees   Paid?
$

A	J	Compliance Agmt.	A	J	E & O	A	J	Proof of ID Aff.	A	J	Adv. Health. Dir.	A	J	SDB Verification
A	J	Correction Agmt.	A	J	Occ. Aff.	A	J	Sig./Name Aff.	A	J	Trust - Irr. / Living	A	J	Vehicle - O+VIN / TT
A	J	DOT / Mortgage	A	J	Own. Aff.	A	J	Survey Aff.	A	J	Will - LWT / Living	A	J	
A	J	Deed - G / QC / W	A	J	POA - L / D	A	J		A	J		A	J	C	Other ▼

7

Notarization Date and Time

Date on Document(s)   Reference #

Fees   Paid?
$

A	J	Compliance Agmt.	A	J	E & O	A	J	Proof of ID Aff.	A	J	Adv. Health. Dir.	A	J	SDB Verification
A	J	Correction Agmt.	A	J	Occ. Aff.	A	J	Sig./Name Aff.	A	J	Trust - Irr. / Living	A	J	Vehicle - O+VIN / TT
A	J	DOT / Mortgage	A	J	Own. Aff.	A	J	Survey Aff.	A	J	Will - LWT / Living	A	J	
A	J	Deed - G / QC / W	A	J	POA - L / D	A	J		A	J		A	J	C	Other ▼

8

Notarization Date and Time

Date on Document(s)   Reference #

Fees   Paid?
$

A	J	Compliance Agmt.	A	J	E & O	A	J	Proof of ID Aff.	A	J	Adv. Health. Dir.	A	J	SDB Verification
A	J	Correction Agmt.	A	J	Occ. Aff.	A	J	Sig./Name Aff.	A	J	Trust - Irr. / Living	A	J	Vehicle - O+VIN / TT
A	J	DOT / Mortgage	A	J	Own. Aff.	A	J	Survey Aff.	A	J	Will - LWT / Living	A	J	
A	J	Deed - G / QC / W	A	J	POA - L / D	A	J		A	J		A	J	C	Other ▼

Signer Name and Address	Method of Identification		Signature and Thumbprint		

8

	□ Driver's License □ Other ID #1 - describe □ Personally Known □ Passport □ Other ID #2 - describe □ Credible Witness(es) Ref. #1 Ref. #2	**X** SIGN HERE	Right Thumbprint	**1**

	□ Driver's License □ Other ID #1 - describe □ Personally Known □ Passport □ Other ID #2 - describe □ Credible Witness(es) Ref. #1 Ref. #2	**X** SIGN HERE	Right Thumbprint	**2**

	□ Driver's License □ Other ID #1 - describe □ Personally Known □ Passport □ Other ID #2 - describe □ Credible Witness(es) Ref. #1 Ref. #2	**X** SIGN HERE	Right Thumbprint	**3**

	□ Driver's License □ Other ID #1 - describe □ Personally Known □ Passport □ Other ID #2 - describe □ Credible Witness(es) Ref. #1 Ref. #2	**X** SIGN HERE	Right Thumbprint	**4**

	□ Driver's License □ Other ID #1 - describe □ Personally Known □ Passport □ Other ID #2 - describe □ Credible Witness(es) Ref. #1 Ref. #2	**X** SIGN HERE	Right Thumbprint	**5**

	□ Driver's License □ Other ID #1 - describe □ Personally Known □ Passport □ Other ID #2 - describe □ Credible Witness(es) Ref. #1 Ref. #2	**X** SIGN HERE	Right Thumbprint	**6**

	□ Driver's License □ Other ID #1 - describe □ Personally Known □ Passport □ Other ID #2 - describe □ Credible Witness(es) Ref. #1 Ref. #2	**X** SIGN HERE	Right Thumbprint	**7**

	□ Driver's License □ Other ID #1 - describe □ Personally Known □ Passport □ Other ID #2 - describe □ Credible Witness(es) Ref. #1 Ref. #2	**X** SIGN HERE	Right Thumbprint	**8**

1

Notarization Date and Time

Date on Document(s)   Reference #

Fees   Paid?
$

A	J	Compliance Agmt.	A	J	E & O	A	J	Proof of ID Aff.	A	J	Adv. Health. Dir.	A	J	SDB Verification
A	J	Correction Agmt.	A	J	Occ. Aff.	A	J	Sig./Name Aff.	A	J	Trust - Irr. / Living	A	J	Vehicle - O+VIN / TT
A	J	DOT / Mortgage	A	J	Own. Aff.	A	J	Survey Aff.	A	J	Will - LWT / Living	A	J	
A	J	Deed - G / QC / W	A	J	POA - L / D	A	J		A	J		A	J	C	Other ▼

2

Notarization Date and Time

Date on Document(s)   Reference #

Fees   Paid?
$

A	J	Compliance Agmt.	A	J	E & O	A	J	Proof of ID Aff.	A	J	Adv. Health. Dir.	A	J	SDB Verification
A	J	Correction Agmt.	A	J	Occ. Aff.	A	J	Sig./Name Aff.	A	J	Trust - Irr. / Living	A	J	Vehicle - O+VIN / TT
A	J	DOT / Mortgage	A	J	Own. Aff.	A	J	Survey Aff.	A	J	Will - LWT / Living	A	J	
A	J	Deed - G / QC / W	A	J	POA - L / D	A	J		A	J		A	J	C	Other ▼

3

Notarization Date and Time

Date on Document(s)   Reference #

Fees   Paid?
$

A	J	Compliance Agmt.	A	J	E & O	A	J	Proof of ID Aff.	A	J	Adv. Health. Dir.	A	J	SDB Verification
A	J	Correction Agmt.	A	J	Occ. Aff.	A	J	Sig./Name Aff.	A	J	Trust - Irr. / Living	A	J	Vehicle - O+VIN / TT
A	J	DOT / Mortgage	A	J	Own. Aff.	A	J	Survey Aff.	A	J	Will - LWT / Living	A	J	
A	J	Deed - G / QC / W	A	J	POA - L / D	A	J		A	J		A	J	C	Other ▼

4

Notarization Date and Time

Date on Document(s)   Reference #

Fees   Paid?
$

A	J	Compliance Agmt.	A	J	E & O	A	J	Proof of ID Aff.	A	J	Adv. Health. Dir.	A	J	SDB Verification
A	J	Correction Agmt.	A	J	Occ. Aff.	A	J	Sig./Name Aff.	A	J	Trust - Irr. / Living	A	J	Vehicle - O+VIN / TT
A	J	DOT / Mortgage	A	J	Own. Aff.	A	J	Survey Aff.	A	J	Will - LWT / Living	A	J	
A	J	Deed - G / QC / W	A	J	POA - L / D	A	J		A	J		A	J	C	Other ▼

5

Notarization Date and Time

Date on Document(s)   Reference #

Fees   Paid?
$

A	J	Compliance Agmt.	A	J	E & O	A	J	Proof of ID Aff.	A	J	Adv. Health. Dir.	A	J	SDB Verification
A	J	Correction Agmt.	A	J	Occ. Aff.	A	J	Sig./Name Aff.	A	J	Trust - Irr. / Living	A	J	Vehicle - O+VIN / TT
A	J	DOT / Mortgage	A	J	Own. Aff.	A	J	Survey Aff.	A	J	Will - LWT / Living	A	J	
A	J	Deed - G / QC / W	A	J	POA - L / D	A	J		A	J		A	J	C	Other ▼

6

Notarization Date and Time

Date on Document(s)   Reference #

Fees   Paid?
$

A	J	Compliance Agmt.	A	J	E & O	A	J	Proof of ID Aff.	A	J	Adv. Health. Dir.	A	J	SDB Verification
A	J	Correction Agmt.	A	J	Occ. Aff.	A	J	Sig./Name Aff.	A	J	Trust - Irr. / Living	A	J	Vehicle - O+VIN / TT
A	J	DOT / Mortgage	A	J	Own. Aff.	A	J	Survey Aff.	A	J	Will - LWT / Living	A	J	
A	J	Deed - G / QC / W	A	J	POA - L / D	A	J		A	J		A	J	C	Other ▼

7

Notarization Date and Time

Date on Document(s)   Reference #

Fees   Paid?
$

A	J	Compliance Agmt.	A	J	E & O	A	J	Proof of ID Aff.	A	J	Adv. Health. Dir.	A	J	SDB Verification
A	J	Correction Agmt.	A	J	Occ. Aff.	A	J	Sig./Name Aff.	A	J	Trust - Irr. / Living	A	J	Vehicle - O+VIN / TT
A	J	DOT / Mortgage	A	J	Own. Aff.	A	J	Survey Aff.	A	J	Will - LWT / Living	A	J	
A	J	Deed - G / QC / W	A	J	POA - L / D	A	J		A	J		A	J	C	Other ▼

8

Notarization Date and Time

Date on Document(s)   Reference #

Fees   Paid?
$

A	J	Compliance Agmt.	A	J	E & O	A	J	Proof of ID Aff.	A	J	Adv. Health. Dir.	A	J	SDB Verification
A	J	Correction Agmt.	A	J	Occ. Aff.	A	J	Sig./Name Aff.	A	J	Trust - Irr. / Living	A	J	Vehicle - O+VIN / TT
A	J	DOT / Mortgage	A	J	Own. Aff.	A	J	Survey Aff.	A	J	Will - LWT / Living	A	J	
A	J	Deed - G / QC / W	A	J	POA - L / D	A	J		A	J		A	J	C	Other ▼

1

Method of Identification
- [ ] Driver's License
- [ ] Passport
- [ ] Other ID #1 - describe
- [ ] Other ID #2 - describe
- [ ] Personally Known
- [ ] Credible Witness(es)

Ref. #1

Ref. #2

X *SIGN HERE*

Right Thumbprint

2

Method of Identification
- [ ] Driver's License
- [ ] Passport
- [ ] Other ID #1 - describe
- [ ] Other ID #2 - describe
- [ ] Personally Known
- [ ] Credible Witness(es)

Ref. #1

Ref. #2

X *SIGN HERE*

Right Thumbprint

3

Method of Identification
- [ ] Driver's License
- [ ] Passport
- [ ] Other ID #1 - describe
- [ ] Other ID #2 - describe
- [ ] Personally Known
- [ ] Credible Witness(es)

Ref. #1

Ref. #2

X *SIGN HERE*

Right Thumbprint

4

Method of Identification
- [ ] Driver's License
- [ ] Passport
- [ ] Other ID #1 - describe
- [ ] Other ID #2 - describe
- [ ] Personally Known
- [ ] Credible Witness(es)

Ref. #1

Ref. #2

X *SIGN HERE*

Right Thumbprint

5

Method of Identification
- [ ] Driver's License
- [ ] Passport
- [ ] Other ID #1 - describe
- [ ] Other ID #2 - describe
- [ ] Personally Known
- [ ] Credible Witness(es)

Ref. #1

Ref. #2

X *SIGN HERE*

Right Thumbprint

6

Method of Identification
- [ ] Driver's License
- [ ] Passport
- [ ] Other ID #1 - describe
- [ ] Other ID #2 - describe
- [ ] Personally Known
- [ ] Credible Witness(es)

Ref. #1

Ref. #2

X *SIGN HERE*

Right Thumbprint

7

Method of Identification
- [ ] Driver's License
- [ ] Passport
- [ ] Other ID #1 - describe
- [ ] Other ID #2 - describe
- [ ] Personally Known
- [ ] Credible Witness(es)

Ref. #1

Ref. #2

X *SIGN HERE*

Right Thumbprint

8

Method of Identification
- [ ] Driver's License
- [ ] Passport
- [ ] Other ID #1 - describe
- [ ] Other ID #2 - describe
- [ ] Personally Known
- [ ] Credible Witness(es)

Ref. #1

Ref. #2

X *SIGN HERE*

Right Thumbprint

11   Dates and Fees   Description of Document(s) or Proceeding   Additional Information

1

Notarization Date and Time

Date on Document(s) | **Reference #**

Fees $ **Paid?** ☐

A J Compliance Agmt.	A J E & O	A J Proof of ID Aff.	A J Adv. Health. Dir.	A J SDB Verification
A J Correction Agmt.	A J Occ. Aff.	A J Sig./Name Aff.	A J Trust - Irr. / Living	A J Vehicle - O+VIN / TT
A J DOT / Mortgage	A J Own. Aff.	A J Survey Aff.	A J Will - LWT / Living	A J
A J Deed - G / QC / W	A J POA - L / D	A J	A J	A J C ☐ Other ▼

2

Notarization Date and Time

Date on Document(s) | **Reference #**

Fees $ **Paid?** ☐

A J Compliance Agmt.	A J E & O	A J Proof of ID Aff.	A J Adv. Health. Dir.	A J SDB Verification
A J Correction Agmt.	A J Occ. Aff.	A J Sig./Name Aff.	A J Trust - Irr. / Living	A J Vehicle - O+VIN / TT
A J DOT / Mortgage	A J Own. Aff.	A J Survey Aff.	A J Will - LWT / Living	A J
A J Deed - G / QC / W	A J POA - L / D	A J	A J	A J C ☐ Other ▼

3

Notarization Date and Time

Date on Document(s) | **Reference #**

Fees $ **Paid?** ☐

A J Compliance Agmt.	A J E & O	A J Proof of ID Aff.	A J Adv. Health. Dir.	A J SDB Verification
A J Correction Agmt.	A J Occ. Aff.	A J Sig./Name Aff.	A J Trust - Irr. / Living	A J Vehicle - O+VIN / TT
A J DOT / Mortgage	A J Own. Aff.	A J Survey Aff.	A J Will - LWT / Living	A J
A J Deed - G / QC / W	A J POA - L / D	A J	A J	A J C ☐ Other ▼

4

Notarization Date and Time

Date on Document(s) | **Reference #**

Fees $ **Paid?** ☐

A J Compliance Agmt.	A J E & O	A J Proof of ID Aff.	A J Adv. Health. Dir.	A J SDB Verification
A J Correction Agmt.	A J Occ. Aff.	A J Sig./Name Aff.	A J Trust - Irr. / Living	A J Vehicle - O+VIN / TT
A J DOT / Mortgage	A J Own. Aff.	A J Survey Aff.	A J Will - LWT / Living	A J
A J Deed - G / QC / W	A J POA - L / D	A J	A J	A J C ☐ Other ▼

5

Notarization Date and Time

Date on Document(s) | **Reference #**

Fees $ **Paid?** ☐

A J Compliance Agmt.	A J E & O	A J Proof of ID Aff.	A J Adv. Health. Dir.	A J SDB Verification
A J Correction Agmt.	A J Occ. Aff.	A J Sig./Name Aff.	A J Trust - Irr. / Living	A J Vehicle - O+VIN / TT
A J DOT / Mortgage	A J Own. Aff.	A J Survey Aff.	A J Will - LWT / Living	A J
A J Deed - G / QC / W	A J POA - L / D	A J	A J	A J C ☐ Other ▼

6

Notarization Date and Time

Date on Document(s) | **Reference #**

Fees $ **Paid?** ☐

A J Compliance Agmt.	A J E & O	A J Proof of ID Aff.	A J Adv. Health. Dir.	A J SDB Verification
A J Correction Agmt.	A J Occ. Aff.	A J Sig./Name Aff.	A J Trust - Irr. / Living	A J Vehicle - O+VIN / TT
A J DOT / Mortgage	A J Own. Aff.	A J Survey Aff.	A J Will - LWT / Living	A J
A J Deed - G / QC / W	A J POA - L / D	A J	A J	A J C ☐ Other ▼

7

Notarization Date and Time

Date on Document(s) | **Reference #**

Fees $ **Paid?** ☐

A J Compliance Agmt.	A J E & O	A J Proof of ID Aff.	A J Adv. Health. Dir.	A J SDB Verification
A J Correction Agmt.	A J Occ. Aff.	A J Sig./Name Aff.	A J Trust - Irr. / Living	A J Vehicle - O+VIN / TT
A J DOT / Mortgage	A J Own. Aff.	A J Survey Aff.	A J Will - LWT / Living	A J
A J Deed - G / QC / W	A J POA - L / D	A J	A J	A J C ☐ Other ▼

8

Notarization Date and Time

Date on Document(s) | **Reference #**

Fees $ **Paid?** ☐

A J Compliance Agmt.	A J E & O	A J Proof of ID Aff.	A J Adv. Health. Dir.	A J SDB Verification
A J Correction Agmt.	A J Occ. Aff.	A J Sig./Name Aff.	A J Trust - Irr. / Living	A J Vehicle - O+VIN / TT
A J DOT / Mortgage	A J Own. Aff.	A J Survey Aff.	A J Will - LWT / Living	A J
A J Deed - G / QC / W	A J POA - L / D	A J	A J	A J C ☐ Other ▼

1

Driver's License ☐ Other ID #1 - describe ☐ Personally Known ☐
Passport ☐ Other ID #2 - describe ☐ Credible Witness(es) ☐

Ref. #1

Ref. #2

x SIGN HERE

Right Thumbprint

2

Driver's License ☐ Other ID #1 - describe ☐ Personally Known ☐
Passport ☐ Other ID #2 - describe ☐ Credible Witness(es) ☐

Ref. #1

Ref. #2

x SIGN HERE

Right Thumbprint

3

Driver's License ☐ Other ID #1 - describe ☐ Personally Known ☐
Passport ☐ Other ID #2 - describe ☐ Credible Witness(es) ☐

Ref. #1

Ref. #2

x SIGN HERE

Right Thumbprint

4

Driver's License ☐ Other ID #1 - describe ☐ Personally Known ☐
Passport ☐ Other ID #2 - describe ☐ Credible Witness(es) ☐

Ref. #1

Ref. #2

x SIGN HERE

Right Thumbprint

5

Driver's License ☐ Other ID #1 - describe ☐ Personally Known ☐
Passport ☐ Other ID #2 - describe ☐ Credible Witness(es) ☐

Ref. #1

Ref. #2

x SIGN HERE

Right Thumbprint

6

Driver's License ☐ Other ID #1 - describe ☐ Personally Known ☐
Passport ☐ Other ID #2 - describe ☐ Credible Witness(es) ☐

Ref. #1

Ref. #2

x SIGN HERE

Right Thumbprint

7

Driver's License ☐ Other ID #1 - describe ☐ Personally Known ☐
Passport ☐ Other ID #2 - describe ☐ Credible Witness(es) ☐

Ref. #1

Ref. #2

x SIGN HERE

Right Thumbprint

8

Driver's License ☐ Other ID #1 - describe ☐ Personally Known ☐
Passport ☐ Other ID #2 - describe ☐ Credible Witness(es) ☐

Ref. #1

Ref. #2

x SIGN HERE

Right Thumbprint

13 | Dates and Fees | Description of Document(s) or Proceeding | Additional Information

1

Notarization Date and Time

Date on Document(s) | **Reference #**

Fees $ | **Paid?** ☐

- A J Compliance Agmt.
- A J Correction Agmt.
- A J DOT / Mortgage
- A J Deed - G / QC / W
- A J E & O
- A J Occ. Aff.
- A J Own. Aff.
- A J POA - L / D
- A J Proof of ID Aff.
- A J Sig./Name Aff.
- A J Survey Aff.
- A J
- A J Adv. Health. Dir.
- A J Trust - Irr. / Living
- A J Will - LWT / Living
- A J
- A J SDB Verification
- A J Vehicle - O+VIN / TT
- A J
- A J C ☐ Other ▼

2

Notarization Date and Time

Date on Document(s) | **Reference #**

Fees $ | **Paid?** ☐

- A J Compliance Agmt.
- A J Correction Agmt.
- A J DOT / Mortgage
- A J Deed - G / QC / W
- A J E & O
- A J Occ. Aff.
- A J Own. Aff.
- A J POA - L / D
- A J Proof of ID Aff.
- A J Sig./Name Aff.
- A J Survey Aff.
- A J
- A J Adv. Health. Dir.
- A J Trust - Irr. / Living
- A J Will - LWT / Living
- A J
- A J SDB Verification
- A J Vehicle - O+VIN / TT
- A J
- A J C ☐ Other ▼

3

Notarization Date and Time

Date on Document(s) | **Reference #**

Fees $ | **Paid?** ☐

- A J Compliance Agmt.
- A J Correction Agmt.
- A J DOT / Mortgage
- A J Deed - G / QC / W
- A J E & O
- A J Occ. Aff.
- A J Own. Aff.
- A J POA - L / D
- A J Proof of ID Aff.
- A J Sig./Name Aff.
- A J Survey Aff.
- A J
- A J Adv. Health. Dir.
- A J Trust - Irr. / Living
- A J Will - LWT / Living
- A J
- A J SDB Verification
- A J Vehicle - O+VIN / TT
- A J
- A J C ☐ Other ▼

4

Notarization Date and Time

Date on Document(s) | **Reference #**

Fees $ | **Paid?** ☐

- A J Compliance Agmt.
- A J Correction Agmt.
- A J DOT / Mortgage
- A J Deed - G / QC / W
- A J E & O
- A J Occ. Aff.
- A J Own. Aff.
- A J POA - L / D
- A J Proof of ID Aff.
- A J Sig./Name Aff.
- A J Survey Aff.
- A J
- A J Adv. Health. Dir.
- A J Trust - Irr. / Living
- A J Will - LWT / Living
- A J
- A J SDB Verification
- A J Vehicle - O+VIN / TT
- A J
- A J C ☐ Other ▼

5

Notarization Date and Time

Date on Document(s) | **Reference #**

Fees $ | **Paid?** ☐

- A J Compliance Agmt.
- A J Correction Agmt.
- A J DOT / Mortgage
- A J Deed - G / QC / W
- A J E & O
- A J Occ. Aff.
- A J Own. Aff.
- A J POA - L / D
- A J Proof of ID Aff.
- A J Sig./Name Aff.
- A J Survey Aff.
- A J
- A J Adv. Health. Dir.
- A J Trust - Irr. / Living
- A J Will - LWT / Living
- A J
- A J SDB Verification
- A J Vehicle - O+VIN / TT
- A J
- A J C ☐ Other ▼

6

Notarization Date and Time

Date on Document(s) | **Reference #**

Fees $ | **Paid?** ☐

- A J Compliance Agmt.
- A J Correction Agmt.
- A J DOT / Mortgage
- A J Deed - G / QC / W
- A J E & O
- A J Occ. Aff.
- A J Own. Aff.
- A J POA - L / D
- A J Proof of ID Aff.
- A J Sig./Name Aff.
- A J Survey Aff.
- A J
- A J Adv. Health. Dir.
- A J Trust - Irr. / Living
- A J Will - LWT / Living
- A J
- A J SDB Verification
- A J Vehicle - O+VIN / TT
- A J
- A J C ☐ Other ▼

7

Notarization Date and Time

Date on Document(s) | **Reference #**

Fees $ | **Paid?** ☐

- A J Compliance Agmt.
- A J Correction Agmt.
- A J DOT / Mortgage
- A J Deed - G / QC / W
- A J E & O
- A J Occ. Aff.
- A J Own. Aff.
- A J POA - L / D
- A J Proof of ID Aff.
- A J Sig./Name Aff.
- A J Survey Aff.
- A J
- A J Adv. Health. Dir.
- A J Trust - Irr. / Living
- A J Will - LWT / Living
- A J
- A J SDB Verification
- A J Vehicle - O+VIN / TT
- A J
- A J C ☐ Other ▼

8

Notarization Date and Time

Date on Document(s) | **Reference #**

Fees $ | **Paid?** ☐

- A J Compliance Agmt.
- A J Correction Agmt.
- A J DOT / Mortgage
- A J Deed - G / QC / W
- A J E & O
- A J Occ. Aff.
- A J Own. Aff.
- A J POA - L / D
- A J Proof of ID Aff.
- A J Sig./Name Aff.
- A J Survey Aff.
- A J
- A J Adv. Health. Dir.
- A J Trust - Irr. / Living
- A J Will - LWT / Living
- A J
- A J SDB Verification
- A J Vehicle - O+VIN / TT
- A J
- A J C ☐ Other ▼

Signer Name and Address	Method of Identification	Signature and Thumbprint	

1

Driver's License □ Other ID #1 - describe □ Personally Known
Passport □ Other ID #2 - describe □ Credible Witness(es)

Ref. #1

Ref. #2

X SIGN HERE

Right Thumbprint

2

Driver's License □ Other ID #1 - describe □ Personally Known
Passport □ Other ID #2 - describe □ Credible Witness(es)

Ref. #1

Ref. #2

X SIGN HERE

Right Thumbprint

3

Driver's License □ Other ID #1 - describe □ Personally Known
Passport □ Other ID #2 - describe □ Credible Witness(es)

Ref. #1

Ref. #2

X SIGN HERE

Right Thumbprint

4

Driver's License □ Other ID #1 - describe □ Personally Known
Passport □ Other ID #2 - describe □ Credible Witness(es)

Ref. #1

Ref. #2

X SIGN HERE

Right Thumbprint

5

Driver's License □ Other ID #1 - describe □ Personally Known
Passport □ Other ID #2 - describe □ Credible Witness(es)

Ref. #1

Ref. #2

X SIGN HERE

Right Thumbprint

6

Driver's License □ Other ID #1 - describe □ Personally Known
Passport □ Other ID #2 - describe □ Credible Witness(es)

Ref. #1

Ref. #2

X SIGN HERE

Right Thumbprint

7

Driver's License □ Other ID #1 - describe □ Personally Known
Passport □ Other ID #2 - describe □ Credible Witness(es)

Ref. #1

Ref. #2

X SIGN HERE

Right Thumbprint

8

Driver's License □ Other ID #1 - describe □ Personally Known
Passport □ Other ID #2 - describe □ Credible Witness(es)

Ref. #1

Ref. #2

X SIGN HERE

Right Thumbprint

15 Dates and Fees | Description of Document(s) or Proceeding | Additional Information

1

Notarization Date and Time

Date on Document(s) | Reference #

Fees $ | Paid? ☐

A J Compliance Agmt.	A J E & O	A J Proof of ID Aff.	A J Adv. Health. Dir.	A J SDB Verification
A J Correction Agmt.	A J Occ. Aff.	A J Sig./Name Aff.	A J Trust - Irr. / Living	A J Vehicle - O+VIN / TT
A J DOT / Mortgage	A J Own. Aff.	A J Survey Aff.	A J Will - LWT / Living	A J
A J Deed - G / QC / W	A J POA - L / D	A J	A J	A J C ☐ Other

2

Notarization Date and Time

Date on Document(s) | Reference #

Fees $ | Paid? ☐

A J Compliance Agmt.	A J E & O	A J Proof of ID Aff.	A J Adv. Health. Dir.	A J SDB Verification
A J Correction Agmt.	A J Occ. Aff.	A J Sig./Name Aff.	A J Trust - Irr. / Living	A J Vehicle - O+VIN / TT
A J DOT / Mortgage	A J Own. Aff.	A J Survey Aff.	A J Will - LWT / Living	A J
A J Deed - G / QC / W	A J POA - L / D	A J	A J	A J C ☐ Other

3

Notarization Date and Time

Date on Document(s) | Reference #

Fees $ | Paid? ☐

A J Compliance Agmt.	A J E & O	A J Proof of ID Aff.	A J Adv. Health. Dir.	A J SDB Verification
A J Correction Agmt.	A J Occ. Aff.	A J Sig./Name Aff.	A J Trust - Irr. / Living	A J Vehicle - O+VIN / TT
A J DOT / Mortgage	A J Own. Aff.	A J Survey Aff.	A J Will - LWT / Living	A J
A J Deed - G / QC / W	A J POA - L / D	A J	A J	A J C ☐ Other

4

Notarization Date and Time

Date on Document(s) | Reference #

Fees $ | Paid? ☐

A J Compliance Agmt.	A J E & O	A J Proof of ID Aff.	A J Adv. Health. Dir.	A J SDB Verification
A J Correction Agmt.	A J Occ. Aff.	A J Sig./Name Aff.	A J Trust - Irr. / Living	A J Vehicle - O+VIN / TT
A J DOT / Mortgage	A J Own. Aff.	A J Survey Aff.	A J Will - LWT / Living	A J
A J Deed - G / QC / W	A J POA - L / D	A J	A J	A J C ☐ Other

5

Notarization Date and Time

Date on Document(s) | Reference #

Fees $ | Paid? ☐

A J Compliance Agmt.	A J E & O	A J Proof of ID Aff.	A J Adv. Health. Dir.	A J SDB Verification
A J Correction Agmt.	A J Occ. Aff.	A J Sig./Name Aff.	A J Trust - Irr. / Living	A J Vehicle - O+VIN / TT
A J DOT / Mortgage	A J Own. Aff.	A J Survey Aff.	A J Will - LWT / Living	A J
A J Deed - G / QC / W	A J POA - L / D	A J	A J	A J C ☐ Other

6

Notarization Date and Time

Date on Document(s) | Reference #

Fees $ | Paid? ☐

A J Compliance Agmt.	A J E & O	A J Proof of ID Aff.	A J Adv. Health. Dir.	A J SDB Verification
A J Correction Agmt.	A J Occ. Aff.	A J Sig./Name Aff.	A J Trust - Irr. / Living	A J Vehicle - O+VIN / TT
A J DOT / Mortgage	A J Own. Aff.	A J Survey Aff.	A J Will - LWT / Living	A J
A J Deed - G / QC / W	A J POA - L / D	A J	A J	A J C ☐ Other

7

Notarization Date and Time

Date on Document(s) | Reference #

Fees $ | Paid? ☐

A J Compliance Agmt.	A J E & O	A J Proof of ID Aff.	A J Adv. Health. Dir.	A J SDB Verification
A J Correction Agmt.	A J Occ. Aff.	A J Sig./Name Aff.	A J Trust - Irr. / Living	A J Vehicle - O+VIN / TT
A J DOT / Mortgage	A J Own. Aff.	A J Survey Aff.	A J Will - LWT / Living	A J
A J Deed - G / QC / W	A J POA - L / D	A J	A J	A J C ☐ Other

8

Notarization Date and Time

Date on Document(s) | Reference #

Fees $ | Paid? ☐

A J Compliance Agmt.	A J E & O	A J Proof of ID Aff.	A J Adv. Health. Dir.	A J SDB Verification
A J Correction Agmt.	A J Occ. Aff.	A J Sig./Name Aff.	A J Trust - Irr. / Living	A J Vehicle - O+VIN / TT
A J DOT / Mortgage	A J Own. Aff.	A J Survey Aff.	A J Will - LWT / Living	A J
A J Deed - G / QC / W	A J POA - L / D	A J	A J	A J C ☐ Other

1

☐ Driver's License ☐ Other ID #1 - describe ☐ Personally Known
☐ Passport ☐ Other ID #2 - describe ☐ Credible Witness(es)

Ref. #1

Ref. #2

Right Thumbprint

X ___SIGN HERE___

2

☐ Driver's License ☐ Other ID #1 - describe ☐ Personally Known
☐ Passport ☐ Other ID #2 - describe ☐ Credible Witness(es)

Ref. #1

Ref. #2

Right Thumbprint

X ___SIGN HERE___

3

☐ Driver's License ☐ Other ID #1 - describe ☐ Personally Known
☐ Passport ☐ Other ID #2 - describe ☐ Credible Witness(es)

Ref. #1

Ref. #2

Right Thumbprint

X ___SIGN HERE___

4

☐ Driver's License ☐ Other ID #1 - describe ☐ Personally Known
☐ Passport ☐ Other ID #2 - describe ☐ Credible Witness(es)

Ref. #1

Ref. #2

Right Thumbprint

X ___SIGN HERE___

5

☐ Driver's License ☐ Other ID #1 - describe ☐ Personally Known
☐ Passport ☐ Other ID #2 - describe ☐ Credible Witness(es)

Ref. #1

Ref. #2

Right Thumbprint

X ___SIGN HERE___

6

☐ Driver's License ☐ Other ID #1 - describe ☐ Personally Known
☐ Passport ☐ Other ID #2 - describe ☐ Credible Witness(es)

Ref. #1

Ref. #2

Right Thumbprint

X ___SIGN HERE___

7

☐ Driver's License ☐ Other ID #1 - describe ☐ Personally Known
☐ Passport ☐ Other ID #2 - describe ☐ Credible Witness(es)

Ref. #1

Ref. #2

Right Thumbprint

X ___SIGN HERE___

8

☐ Driver's License ☐ Other ID #1 - describe ☐ Personally Known
☐ Passport ☐ Other ID #2 - describe ☐ Credible Witness(es)

Ref. #1

Ref. #2

Right Thumbprint

X ___SIGN HERE___

1

Notarization Date and Time

Date on Document(s)   Reference #

Fees   Paid?
$

- [ ] A [ ] J Compliance Agmt.   [ ] A [ ] J E & O   [ ] A [ ] J Proof of ID Aff.   [ ] A [ ] J Adv. Health. Dir.   [ ] A [ ] J SDB Verification
- [ ] A [ ] J Correction Agmt.   [ ] A [ ] J Occ. Aff.   [ ] A [ ] J Sig./Name Aff.   [ ] A [ ] J Trust - Irr. / Living   [ ] A [ ] J Vehicle - O+VIN / TT
- [ ] A [ ] J DOT / Mortgage   [ ] A [ ] J Own. Aff.   [ ] A [ ] J Survey Aff.   [ ] A [ ] J Will - LWT / Living   [ ] A [ ] J
- [ ] A [ ] J Deed - G / QC / W   [ ] A [ ] J POA - L / D   [ ] A [ ] J   [ ] A [ ] J   [ ] A [ ] J [ ] C [ ] Other ▼

2

Notarization Date and Time

Date on Document(s)   Reference #

Fees   Paid?
$

- [ ] A [ ] J Compliance Agmt.   [ ] A [ ] J E & O   [ ] A [ ] J Proof of ID Aff.   [ ] A [ ] J Adv. Health. Dir.   [ ] A [ ] J SDB Verification
- [ ] A [ ] J Correction Agmt.   [ ] A [ ] J Occ. Aff.   [ ] A [ ] J Sig./Name Aff.   [ ] A [ ] J Trust - Irr. / Living   [ ] A [ ] J Vehicle - O+VIN / TT
- [ ] A [ ] J DOT / Mortgage   [ ] A [ ] J Own. Aff.   [ ] A [ ] J Survey Aff.   [ ] A [ ] J Will - LWT / Living   [ ] A [ ] J
- [ ] A [ ] J Deed - G / QC / W   [ ] A [ ] J POA - L / D   [ ] A [ ] J   [ ] A [ ] J   [ ] A [ ] J [ ] C [ ] Other ▼

3

Notarization Date and Time

Date on Document(s)   Reference #

Fees   Paid?
$

- [ ] A [ ] J Compliance Agmt.   [ ] A [ ] J E & O   [ ] A [ ] J Proof of ID Aff.   [ ] A [ ] J Adv. Health. Dir.   [ ] A [ ] J SDB Verification
- [ ] A [ ] J Correction Agmt.   [ ] A [ ] J Occ. Aff.   [ ] A [ ] J Sig./Name Aff.   [ ] A [ ] J Trust - Irr. / Living   [ ] A [ ] J Vehicle - O+VIN / TT
- [ ] A [ ] J DOT / Mortgage   [ ] A [ ] J Own. Aff.   [ ] A [ ] J Survey Aff.   [ ] A [ ] J Will - LWT / Living   [ ] A [ ] J
- [ ] A [ ] J Deed - G / QC / W   [ ] A [ ] J POA - L / D   [ ] A [ ] J   [ ] A [ ] J   [ ] A [ ] J [ ] C [ ] Other ▼

4

Notarization Date and Time

Date on Document(s)   Reference #

Fees   Paid?
$

- [ ] A [ ] J Compliance Agmt.   [ ] A [ ] J E & O   [ ] A [ ] J Proof of ID Aff.   [ ] A [ ] J Adv. Health. Dir.   [ ] A [ ] J SDB Verification
- [ ] A [ ] J Correction Agmt.   [ ] A [ ] J Occ. Aff.   [ ] A [ ] J Sig./Name Aff.   [ ] A [ ] J Trust - Irr. / Living   [ ] A [ ] J Vehicle - O+VIN / TT
- [ ] A [ ] J DOT / Mortgage   [ ] A [ ] J Own. Aff.   [ ] A [ ] J Survey Aff.   [ ] A [ ] J Will - LWT / Living   [ ] A [ ] J
- [ ] A [ ] J Deed - G / QC / W   [ ] A [ ] J POA - L / D   [ ] A [ ] J   [ ] A [ ] J   [ ] A [ ] J [ ] C [ ] Other ▼

5

Notarization Date and Time

Date on Document(s)   Reference #

Fees   Paid?
$

- [ ] A [ ] J Compliance Agmt.   [ ] A [ ] J E & O   [ ] A [ ] J Proof of ID Aff.   [ ] A [ ] J Adv. Health. Dir.   [ ] A [ ] J SDB Verification
- [ ] A [ ] J Correction Agmt.   [ ] A [ ] J Occ. Aff.   [ ] A [ ] J Sig./Name Aff.   [ ] A [ ] J Trust - Irr. / Living   [ ] A [ ] J Vehicle - O+VIN / TT
- [ ] A [ ] J DOT / Mortgage   [ ] A [ ] J Own. Aff.   [ ] A [ ] J Survey Aff.   [ ] A [ ] J Will - LWT / Living   [ ] A [ ] J
- [ ] A [ ] J Deed - G / QC / W   [ ] A [ ] J POA - L / D   [ ] A [ ] J   [ ] A [ ] J   [ ] A [ ] J [ ] C [ ] Other ▼

6

Notarization Date and Time

Date on Document(s)   Reference #

Fees   Paid?
$

- [ ] A [ ] J Compliance Agmt.   [ ] A [ ] J E & O   [ ] A [ ] J Proof of ID Aff.   [ ] A [ ] J Adv. Health. Dir.   [ ] A [ ] J SDB Verification
- [ ] A [ ] J Correction Agmt.   [ ] A [ ] J Occ. Aff.   [ ] A [ ] J Sig./Name Aff.   [ ] A [ ] J Trust - Irr. / Living   [ ] A [ ] J Vehicle - O+VIN / TT
- [ ] A [ ] J DOT / Mortgage   [ ] A [ ] J Own. Aff.   [ ] A [ ] J Survey Aff.   [ ] A [ ] J Will - LWT / Living   [ ] A [ ] J
- [ ] A [ ] J Deed - G / QC / W   [ ] A [ ] J POA - L / D   [ ] A [ ] J   [ ] A [ ] J   [ ] A [ ] J [ ] C [ ] Other ▼

7

Notarization Date and Time

Date on Document(s)   Reference #

Fees   Paid?
$

- [ ] A [ ] J Compliance Agmt.   [ ] A [ ] J E & O   [ ] A [ ] J Proof of ID Aff.   [ ] A [ ] J Adv. Health. Dir.   [ ] A [ ] J SDB Verification
- [ ] A [ ] J Correction Agmt.   [ ] A [ ] J Occ. Aff.   [ ] A [ ] J Sig./Name Aff.   [ ] A [ ] J Trust - Irr. / Living   [ ] A [ ] J Vehicle - O+VIN / TT
- [ ] A [ ] J DOT / Mortgage   [ ] A [ ] J Own. Aff.   [ ] A [ ] J Survey Aff.   [ ] A [ ] J Will - LWT / Living   [ ] A [ ] J
- [ ] A [ ] J Deed - G / QC / W   [ ] A [ ] J POA - L / D   [ ] A [ ] J   [ ] A [ ] J   [ ] A [ ] J [ ] C [ ] Other ▼

8

Notarization Date and Time

Date on Document(s)   Reference #

Fees   Paid?
$

- [ ] A [ ] J Compliance Agmt.   [ ] A [ ] J E & O   [ ] A [ ] J Proof of ID Aff.   [ ] A [ ] J Adv. Health. Dir.   [ ] A [ ] J SDB Verification
- [ ] A [ ] J Correction Agmt.   [ ] A [ ] J Occ. Aff.   [ ] A [ ] J Sig./Name Aff.   [ ] A [ ] J Trust - Irr. / Living   [ ] A [ ] J Vehicle - O+VIN / TT
- [ ] A [ ] J DOT / Mortgage   [ ] A [ ] J Own. Aff.   [ ] A [ ] J Survey Aff.   [ ] A [ ] J Will - LWT / Living   [ ] A [ ] J
- [ ] A [ ] J Deed - G / QC / W   [ ] A [ ] J POA - L / D   [ ] A [ ] J   [ ] A [ ] J   [ ] A [ ] J [ ] C [ ] Other ▼

1

☐ Driver's License   ☐ Other ID #1 - describe   ☐ Personally Known
☐ Passport   ☐ Other ID #2 - describe   ☐ Credible Witness(es)

Ref. #1

Ref. #2

X **SIGN HERE**

Right Thumbprint

2

☐ Driver's License   ☐ Other ID #1 - describe   ☐ Personally Known
☐ Passport   ☐ Other ID #2 - describe   ☐ Credible Witness(es)

Ref. #1

Ref. #2

X **SIGN HERE**

Right Thumbprint

3

☐ Driver's License   ☐ Other ID #1 - describe   ☐ Personally Known
☐ Passport   ☐ Other ID #2 - describe   ☐ Credible Witness(es)

Ref. #1

Ref. #2

X **SIGN HERE**

Right Thumbprint

4

☐ Driver's License   ☐ Other ID #1 - describe   ☐ Personally Known
☐ Passport   ☐ Other ID #2 - describe   ☐ Credible Witness(es)

Ref. #1

Ref. #2

X **SIGN HERE**

Right Thumbprint

5

☐ Driver's License   ☐ Other ID #1 - describe   ☐ Personally Known
☐ Passport   ☐ Other ID #2 - describe   ☐ Credible Witness(es)

Ref. #1

Ref. #2

X **SIGN HERE**

Right Thumbprint

6

☐ Driver's License   ☐ Other ID #1 - describe   ☐ Personally Known
☐ Passport   ☐ Other ID #2 - describe   ☐ Credible Witness(es)

Ref. #1

Ref. #2

X **SIGN HERE**

Right Thumbprint

7

☐ Driver's License   ☐ Other ID #1 - describe   ☐ Personally Known
☐ Passport   ☐ Other ID #2 - describe   ☐ Credible Witness(es)

Ref. #1

Ref. #2

X **SIGN HERE**

Right Thumbprint

8

☐ Driver's License   ☐ Other ID #1 - describe   ☐ Personally Known
☐ Passport   ☐ Other ID #2 - describe   ☐ Credible Witness(es)

Ref. #1

Ref. #2

X **SIGN HERE**

Right Thumbprint

1

Notarization Date and Time

Date on Document(s)   Reference #

Fees $ Paid? ☐

A J Compliance Agmt.	A J E & O	A J Proof of ID Aff.	A J Adv. Health. Dir.	A J SDB Verification
A J Correction Agmt.	A J Occ. Aff.	A J Sig./Name Aff.	A J Trust - Irr. / Living	A J Vehicle - O+VIN / TT
A J DOT / Mortgage	A J Own. Aff.	A J Survey Aff.	A J Will - LWT / Living	A J
A J Deed - G / QC / W	A J POA - L / D	A J	A J	A J C ☐ Other ▼

2

Notarization Date and Time

Date on Document(s)   Reference #

Fees $ Paid? ☐

A J Compliance Agmt.	A J E & O	A J Proof of ID Aff.	A J Adv. Health. Dir.	A J SDB Verification
A J Correction Agmt.	A J Occ. Aff.	A J Sig./Name Aff.	A J Trust - Irr. / Living	A J Vehicle - O+VIN / TT
A J DOT / Mortgage	A J Own. Aff.	A J Survey Aff.	A J Will - LWT / Living	A J
A J Deed - G / QC / W	A J POA - L / D	A J	A J	A J C ☐ Other ▼

3

Notarization Date and Time

Date on Document(s)   Reference #

Fees $ Paid? ☐

A J Compliance Agmt.	A J E & O	A J Proof of ID Aff.	A J Adv. Health. Dir.	A J SDB Verification
A J Correction Agmt.	A J Occ. Aff.	A J Sig./Name Aff.	A J Trust - Irr. / Living	A J Vehicle - O+VIN / TT
A J DOT / Mortgage	A J Own. Aff.	A J Survey Aff.	A J Will - LWT / Living	A J
A J Deed - G / QC / W	A J POA - L / D	A J	A J	A J C ☐ Other ▼

4

Notarization Date and Time

Date on Document(s)   Reference #

Fees $ Paid? ☐

A J Compliance Agmt.	A J E & O	A J Proof of ID Aff.	A J Adv. Health. Dir.	A J SDB Verification
A J Correction Agmt.	A J Occ. Aff.	A J Sig./Name Aff.	A J Trust - Irr. / Living	A J Vehicle - O+VIN / TT
A J DOT / Mortgage	A J Own. Aff.	A J Survey Aff.	A J Will - LWT / Living	A J
A J Deed - G / QC / W	A J POA - L / D	A J	A J	A J C ☐ Other ▼

5

Notarization Date and Time

Date on Document(s)   Reference #

Fees $ Paid? ☐

A J Compliance Agmt.	A J E & O	A J Proof of ID Aff.	A J Adv. Health. Dir.	A J SDB Verification
A J Correction Agmt.	A J Occ. Aff.	A J Sig./Name Aff.	A J Trust - Irr. / Living	A J Vehicle - O+VIN / TT
A J DOT / Mortgage	A J Own. Aff.	A J Survey Aff.	A J Will - LWT / Living	A J
A J Deed - G / QC / W	A J POA - L / D	A J	A J	A J C ☐ Other ▼

6

Notarization Date and Time

Date on Document(s)   Reference #

Fees $ Paid? ☐

A J Compliance Agmt.	A J E & O	A J Proof of ID Aff.	A J Adv. Health. Dir.	A J SDB Verification
A J Correction Agmt.	A J Occ. Aff.	A J Sig./Name Aff.	A J Trust - Irr. / Living	A J Vehicle - O+VIN / TT
A J DOT / Mortgage	A J Own. Aff.	A J Survey Aff.	A J Will - LWT / Living	A J
A J Deed - G / QC / W	A J POA - L / D	A J	A J	A J C ☐ Other ▼

7

Notarization Date and Time

Date on Document(s)   Reference #

Fees $ Paid? ☐

A J Compliance Agmt.	A J E & O	A J Proof of ID Aff.	A J Adv. Health. Dir.	A J SDB Verification
A J Correction Agmt.	A J Occ. Aff.	A J Sig./Name Aff.	A J Trust - Irr. / Living	A J Vehicle - O+VIN / TT
A J DOT / Mortgage	A J Own. Aff.	A J Survey Aff.	A J Will - LWT / Living	A J
A J Deed - G / QC / W	A J POA - L / D	A J	A J	A J C ☐ Other ▼

8

Notarization Date and Time

Date on Document(s)   Reference #

Fees $ Paid? ☐

A J Compliance Agmt.	A J E & O	A J Proof of ID Aff.	A J Adv. Health. Dir.	A J SDB Verification
A J Correction Agmt.	A J Occ. Aff.	A J Sig./Name Aff.	A J Trust - Irr. / Living	A J Vehicle - O+VIN / TT
A J DOT / Mortgage	A J Own. Aff.	A J Survey Aff.	A J Will - LWT / Living	A J
A J Deed - G / QC / W	A J POA - L / D	A J	A J	A J C ☐ Other ▼

1

☐ Driver's License ☐ Other ID #1 - describe ☐ Personally Known
☐ Passport ☐ Other ID #2 - describe ☐ Credible Witness(es)

Ref. #1

Ref. #2

Right Thumbprint

X _____ SIGN HERE

2

☐ Driver's License ☐ Other ID #1 - describe ☐ Personally Known
☐ Passport ☐ Other ID #2 - describe ☐ Credible Witness(es)

Ref. #1

Ref. #2

Right Thumbprint

X _____ SIGN HERE

3

☐ Driver's License ☐ Other ID #1 - describe ☐ Personally Known
☐ Passport ☐ Other ID #2 - describe ☐ Credible Witness(es)

Ref. #1

Ref. #2

Right Thumbprint

X _____ SIGN HERE

4

☐ Driver's License ☐ Other ID #1 - describe ☐ Personally Known
☐ Passport ☐ Other ID #2 - describe ☐ Credible Witness(es)

Ref. #1

Ref. #2

Right Thumbprint

X _____ SIGN HERE

5

☐ Driver's License ☐ Other ID #1 - describe ☐ Personally Known
☐ Passport ☐ Other ID #2 - describe ☐ Credible Witness(es)

Ref. #1

Ref. #2

Right Thumbprint

X _____ SIGN HERE

6

☐ Driver's License ☐ Other ID #1 - describe ☐ Personally Known
☐ Passport ☐ Other ID #2 - describe ☐ Credible Witness(es)

Ref. #1

Ref. #2

Right Thumbprint

X _____ SIGN HERE

7

☐ Driver's License ☐ Other ID #1 - describe ☐ Personally Known
☐ Passport ☐ Other ID #2 - describe ☐ Credible Witness(es)

Ref. #1

Ref. #2

Right Thumbprint

X _____ SIGN HERE

8

☐ Driver's License ☐ Other ID #1 - describe ☐ Personally Known
☐ Passport ☐ Other ID #2 - describe ☐ Credible Witness(es)

Ref. #1

Ref. #2

Right Thumbprint

X _____ SIGN HERE

Entry 1

Dates and Fees:
- Notarization Date and Time
- Date on Document(s) — Reference #
- Fees: $ — Paid? ☐

Description of Document(s) or Proceeding:
A / J	A / J	A / J	A / J	A / J
Compliance Agmt.	E & O	Proof of ID Aff.	Adv. Health. Dir.	SDB Verification
Correction Agmt.	Occ. Aff.	Sig./Name Aff.	Trust - Irr. / Living	Vehicle - O+VIN / TT
DOT / Mortgage	Own. Aff.	Survey Aff.	Will - LWT / Living	
Deed - G / QC / W	POA - L / D			Other ▼ (A / J / C ☐)

Entry 2

Dates and Fees:
- Notarization Date and Time
- Date on Document(s) — Reference #
- Fees: $ — Paid? ☐

Description of Document(s) or Proceeding:
A / J	A / J	A / J	A / J	A / J
Compliance Agmt.	E & O	Proof of ID Aff.	Adv. Health. Dir.	SDB Verification
Correction Agmt.	Occ. Aff.	Sig./Name Aff.	Trust - Irr. / Living	Vehicle - O+VIN / TT
DOT / Mortgage	Own. Aff.	Survey Aff.	Will - LWT / Living	
Deed - G / QC / W	POA - L / D			Other ▼ (A / J / C ☐)

Entry 3

Dates and Fees:
- Notarization Date and Time
- Date on Document(s) — Reference #
- Fees: $ — Paid? ☐

Description of Document(s) or Proceeding:
A / J	A / J	A / J	A / J	A / J
Compliance Agmt.	E & O	Proof of ID Aff.	Adv. Health. Dir.	SDB Verification
Correction Agmt.	Occ. Aff.	Sig./Name Aff.	Trust - Irr. / Living	Vehicle - O+VIN / TT
DOT / Mortgage	Own. Aff.	Survey Aff.	Will - LWT / Living	
Deed - G / QC / W	POA - L / D			Other ▼ (A / J / C ☐)

Entry 4

Dates and Fees:
- Notarization Date and Time
- Date on Document(s) — Reference #
- Fees: $ — Paid? ☐

Description of Document(s) or Proceeding:
A / J	A / J	A / J	A / J	A / J
Compliance Agmt.	E & O	Proof of ID Aff.	Adv. Health. Dir.	SDB Verification
Correction Agmt.	Occ. Aff.	Sig./Name Aff.	Trust - Irr. / Living	Vehicle - O+VIN / TT
DOT / Mortgage	Own. Aff.	Survey Aff.	Will - LWT / Living	
Deed - G / QC / W	POA - L / D			Other ▼ (A / J / C ☐)

Entry 5

Dates and Fees:
- Notarization Date and Time
- Date on Document(s) — Reference #
- Fees: $ — Paid? ☐

Description of Document(s) or Proceeding:
A / J	A / J	A / J	A / J	A / J
Compliance Agmt.	E & O	Proof of ID Aff.	Adv. Health. Dir.	SDB Verification
Correction Agmt.	Occ. Aff.	Sig./Name Aff.	Trust - Irr. / Living	Vehicle - O+VIN / TT
DOT / Mortgage	Own. Aff.	Survey Aff.	Will - LWT / Living	
Deed - G / QC / W	POA - L / D			Other ▼ (A / J / C ☐)

Entry 6

Dates and Fees:
- Notarization Date and Time
- Date on Document(s) — Reference #
- Fees: $ — Paid? ☐

Description of Document(s) or Proceeding:
A / J	A / J	A / J	A / J	A / J
Compliance Agmt.	E & O	Proof of ID Aff.	Adv. Health. Dir.	SDB Verification
Correction Agmt.	Occ. Aff.	Sig./Name Aff.	Trust - Irr. / Living	Vehicle - O+VIN / TT
DOT / Mortgage	Own. Aff.	Survey Aff.	Will - LWT / Living	
Deed - G / QC / W	POA - L / D			Other ▼ (A / J / C ☐)

Entry 7

Dates and Fees:
- Notarization Date and Time
- Date on Document(s) — Reference #
- Fees: $ — Paid? ☐

Description of Document(s) or Proceeding:
A / J	A / J	A / J	A / J	A / J
Compliance Agmt.	E & O	Proof of ID Aff.	Adv. Health. Dir.	SDB Verification
Correction Agmt.	Occ. Aff.	Sig./Name Aff.	Trust - Irr. / Living	Vehicle - O+VIN / TT
DOT / Mortgage	Own. Aff.	Survey Aff.	Will - LWT / Living	
Deed - G / QC / W	POA - L / D			Other ▼ (A / J / C ☐)

Entry 8

Dates and Fees:
- Notarization Date and Time
- Date on Document(s) — Reference #
- Fees: $ — Paid? ☐

Description of Document(s) or Proceeding:
A / J	A / J	A / J	A / J	A / J
Compliance Agmt.	E & O	Proof of ID Aff.	Adv. Health. Dir.	SDB Verification
Correction Agmt.	Occ. Aff.	Sig./Name Aff.	Trust - Irr. / Living	Vehicle - O+VIN / TT
DOT / Mortgage	Own. Aff.	Survey Aff.	Will - LWT / Living	
Deed - G / QC / W	POA - L / D			Other ▼ (A / J / C ☐)

1

Method of Identification:
- [ ] Driver's License
- [ ] Passport
- [ ] Other ID #1 - describe
- [ ] Other ID #2 - describe
- [ ] Personally Known
- [ ] Credible Witness(es)

Ref. #1

Ref. #2

X _SIGN HERE_

Right Thumbprint

2

Method of Identification:
- [ ] Driver's License
- [ ] Passport
- [ ] Other ID #1 - describe
- [ ] Other ID #2 - describe
- [ ] Personally Known
- [ ] Credible Witness(es)

Ref. #1

Ref. #2

X _SIGN HERE_

Right Thumbprint

3

Method of Identification:
- [ ] Driver's License
- [ ] Passport
- [ ] Other ID #1 - describe
- [ ] Other ID #2 - describe
- [ ] Personally Known
- [ ] Credible Witness(es)

Ref. #1

Ref. #2

X _SIGN HERE_

Right Thumbprint

4

Method of Identification:
- [ ] Driver's License
- [ ] Passport
- [ ] Other ID #1 - describe
- [ ] Other ID #2 - describe
- [ ] Personally Known
- [ ] Credible Witness(es)

Ref. #1

Ref. #2

X _SIGN HERE_

Right Thumbprint

5

Method of Identification:
- [ ] Driver's License
- [ ] Passport
- [ ] Other ID #1 - describe
- [ ] Other ID #2 - describe
- [ ] Personally Known
- [ ] Credible Witness(es)

Ref. #1

Ref. #2

X _SIGN HERE_

Right Thumbprint

6

Method of Identification:
- [ ] Driver's License
- [ ] Passport
- [ ] Other ID #1 - describe
- [ ] Other ID #2 - describe
- [ ] Personally Known
- [ ] Credible Witness(es)

Ref. #1

Ref. #2

X _SIGN HERE_

Right Thumbprint

7

Method of Identification:
- [ ] Driver's License
- [ ] Passport
- [ ] Other ID #1 - describe
- [ ] Other ID #2 - describe
- [ ] Personally Known
- [ ] Credible Witness(es)

Ref. #1

Ref. #2

X _SIGN HERE_

Right Thumbprint

8

Method of Identification:
- [ ] Driver's License
- [ ] Passport
- [ ] Other ID #1 - describe
- [ ] Other ID #2 - describe
- [ ] Personally Known
- [ ] Credible Witness(es)

Ref. #1

Ref. #2

X _SIGN HERE_

Right Thumbprint

1

Notarization Date and Time

Date on Document(s)   Reference #

Fees   Paid?
$

A J Compliance Agmt.	A J E & O	A J Proof of ID Aff.	A J Adv. Health. Dir.	A J SDB Verification
A J Correction Agmt.	A J Occ. Aff.	A J Sig./Name Aff.	A J Trust - Irr. / Living	A J Vehicle - O+VIN / TT
A J DOT / Mortgage	A J Own. Aff.	A J Survey Aff.	A J Will - LWT / Living	A J
A J Deed - G / QC / W	A J POA - L / D	A J	A J	A J C Other ▼

2

Notarization Date and Time

Date on Document(s)   Reference #

Fees   Paid?
$

A J Compliance Agmt.	A J E & O	A J Proof of ID Aff.	A J Adv. Health. Dir.	A J SDB Verification
A J Correction Agmt.	A J Occ. Aff.	A J Sig./Name Aff.	A J Trust - Irr. / Living	A J Vehicle - O+VIN / TT
A J DOT / Mortgage	A J Own. Aff.	A J Survey Aff.	A J Will - LWT / Living	A J
A J Deed - G / QC / W	A J POA - L / D	A J	A J	A J C Other ▼

3

Notarization Date and Time

Date on Document(s)   Reference #

Fees   Paid?
$

A J Compliance Agmt.	A J E & O	A J Proof of ID Aff.	A J Adv. Health. Dir.	A J SDB Verification
A J Correction Agmt.	A J Occ. Aff.	A J Sig./Name Aff.	A J Trust - Irr. / Living	A J Vehicle - O+VIN / TT
A J DOT / Mortgage	A J Own. Aff.	A J Survey Aff.	A J Will - LWT / Living	A J
A J Deed - G / QC / W	A J POA - L / D	A J	A J	A J C Other ▼

4

Notarization Date and Time

Date on Document(s)   Reference #

Fees   Paid?
$

A J Compliance Agmt.	A J E & O	A J Proof of ID Aff.	A J Adv. Health. Dir.	A J SDB Verification
A J Correction Agmt.	A J Occ. Aff.	A J Sig./Name Aff.	A J Trust - Irr. / Living	A J Vehicle - O+VIN / TT
A J DOT / Mortgage	A J Own. Aff.	A J Survey Aff.	A J Will - LWT / Living	A J
A J Deed - G / QC / W	A J POA - L / D	A J	A J	A J C Other ▼

5

Notarization Date and Time

Date on Document(s)   Reference #

Fees   Paid?
$

A J Compliance Agmt.	A J E & O	A J Proof of ID Aff.	A J Adv. Health. Dir.	A J SDB Verification
A J Correction Agmt.	A J Occ. Aff.	A J Sig./Name Aff.	A J Trust - Irr. / Living	A J Vehicle - O+VIN / TT
A J DOT / Mortgage	A J Own. Aff.	A J Survey Aff.	A J Will - LWT / Living	A J
A J Deed - G / QC / W	A J POA - L / D	A J	A J	A J C Other ▼

6

Notarization Date and Time

Date on Document(s)   Reference #

Fees   Paid?
$

A J Compliance Agmt.	A J E & O	A J Proof of ID Aff.	A J Adv. Health. Dir.	A J SDB Verification
A J Correction Agmt.	A J Occ. Aff.	A J Sig./Name Aff.	A J Trust - Irr. / Living	A J Vehicle - O+VIN / TT
A J DOT / Mortgage	A J Own. Aff.	A J Survey Aff.	A J Will - LWT / Living	A J
A J Deed - G / QC / W	A J POA - L / D	A J	A J	A J C Other ▼

7

Notarization Date and Time

Date on Document(s)   Reference #

Fees   Paid?
$

A J Compliance Agmt.	A J E & O	A J Proof of ID Aff.	A J Adv. Health. Dir.	A J SDB Verification
A J Correction Agmt.	A J Occ. Aff.	A J Sig./Name Aff.	A J Trust - Irr. / Living	A J Vehicle - O+VIN / TT
A J DOT / Mortgage	A J Own. Aff.	A J Survey Aff.	A J Will - LWT / Living	A J
A J Deed - G / QC / W	A J POA - L / D	A J	A J	A J C Other ▼

8

Notarization Date and Time

Date on Document(s)   Reference #

Fees   Paid?
$

A J Compliance Agmt.	A J E & O	A J Proof of ID Aff.	A J Adv. Health. Dir.	A J SDB Verification
A J Correction Agmt.	A J Occ. Aff.	A J Sig./Name Aff.	A J Trust - Irr. / Living	A J Vehicle - O+VIN / TT
A J DOT / Mortgage	A J Own. Aff.	A J Survey Aff.	A J Will - LWT / Living	A J
A J Deed - G / QC / W	A J POA - L / D	A J	A J	A J C Other ▼

1

Method of Identification:
- ☐ Driver's License ☐ Other ID #1 - describe ☐ Personally Known
- ☐ Passport ☐ Other ID #2 - describe ☐ Credible Witness(es)

Ref. #1

Ref. #2

X SIGN HERE

Right Thumbprint

2

Method of Identification:
- ☐ Driver's License ☐ Other ID #1 - describe ☐ Personally Known
- ☐ Passport ☐ Other ID #2 - describe ☐ Credible Witness(es)

Ref. #1

Ref. #2

X SIGN HERE

Right Thumbprint

3

Method of Identification:
- ☐ Driver's License ☐ Other ID #1 - describe ☐ Personally Known
- ☐ Passport ☐ Other ID #2 - describe ☐ Credible Witness(es)

Ref. #1

Ref. #2

X SIGN HERE

Right Thumbprint

4

Method of Identification:
- ☐ Driver's License ☐ Other ID #1 - describe ☐ Personally Known
- ☐ Passport ☐ Other ID #2 - describe ☐ Credible Witness(es)

Ref. #1

Ref. #2

X SIGN HERE

Right Thumbprint

5

Method of Identification:
- ☐ Driver's License ☐ Other ID #1 - describe ☐ Personally Known
- ☐ Passport ☐ Other ID #2 - describe ☐ Credible Witness(es)

Ref. #1

Ref. #2

X SIGN HERE

Right Thumbprint

6

Method of Identification:
- ☐ Driver's License ☐ Other ID #1 - describe ☐ Personally Known
- ☐ Passport ☐ Other ID #2 - describe ☐ Credible Witness(es)

Ref. #1

Ref. #2

X SIGN HERE

Right Thumbprint

7

Method of Identification:
- ☐ Driver's License ☐ Other ID #1 - describe ☐ Personally Known
- ☐ Passport ☐ Other ID #2 - describe ☐ Credible Witness(es)

Ref. #1

Ref. #2

X SIGN HERE

Right Thumbprint

8

Method of Identification:
- ☐ Driver's License ☐ Other ID #1 - describe ☐ Personally Known
- ☐ Passport ☐ Other ID #2 - describe ☐ Credible Witness(es)

Ref. #1

Ref. #2

X SIGN HERE

Right Thumbprint

25 | Dates and Fees | Description of Document(s) or Proceeding | Additional Information

1
Notarization Date and Time

Date on Document(s)   Reference #

Fees   Paid?
$

Checkboxes (A / J):
- Compliance Agmt.
- Correction Agmt.
- DOT / Mortgage
- Deed - G / QC / W
- E & O
- Occ. Aff.
- Own. Aff.
- POA - L / D
- Proof of ID Aff.
- Sig./Name Aff.
- Survey Aff.
- Adv. Health. Dir.
- Trust - Irr. / Living
- Will - LWT / Living
- SDB Verification
- Vehicle - O+VIN / TT
- Other (A / J / C)

2
Notarization Date and Time

Date on Document(s)   Reference #

Fees   Paid?
$

Checkboxes (A / J):
- Compliance Agmt.
- Correction Agmt.
- DOT / Mortgage
- Deed - G / QC / W
- E & O
- Occ. Aff.
- Own. Aff.
- POA - L / D
- Proof of ID Aff.
- Sig./Name Aff.
- Survey Aff.
- Adv. Health. Dir.
- Trust - Irr. / Living
- Will - LWT / Living
- SDB Verification
- Vehicle - O+VIN / TT
- Other (A / J / C)

3
Notarization Date and Time

Date on Document(s)   Reference #

Fees   Paid?
$

Checkboxes (A / J):
- Compliance Agmt.
- Correction Agmt.
- DOT / Mortgage
- Deed - G / QC / W
- E & O
- Occ. Aff.
- Own. Aff.
- POA - L / D
- Proof of ID Aff.
- Sig./Name Aff.
- Survey Aff.
- Adv. Health. Dir.
- Trust - Irr. / Living
- Will - LWT / Living
- SDB Verification
- Vehicle - O+VIN / TT
- Other (A / J / C)

4
Notarization Date and Time

Date on Document(s)   Reference #

Fees   Paid?
$

Checkboxes (A / J):
- Compliance Agmt.
- Correction Agmt.
- DOT / Mortgage
- Deed - G / QC / W
- E & O
- Occ. Aff.
- Own. Aff.
- POA - L / D
- Proof of ID Aff.
- Sig./Name Aff.
- Survey Aff.
- Adv. Health. Dir.
- Trust - Irr. / Living
- Will - LWT / Living
- SDB Verification
- Vehicle - O+VIN / TT
- Other (A / J / C)

5
Notarization Date and Time

Date on Document(s)   Reference #

Fees   Paid?
$

Checkboxes (A / J):
- Compliance Agmt.
- Correction Agmt.
- DOT / Mortgage
- Deed - G / QC / W
- E & O
- Occ. Aff.
- Own. Aff.
- POA - L / D
- Proof of ID Aff.
- Sig./Name Aff.
- Survey Aff.
- Adv. Health. Dir.
- Trust - Irr. / Living
- Will - LWT / Living
- SDB Verification
- Vehicle - O+VIN / TT
- Other (A / J / C)

6
Notarization Date and Time

Date on Document(s)   Reference #

Fees   Paid?
$

Checkboxes (A / J):
- Compliance Agmt.
- Correction Agmt.
- DOT / Mortgage
- Deed - G / QC / W
- E & O
- Occ. Aff.
- Own. Aff.
- POA - L / D
- Proof of ID Aff.
- Sig./Name Aff.
- Survey Aff.
- Adv. Health. Dir.
- Trust - Irr. / Living
- Will - LWT / Living
- SDB Verification
- Vehicle - O+VIN / TT
- Other (A / J / C)

7
Notarization Date and Time

Date on Document(s)   Reference #

Fees   Paid?
$

Checkboxes (A / J):
- Compliance Agmt.
- Correction Agmt.
- DOT / Mortgage
- Deed - G / QC / W
- E & O
- Occ. Aff.
- Own. Aff.
- POA - L / D
- Proof of ID Aff.
- Sig./Name Aff.
- Survey Aff.
- Adv. Health. Dir.
- Trust - Irr. / Living
- Will - LWT / Living
- SDB Verification
- Vehicle - O+VIN / TT
- Other (A / J / C)

8
Notarization Date and Time

Date on Document(s)   Reference #

Fees   Paid?
$

Checkboxes (A / J):
- Compliance Agmt.
- Correction Agmt.
- DOT / Mortgage
- Deed - G / QC / W
- E & O
- Occ. Aff.
- Own. Aff.
- POA - L / D
- Proof of ID Aff.
- Sig./Name Aff.
- Survey Aff.
- Adv. Health. Dir.
- Trust - Irr. / Living
- Will - LWT / Living
- SDB Verification
- Vehicle - O+VIN / TT
- Other (A / J / C)

1

☐ Driver's License ☐ Other ID #1 - describe ☐ Personally Known
☐ Passport ☐ Other ID #2 - describe ☐ Credible Witness(es)

Ref. #1

Ref. #2

Right Thumbprint

X SIGN HERE

2

☐ Driver's License ☐ Other ID #1 - describe ☐ Personally Known
☐ Passport ☐ Other ID #2 - describe ☐ Credible Witness(es)

Ref. #1

Ref. #2

Right Thumbprint

X SIGN HERE

3

☐ Driver's License ☐ Other ID #1 - describe ☐ Personally Known
☐ Passport ☐ Other ID #2 - describe ☐ Credible Witness(es)

Ref. #1

Ref. #2

Right Thumbprint

X SIGN HERE

4

☐ Driver's License ☐ Other ID #1 - describe ☐ Personally Known
☐ Passport ☐ Other ID #2 - describe ☐ Credible Witness(es)

Ref. #1

Ref. #2

Right Thumbprint

X SIGN HERE

5

☐ Driver's License ☐ Other ID #1 - describe ☐ Personally Known
☐ Passport ☐ Other ID #2 - describe ☐ Credible Witness(es)

Ref. #1

Ref. #2

Right Thumbprint

X SIGN HERE

6

☐ Driver's License ☐ Other ID #1 - describe ☐ Personally Known
☐ Passport ☐ Other ID #2 - describe ☐ Credible Witness(es)

Ref. #1

Ref. #2

Right Thumbprint

X SIGN HERE

7

☐ Driver's License ☐ Other ID #1 - describe ☐ Personally Known
☐ Passport ☐ Other ID #2 - describe ☐ Credible Witness(es)

Ref. #1

Ref. #2

Right Thumbprint

X SIGN HERE

8

☐ Driver's License ☐ Other ID #1 - describe ☐ Personally Known
☐ Passport ☐ Other ID #2 - describe ☐ Credible Witness(es)

Ref. #1

Ref. #2

Right Thumbprint

X SIGN HERE

27   Dates and Fees   Description of Document(s) or Proceeding   Additional Information

1

Notarization Date and Time

Date on Document(s)   Reference #

Fees   Paid?

$

A	J	Compliance Agmt.	A	J	E & O	A	J	Proof of ID Aff.	A	J	Adv. Health. Dir.	A	J	SDB Verification
A	J	Correction Agmt.	A	J	Occ. Aff.	A	J	Sig./Name Aff.	A	J	Trust - Irr. / Living	A	J	Vehicle - O+VIN / TT
A	J	DOT / Mortgage	A	J	Own. Aff.	A	J	Survey Aff.	A	J	Will - LWT / Living	A	J	
A	J	Deed - G / QC / W	A	J	POA - L / D	A	J		A	J		A	J	C	Other

2

Notarization Date and Time

Date on Document(s)   Reference #

Fees   Paid?

$

A	J	Compliance Agmt.	A	J	E & O	A	J	Proof of ID Aff.	A	J	Adv. Health. Dir.	A	J	SDB Verification
A	J	Correction Agmt.	A	J	Occ. Aff.	A	J	Sig./Name Aff.	A	J	Trust - Irr. / Living	A	J	Vehicle - O+VIN / TT
A	J	DOT / Mortgage	A	J	Own. Aff.	A	J	Survey Aff.	A	J	Will - LWT / Living	A	J	
A	J	Deed - G / QC / W	A	J	POA - L / D	A	J		A	J		A	J	C	Other

3

Notarization Date and Time

Date on Document(s) Reference #

Fees   Paid?

$

A	J	Compliance Agmt.	A	J	E & O	A	J	Proof of ID Aff.	A	J	Adv. Health. Dir.	A	J	SDB Verification
A	J	Correction Agmt.	A	J	Occ. Aff.	A	J	Sig./Name Aff.	A	J	Trust - Irr. / Living	A	J	Vehicle - O+VIN / TT
A	J	DOT / Mortgage	A	J	Own. Aff.	A	J	Survey Aff.	A	J	Will - LWT / Living	A	J	
A	J	Deed - G / QC / W	A	J	POA - L / D	A	J		A	J		A	J	C	Other

4

Notarization Date and Time

Date on Document(s) Reference #

Fees   Paid?

$

A	J	Compliance Agmt.	A	J	E & O	A	J	Proof of ID Aff.	A	J	Adv. Health. Dir.	A	J	SDB Verification
A	J	Correction Agmt.	A	J	Occ. Aff.	A	J	Sig./Name Aff.	A	J	Trust - Irr. / Living	A	J	Vehicle - O+VIN / TT
A	J	DOT / Mortgage	A	J	Own. Aff.	A	J	Survey Aff.	A	J	Will - LWT / Living	A	J	
A	J	Deed - G / QC / W	A	J	POA - L / D	A	J		A	J		A	J	C	Other

5

Notarization Date and Time

Date on Document(s) Reference #

Fees   Paid?

$

A	J	Compliance Agmt.	A	J	E & O	A	J	Proof of ID Aff.	A	J	Adv. Health. Dir.	A	J	SDB Verification
A	J	Correction Agmt.	A	J	Occ. Aff.	A	J	Sig./Name Aff.	A	J	Trust - Irr. / Living	A	J	Vehicle - O+VIN / TT
A	J	DOT / Mortgage	A	J	Own. Aff.	A	J	Survey Aff.	A	J	Will - LWT / Living	A	J	
A	J	Deed - G / QC / W	A	J	POA - L / D	A	J		A	J		A	J	C	Other

6

Notarization Date and Time

Date on Document(s) Reference #

Fees   Paid?

$

A	J	Compliance Agmt.	A	J	E & O	A	J	Proof of ID Aff.	A	J	Adv. Health. Dir.	A	J	SDB Verification
A	J	Correction Agmt.	A	J	Occ. Aff.	A	J	Sig./Name Aff.	A	J	Trust - Irr. / Living	A	J	Vehicle - O+VIN / TT
A	J	DOT / Mortgage	A	J	Own. Aff.	A	J	Survey Aff.	A	J	Will - LWT / Living	A	J	
A	J	Deed - G / QC / W	A	J	POA - L / D	A	J		A	J		A	J	C	Other

7

Notarization Date and Time

Date on Document(s) Reference #

Fees   Paid?

$

A	J	Compliance Agmt.	A	J	E & O	A	J	Proof of ID Aff.	A	J	Adv. Health. Dir.	A	J	SDB Verification
A	J	Correction Agmt.	A	J	Occ. Aff.	A	J	Sig./Name Aff.	A	J	Trust - Irr. / Living	A	J	Vehicle - O+VIN / TT
A	J	DOT / Mortgage	A	J	Own. Aff.	A	J	Survey Aff.	A	J	Will - LWT / Living	A	J	
A	J	Deed - G / QC / W	A	J	POA - L / D	A	J		A	J		A	J	C	Other

8

Notarization Date and Time

Date on Document(s) Reference #

Fees   Paid?

$

A	J	Compliance Agmt.	A	J	E & O	A	J	Proof of ID Aff.	A	J	Adv. Health. Dir.	A	J	SDB Verification
A	J	Correction Agmt.	A	J	Occ. Aff.	A	J	Sig./Name Aff.	A	J	Trust - Irr. / Living	A	J	Vehicle - O+VIN / TT
A	J	DOT / Mortgage	A	J	Own. Aff.	A	J	Survey Aff.	A	J	Will - LWT / Living	A	J	
A	J	Deed - G / QC / W	A	J	POA - L / D	A	J		A	J		A	J	C	Other

Signer Name and Address	Method of Identification	Signature and Thumbprint	28

Entry 1
- Method of Identification: ☐ Driver's License ☐ Passport ☐ Other ID #1 - describe ☐ Other ID #2 - describe ☐ Personally Known ☐ Credible Witness(es)
- Ref. #1
- Ref. #2
- X SIGN HERE
- Right Thumbprint

Entry 2
- Method of Identification: ☐ Driver's License ☐ Passport ☐ Other ID #1 - describe ☐ Other ID #2 - describe ☐ Personally Known ☐ Credible Witness(es)
- Ref. #1
- Ref. #2
- X SIGN HERE
- Right Thumbprint

Entry 3
- Method of Identification: ☐ Driver's License ☐ Passport ☐ Other ID #1 - describe ☐ Other ID #2 - describe ☐ Personally Known ☐ Credible Witness(es)
- Ref. #1
- Ref. #2
- X SIGN HERE
- Right Thumbprint

Entry 4
- Method of Identification: ☐ Driver's License ☐ Passport ☐ Other ID #1 - describe ☐ Other ID #2 - describe ☐ Personally Known ☐ Credible Witness(es)
- Ref. #1
- Ref. #2
- X SIGN HERE
- Right Thumbprint

Entry 5
- Method of Identification: ☐ Driver's License ☐ Passport ☐ Other ID #1 - describe ☐ Other ID #2 - describe ☐ Personally Known ☐ Credible Witness(es)
- Ref. #1
- Ref. #2
- X SIGN HERE
- Right Thumbprint

Entry 6
- Method of Identification: ☐ Driver's License ☐ Passport ☐ Other ID #1 - describe ☐ Other ID #2 - describe ☐ Personally Known ☐ Credible Witness(es)
- Ref. #1
- Ref. #2
- X SIGN HERE
- Right Thumbprint

Entry 7
- Method of Identification: ☐ Driver's License ☐ Passport ☐ Other ID #1 - describe ☐ Other ID #2 - describe ☐ Personally Known ☐ Credible Witness(es)
- Ref. #1
- Ref. #2
- X SIGN HERE
- Right Thumbprint

Entry 8
- Method of Identification: ☐ Driver's License ☐ Passport ☐ Other ID #1 - describe ☐ Other ID #2 - describe ☐ Personally Known ☐ Credible Witness(es)
- Ref. #1
- Ref. #2
- X SIGN HERE
- Right Thumbprint

| 29 | Dates and Fees | Description of Document(s) or Proceeding | Additional Information |

1

Notarization Date and Time

Date on Document(s) | Reference #

Fees: $ | Paid? ☐

- [A][J] Compliance Agmt.
- [A][J] Correction Agmt.
- [A][J] DOT / Mortgage
- [A][J] Deed - G / QC / W
- [A][J] E & O
- [A][J] Occ. Aff.
- [A][J] Own. Aff.
- [A][J] POA - L / D
- [A][J] Proof of ID Aff.
- [A][J] Sig./Name Aff.
- [A][J] Survey Aff.
- [A][J]
- [A][J] Adv. Health. Dir.
- [A][J] Trust - Irr. / Living
- [A][J] Will - LWT / Living
- [A][J]
- [A][J] SDB Verification
- [A][J] Vehicle - O+VIN / TT
- [A][J]
- [A][J][C] Other ▼

2

Notarization Date and Time

Date on Document(s) | Reference #

Fees: $ | Paid? ☐

- [A][J] Compliance Agmt.
- [A][J] Correction Agmt.
- [A][J] DOT / Mortgage
- [A][J] Deed - G / QC / W
- [A][J] E & O
- [A][J] Occ. Aff.
- [A][J] Own. Aff.
- [A][J] POA - L / D
- [A][J] Proof of ID Aff.
- [A][J] Sig./Name Aff.
- [A][J] Survey Aff.
- [A][J]
- [A][J] Adv. Health. Dir.
- [A][J] Trust - Irr. / Living
- [A][J] Will - LWT / Living
- [A][J]
- [A][J] SDB Verification
- [A][J] Vehicle - O+VIN / TT
- [A][J]
- [A][J][C] Other ▼

3

Notarization Date and Time

Date on Document(s) | Reference #

Fees: $ | Paid? ☐

- [A][J] Compliance Agmt.
- [A][J] Correction Agmt.
- [A][J] DOT / Mortgage
- [A][J] Deed - G / QC / W
- [A][J] E & O
- [A][J] Occ. Aff.
- [A][J] Own. Aff.
- [A][J] POA - L / D
- [A][J] Proof of ID Aff.
- [A][J] Sig./Name Aff.
- [A][J] Survey Aff.
- [A][J]
- [A][J] Adv. Health. Dir.
- [A][J] Trust - Irr. / Living
- [A][J] Will - LWT / Living
- [A][J]
- [A][J] SDB Verification
- [A][J] Vehicle - O+VIN / TT
- [A][J]
- [A][J][C] Other ▼

4

Notarization Date and Time

Date on Document(s) | Reference #

Fees: $ | Paid? ☐

- [A][J] Compliance Agmt.
- [A][J] Correction Agmt.
- [A][J] DOT / Mortgage
- [A][J] Deed - G / QC / W
- [A][J] E & O
- [A][J] Occ. Aff.
- [A][J] Own. Aff.
- [A][J] POA - L / D
- [A][J] Proof of ID Aff.
- [A][J] Sig./Name Aff.
- [A][J] Survey Aff.
- [A][J]
- [A][J] Adv. Health. Dir.
- [A][J] Trust - Irr. / Living
- [A][J] Will - LWT / Living
- [A][J]
- [A][J] SDB Verification
- [A][J] Vehicle - O+VIN / TT
- [A][J]
- [A][J][C] Other ▼

5

Notarization Date and Time

Date on Document(s) | Reference #

Fees: $ | Paid? ☐

- [A][J] Compliance Agmt.
- [A][J] Correction Agmt.
- [A][J] DOT / Mortgage
- [A][J] Deed - G / QC / W
- [A][J] E & O
- [A][J] Occ. Aff.
- [A][J] Own. Aff.
- [A][J] POA - L / D
- [A][J] Proof of ID Aff.
- [A][J] Sig./Name Aff.
- [A][J] Survey Aff.
- [A][J]
- [A][J] Adv. Health. Dir.
- [A][J] Trust - Irr. / Living
- [A][J] Will - LWT / Living
- [A][J]
- [A][J] SDB Verification
- [A][J] Vehicle - O+VIN / TT
- [A][J]
- [A][J][C] Other ▼

6

Notarization Date and Time

Date on Document(s) | Reference #

Fees: $ | Paid? ☐

- [A][J] Compliance Agmt.
- [A][J] Correction Agmt.
- [A][J] DOT / Mortgage
- [A][J] Deed - G / QC / W
- [A][J] E & O
- [A][J] Occ. Aff.
- [A][J] Own. Aff.
- [A][J] POA - L / D
- [A][J] Proof of ID Aff.
- [A][J] Sig./Name Aff.
- [A][J] Survey Aff.
- [A][J]
- [A][J] Adv. Health. Dir.
- [A][J] Trust - Irr. / Living
- [A][J] Will - LWT / Living
- [A][J]
- [A][J] SDB Verification
- [A][J] Vehicle - O+VIN / TT
- [A][J]
- [A][J][C] Other ▼

7

Notarization Date and Time

Date on Document(s) | Reference #

Fees: $ | Paid? ☐

- [A][J] Compliance Agmt.
- [A][J] Correction Agmt.
- [A][J] DOT / Mortgage
- [A][J] Deed - G / QC / W
- [A][J] E & O
- [A][J] Occ. Aff.
- [A][J] Own. Aff.
- [A][J] POA - L / D
- [A][J] Proof of ID Aff.
- [A][J] Sig./Name Aff.
- [A][J] Survey Aff.
- [A][J]
- [A][J] Adv. Health. Dir.
- [A][J] Trust - Irr. / Living
- [A][J] Will - LWT / Living
- [A][J]
- [A][J] SDB Verification
- [A][J] Vehicle - O+VIN / TT
- [A][J]
- [A][J][C] Other ▼

8

Notarization Date and Time

Date on Document(s) | Reference #

Fees: $ | Paid? ☐

- [A][J] Compliance Agmt.
- [A][J] Correction Agmt.
- [A][J] DOT / Mortgage
- [A][J] Deed - G / QC / W
- [A][J] E & O
- [A][J] Occ. Aff.
- [A][J] Own. Aff.
- [A][J] POA - L / D
- [A][J] Proof of ID Aff.
- [A][J] Sig./Name Aff.
- [A][J] Survey Aff.
- [A][J]
- [A][J] Adv. Health. Dir.
- [A][J] Trust - Irr. / Living
- [A][J] Will - LWT / Living
- [A][J]
- [A][J] SDB Verification
- [A][J] Vehicle - O+VIN / TT
- [A][J]
- [A][J][C] Other ▼

Entry 1

- ☐ Driver's License ☐ Other ID #1 - describe ☐ Personally Known
- ☐ Passport ☐ Other ID #2 - describe ☐ Credible Witness(es)

Ref. #1

Ref. #2

X _____ SIGN HERE

Right Thumbprint

Entry 2

- ☐ Driver's License ☐ Other ID #1 - describe ☐ Personally Known
- ☐ Passport ☐ Other ID #2 - describe ☐ Credible Witness(es)

Ref. #1

Ref. #2

X _____ SIGN HERE

Right Thumbprint

Entry 3

- ☐ Driver's License ☐ Other ID #1 - describe ☐ Personally Known
- ☐ Passport ☐ Other ID #2 - describe ☐ Credible Witness(es)

Ref. #1

Ref. #2

X _____ SIGN HERE

Right Thumbprint

Entry 4

- ☐ Driver's License ☐ Other ID #1 - describe ☐ Personally Known
- ☐ Passport ☐ Other ID #2 - describe ☐ Credible Witness(es)

Ref. #1

Ref. #2

X _____ SIGN HERE

Right Thumbprint

Entry 5

- ☐ Driver's License ☐ Other ID #1 - describe ☐ Personally Known
- ☐ Passport ☐ Other ID #2 - describe ☐ Credible Witness(es)

Ref. #1

Ref. #2

X _____ SIGN HERE

Right Thumbprint

Entry 6

- ☐ Driver's License ☐ Other ID #1 - describe ☐ Personally Known
- ☐ Passport ☐ Other ID #2 - describe ☐ Credible Witness(es)

Ref. #1

Ref. #2

X _____ SIGN HERE

Right Thumbprint

Entry 7

- ☐ Driver's License ☐ Other ID #1 - describe ☐ Personally Known
- ☐ Passport ☐ Other ID #2 - describe ☐ Credible Witness(es)

Ref. #1

Ref. #2

X _____ SIGN HERE

Right Thumbprint

Entry 8

- ☐ Driver's License ☐ Other ID #1 - describe ☐ Personally Known
- ☐ Passport ☐ Other ID #2 - describe ☐ Credible Witness(es)

Ref. #1

Ref. #2

X _____ SIGN HERE

Right Thumbprint

1

Notarization Date and Time

Date on Document(s)   Reference #

Fees   Paid?
$

A J Compliance Agmt.	A J E & O	A J Proof of ID Aff.	A J Adv. Health. Dir.	A J SDB Verification
A J Correction Agmt.	A J Occ. Aff.	A J Sig./Name Aff.	A J Trust - Irr. / Living	A J Vehicle - O+VIN / TT
A J DOT / Mortgage	A J Own. Aff.	A J Survey Aff.	A J Will - LWT / Living	A J
A J Deed - G / QC / W	A J POA - L / D	A J	A J	A J C Other ▼

2

Notarization Date and Time

Date on Document(s)   Reference #

Fees   Paid?
$

A J Compliance Agmt.	A J E & O	A J Proof of ID Aff.	A J Adv. Health. Dir.	A J SDB Verification
A J Correction Agmt.	A J Occ. Aff.	A J Sig./Name Aff.	A J Trust - Irr. / Living	A J Vehicle - O+VIN / TT
A J DOT / Mortgage	A J Own. Aff.	A J Survey Aff.	A J Will - LWT / Living	A J
A J Deed - G / QC / W	A J POA - L / D	A J	A J	A J C Other ▼

3

Notarization Date and Time

Date on Document(s)   Reference #

Fees   Paid?
$

A J Compliance Agmt.	A J E & O	A J Proof of ID Aff.	A J Adv. Health. Dir.	A J SDB Verification
A J Correction Agmt.	A J Occ. Aff.	A J Sig./Name Aff.	A J Trust - Irr. / Living	A J Vehicle - O+VIN / TT
A J DOT / Mortgage	A J Own. Aff.	A J Survey Aff.	A J Will - LWT / Living	A J
A J Deed - G / QC / W	A J POA - L / D	A J	A J	A J C Other ▼

4

Notarization Date and Time

Date on Document(s)   Reference #

Fees   Paid?
$

A J Compliance Agmt.	A J E & O	A J Proof of ID Aff.	A J Adv. Health. Dir.	A J SDB Verification
A J Correction Agmt.	A J Occ. Aff.	A J Sig./Name Aff.	A J Trust - Irr. / Living	A J Vehicle - O+VIN / TT
A J DOT / Mortgage	A J Own. Aff.	A J Survey Aff.	A J Will - LWT / Living	A J
A J Deed - G / QC / W	A J POA - L / D	A J	A J	A J C Other ▼

5

Notarization Date and Time

Date on Document(s)   Reference #

Fees   Paid?
$

A J Compliance Agmt.	A J E & O	A J Proof of ID Aff.	A J Adv. Health. Dir.	A J SDB Verification
A J Correction Agmt.	A J Occ. Aff.	A J Sig./Name Aff.	A J Trust - Irr. / Living	A J Vehicle - O+VIN / TT
A J DOT / Mortgage	A J Own. Aff.	A J Survey Aff.	A J Will - LWT / Living	A J
A J Deed - G / QC / W	A J POA - L / D	A J	A J	A J C Other ▼

6

Notarization Date and Time

Date on Document(s)   Reference #

Fees   Paid?
$

A J Compliance Agmt.	A J E & O	A J Proof of ID Aff.	A J Adv. Health. Dir.	A J SDB Verification
A J Correction Agmt.	A J Occ. Aff.	A J Sig./Name Aff.	A J Trust - Irr. / Living	A J Vehicle - O+VIN / TT
A J DOT / Mortgage	A J Own. Aff.	A J Survey Aff.	A J Will - LWT / Living	A J
A J Deed - G / QC / W	A J POA - L / D	A J	A J	A J C Other ▼

7

Notarization Date and Time

Date on Document(s)   Reference #

Fees   Paid?
$

A J Compliance Agmt.	A J E & O	A J Proof of ID Aff.	A J Adv. Health. Dir.	A J SDB Verification
A J Correction Agmt.	A J Occ. Aff.	A J Sig./Name Aff.	A J Trust - Irr. / Living	A J Vehicle - O+VIN / TT
A J DOT / Mortgage	A J Own. Aff.	A J Survey Aff.	A J Will - LWT / Living	A J
A J Deed - G / QC / W	A J POA - L / D	A J	A J	A J C Other ▼

8

Notarization Date and Time

Date on Document(s)   Reference #

Fees   Paid?
$

A J Compliance Agmt.	A J E & O	A J Proof of ID Aff.	A J Adv. Health. Dir.	A J SDB Verification
A J Correction Agmt.	A J Occ. Aff.	A J Sig./Name Aff.	A J Trust - Irr. / Living	A J Vehicle - O+VIN / TT
A J DOT / Mortgage	A J Own. Aff.	A J Survey Aff.	A J Will - LWT / Living	A J
A J Deed - G / QC / W	A J POA - L / D	A J	A J	A J C Other ▼

1

☐ Driver's License ☐ Other ID #1 - describe ☐ Personally Known
☐ Passport ☐ Other ID #2 - describe ☐ Credible Witness(es)

Ref. #1

Ref. #2

x SIGN HERE

Right Thumbprint

2

☐ Driver's License ☐ Other ID #1 - describe ☐ Personally Known
☐ Passport ☐ Other ID #2 - describe ☐ Credible Witness(es)

Ref. #1

Ref. #2

x SIGN HERE

Right Thumbprint

3

☐ Driver's License ☐ Other ID #1 - describe ☐ Personally Known
☐ Passport ☐ Other ID #2 - describe ☐ Credible Witness(es)

Ref. #1

Ref. #2

x SIGN HERE

Right Thumbprint

4

☐ Driver's License ☐ Other ID #1 - describe ☐ Personally Known
☐ Passport ☐ Other ID #2 - describe ☐ Credible Witness(es)

Ref. #1

Ref. #2

x SIGN HERE

Right Thumbprint

5

☐ Driver's License ☐ Other ID #1 - describe ☐ Personally Known
☐ Passport ☐ Other ID #2 - describe ☐ Credible Witness(es)

Ref. #1

Ref. #2

x SIGN HERE

Right Thumbprint

6

☐ Driver's License ☐ Other ID #1 - describe ☐ Personally Known
☐ Passport ☐ Other ID #2 - describe ☐ Credible Witness(es)

Ref. #1

Ref. #2

x SIGN HERE

Right Thumbprint

7

☐ Driver's License ☐ Other ID #1 - describe ☐ Personally Known
☐ Passport ☐ Other ID #2 - describe ☐ Credible Witness(es)

Ref. #1

Ref. #2

x SIGN HERE

Right Thumbprint

8

☐ Driver's License ☐ Other ID #1 - describe ☐ Personally Known
☐ Passport ☐ Other ID #2 - describe ☐ Credible Witness(es)

Ref. #1

Ref. #2

x SIGN HERE

Right Thumbprint

33   Dates and Fees   Description of Document(s) or Proceeding   Additional Information

1

Notarization Date and Time

Date on Document(s) Reference #

Fees   Paid?
$

A J Compliance Agmt.   A J E & O   A J Proof of ID Aff.   A J Adv. Health. Dir.   A J SDB Verification
A J Correction Agmt.   A J Occ. Aff.   A J Sig./Name Aff.   A J Trust - Irr. / Living   A J Vehicle - O+VIN / TT
A J DOT / Mortgage   A J Own. Aff.   A J Survey Aff.   A J Will - LWT / Living   A J
A J Deed - G / QC / W   A J POA - L / D   A J   A J   A J C Other ▼

2

Notarization Date and Time

Date on Document(s) Reference #

Fees   Paid?
$

A J Compliance Agmt.   A J E & O   A J Proof of ID Aff.   A J Adv. Health. Dir.   A J SDB Verification
A J Correction Agmt.   A J Occ. Aff.   A J Sig./Name Aff.   A J Trust - Irr. / Living   A J Vehicle - O+VIN / TT
A J DOT / Mortgage   A J Own. Aff.   A J Survey Aff.   A J Will - LWT / Living   A J
A J Deed - G / QC / W   A J POA - L / D   A J   A J   A J C Other ▼

3

Notarization Date and Time

Date on Document(s) Reference #

Fees   Paid?
$

A J Compliance Agmt.   A J E & O   A J Proof of ID Aff.   A J Adv. Health. Dir.   A J SDB Verification
A J Correction Agmt.   A J Occ. Aff.   A J Sig./Name Aff.   A J Trust - Irr. / Living   A J Vehicle - O+VIN / TT
A J DOT / Mortgage   A J Own. Aff.   A J Survey Aff.   A J Will - LWT / Living   A J
A J Deed - G / QC / W   A J POA - L / D   A J   A J   A J C Other ▼

4

Notarization Date and Time

Date on Document(s) Reference #

Fees   Paid?
$

A J Compliance Agmt.   A J E & O   A J Proof of ID Aff.   A J Adv. Health. Dir.   A J SDB Verification
A J Correction Agmt.   A J Occ. Aff.   A J Sig./Name Aff.   A J Trust - Irr. / Living   A J Vehicle - O+VIN / TT
A J DOT / Mortgage   A J Own. Aff.   A J Survey Aff.   A J Will - LWT / Living   A J
A J Deed - G / QC / W   A J POA - L / D   A J   A J   A J C Other ▼

5

Notarization Date and Time

Date on Document(s) Reference #

Fees   Paid?
$

A J Compliance Agmt.   A J E & O   A J Proof of ID Aff.   A J Adv. Health. Dir.   A J SDB Verification
A J Correction Agmt.   A J Occ. Aff.   A J Sig./Name Aff.   A J Trust - Irr. / Living   A J Vehicle - O+VIN / TT
A J DOT / Mortgage   A J Own. Aff.   A J Survey Aff.   A J Will - LWT / Living   A J
A J Deed - G / QC / W   A J POA - L / D   A J   A J   A J C Other ▼

6

Notarization Date and Time

Date on Document(s) Reference #

Fees   Paid?
$

A J Compliance Agmt.   A J E & O   A J Proof of ID Aff.   A J Adv. Health. Dir.   A J SDB Verification
A J Correction Agmt.   A J Occ. Aff.   A J Sig./Name Aff.   A J Trust - Irr. / Living   A J Vehicle - O+VIN / TT
A J DOT / Mortgage   A J Own. Aff.   A J Survey Aff.   A J Will - LWT / Living   A J
A J Deed - G / QC / W   A J POA - L / D   A J   A J   A J C Other ▼

7

Notarization Date and Time

Date on Document(s) Reference #

Fees   Paid?
$

A J Compliance Agmt.   A J E & O   A J Proof of ID Aff.   A J Adv. Health. Dir.   A J SDB Verification
A J Correction Agmt.   A J Occ. Aff.   A J Sig./Name Aff.   A J Trust - Irr. / Living   A J Vehicle - O+VIN / TT
A J DOT / Mortgage   A J Own. Aff.   A J Survey Aff.   A J Will - LWT / Living   A J
A J Deed - G / QC / W   A J POA - L / D   A J   A J   A J C Other ▼

8

Notarization Date and Time

Date on Document(s) Reference #

Fees   Paid?
$

A J Compliance Agmt.   A J E & O   A J Proof of ID Aff.   A J Adv. Health. Dir.   A J SDB Verification
A J Correction Agmt.   A J Occ. Aff.   A J Sig./Name Aff.   A J Trust - Irr. / Living   A J Vehicle - O+VIN / TT
A J DOT / Mortgage   A J Own. Aff.   A J Survey Aff.   A J Will - LWT / Living   A J
A J Deed - G / QC / W   A J POA - L / D   A J   A J   A J C Other ▼

Signer Name and Address	Method of Identification	Signature and Thumbprint	
	☐ Driver's License ☐ Other ID #1 - describe ☐ Personally Known ☐ Passport ☐ Other ID #2 - describe ☐ Credible Witness(es) Ref. #1 Ref. #2	x _SIGN HERE_	Right Thumbprint **1**
	☐ Driver's License ☐ Other ID #1 - describe ☐ Personally Known ☐ Passport ☐ Other ID #2 - describe ☐ Credible Witness(es) Ref. #1 Ref. #2	x _SIGN HERE_	Right Thumbprint **2**
	☐ Driver's License ☐ Other ID #1 - describe ☐ Personally Known ☐ Passport ☐ Other ID #2 - describe ☐ Credible Witness(es) Ref. #1 Ref. #2	x _SIGN HERE_	Right Thumbprint **3**
	☐ Driver's License ☐ Other ID #1 - describe ☐ Personally Known ☐ Passport ☐ Other ID #2 - describe ☐ Credible Witness(es) Ref. #1 Ref. #2	x _SIGN HERE_	Right Thumbprint **4**
	☐ Driver's License ☐ Other ID #1 - describe ☐ Personally Known ☐ Passport ☐ Other ID #2 - describe ☐ Credible Witness(es) Ref. #1 Ref. #2	x _SIGN HERE_	Right Thumbprint **5**
	☐ Driver's License ☐ Other ID #1 - describe ☐ Personally Known ☐ Passport ☐ Other ID #2 - describe ☐ Credible Witness(es) Ref. #1 Ref. #2	x _SIGN HERE_	Right Thumbprint **6**
	☐ Driver's License ☐ Other ID #1 - describe ☐ Personally Known ☐ Passport ☐ Other ID #2 - describe ☐ Credible Witness(es) Ref. #1 Ref. #2	x _SIGN HERE_	Right Thumbprint **7**
	☐ Driver's License ☐ Other ID #1 - describe ☐ Personally Known ☐ Passport ☐ Other ID #2 - describe ☐ Credible Witness(es) Ref. #1 Ref. #2	x _SIGN HERE_	Right Thumbprint **8**

Entry 1

Notarization Date and Time

Date on Document(s)   Reference #

Fees $ Paid? ☐

A J	Compliance Agmt.	A J	E & O	A J	Proof of ID Aff.	A J	Adv. Health. Dir.	A J	SDB Verification
A J	Correction Agmt.	A J	Occ. Aff.	A J	Sig./Name Aff.	A J	Trust - Irr. / Living	A J	Vehicle - O+VIN / TT
A J	DOT / Mortgage	A J	Own. Aff.	A J	Survey Aff.	A J	Will - LWT / Living	A J	
A J	Deed - G / QC / W	A J	POA - L / D	A J		A J		A J C ☐	Other ▼

Entry 2

Notarization Date and Time

Date on Document(s)   Reference #

Fees $ Paid? ☐

A J	Compliance Agmt.	A J	E & O	A J	Proof of ID Aff.	A J	Adv. Health. Dir.	A J	SDB Verification
A J	Correction Agmt.	A J	Occ. Aff.	A J	Sig./Name Aff.	A J	Trust - Irr. / Living	A J	Vehicle - O+VIN / TT
A J	DOT / Mortgage	A J	Own. Aff.	A J	Survey Aff.	A J	Will - LWT / Living	A J	
A J	Deed - G / QC / W	A J	POA - L / D	A J		A J		A J C ☐	Other ▼

Entry 3

Notarization Date and Time

Date on Document(s)   Reference #

Fees $ Paid? ☐

A J	Compliance Agmt.	A J	E & O	A J	Proof of ID Aff.	A J	Adv. Health. Dir.	A J	SDB Verification
A J	Correction Agmt.	A J	Occ. Aff.	A J	Sig./Name Aff.	A J	Trust - Irr. / Living	A J	Vehicle - O+VIN / TT
A J	DOT / Mortgage	A J	Own. Aff.	A J	Survey Aff.	A J	Will - LWT / Living	A J	
A J	Deed - G / QC / W	A J	POA - L / D	A J		A J		A J C ☐	Other ▼

Entry 4

Notarization Date and Time

Date on Document(s)   Reference #

Fees $ Paid? ☐

A J	Compliance Agmt.	A J	E & O	A J	Proof of ID Aff.	A J	Adv. Health. Dir.	A J	SDB Verification
A J	Correction Agmt.	A J	Occ. Aff.	A J	Sig./Name Aff.	A J	Trust - Irr. / Living	A J	Vehicle - O+VIN / TT
A J	DOT / Mortgage	A J	Own. Aff.	A J	Survey Aff.	A J	Will - LWT / Living	A J	
A J	Deed - G / QC / W	A J	POA - L / D	A J		A J		A J C ☐	Other ▼

Entry 5

Notarization Date and Time

Date on Document(s)   Reference #

Fees $ Paid? ☐

A J	Compliance Agmt.	A J	E & O	A J	Proof of ID Aff.	A J	Adv. Health. Dir.	A J	SDB Verification
A J	Correction Agmt.	A J	Occ. Aff.	A J	Sig./Name Aff.	A J	Trust - Irr. / Living	A J	Vehicle - O+VIN / TT
A J	DOT / Mortgage	A J	Own. Aff.	A J	Survey Aff.	A J	Will - LWT / Living	A J	
A J	Deed - G / QC / W	A J	POA - L / D	A J		A J		A J C ☐	Other ▼

Entry 6

Notarization Date and Time

Date on Document(s)   Reference #

Fees $ Paid? ☐

A J	Compliance Agmt.	A J	E & O	A J	Proof of ID Aff.	A J	Adv. Health. Dir.	A J	SDB Verification
A J	Correction Agmt.	A J	Occ. Aff.	A J	Sig./Name Aff.	A J	Trust - Irr. / Living	A J	Vehicle - O+VIN / TT
A J	DOT / Mortgage	A J	Own. Aff.	A J	Survey Aff.	A J	Will - LWT / Living	A J	
A J	Deed - G / QC / W	A J	POA - L / D	A J		A J		A J C ☐	Other ▼

Entry 7

Notarization Date and Time

Date on Document(s)   Reference #

Fees $ Paid? ☐

A J	Compliance Agmt.	A J	E & O	A J	Proof of ID Aff.	A J	Adv. Health. Dir.	A J	SDB Verification
A J	Correction Agmt.	A J	Occ. Aff.	A J	Sig./Name Aff.	A J	Trust - Irr. / Living	A J	Vehicle - O+VIN / TT
A J	DOT / Mortgage	A J	Own. Aff.	A J	Survey Aff.	A J	Will - LWT / Living	A J	
A J	Deed - G / QC / W	A J	POA - L / D	A J		A J		A J C ☐	Other ▼

Entry 8

Notarization Date and Time

Date on Document(s)   Reference #

Fees $ Paid? ☐

A J	Compliance Agmt.	A J	E & O	A J	Proof of ID Aff.	A J	Adv. Health. Dir.	A J	SDB Verification
A J	Correction Agmt.	A J	Occ. Aff.	A J	Sig./Name Aff.	A J	Trust - Irr. / Living	A J	Vehicle - O+VIN / TT
A J	DOT / Mortgage	A J	Own. Aff.	A J	Survey Aff.	A J	Will - LWT / Living	A J	
A J	Deed - G / QC / W	A J	POA - L / D	A J		A J		A J C ☐	Other ▼

1

- [ ] Driver's License
- [ ] Passport
- [ ] Other ID #1 - describe
- [ ] Other ID #2 - describe
- [ ] Personally Known
- [ ] Credible Witness(es)

Ref. #1

Ref. #2

X SIGN HERE

Right Thumbprint

2

- [ ] Driver's License
- [ ] Passport
- [ ] Other ID #1 - describe
- [ ] Other ID #2 - describe
- [ ] Personally Known
- [ ] Credible Witness(es)

Ref. #1

Ref. #2

X SIGN HERE

Right Thumbprint

3

- [ ] Driver's License
- [ ] Passport
- [ ] Other ID #1 - describe
- [ ] Other ID #2 - describe
- [ ] Personally Known
- [ ] Credible Witness(es)

Ref. #1

Ref. #2

X SIGN HERE

Right Thumbprint

4

- [ ] Driver's License
- [ ] Passport
- [ ] Other ID #1 - describe
- [ ] Other ID #2 - describe
- [ ] Personally Known
- [ ] Credible Witness(es)

Ref. #1

Ref. #2

X SIGN HERE

Right Thumbprint

5

- [ ] Driver's License
- [ ] Passport
- [ ] Other ID #1 - describe
- [ ] Other ID #2 - describe
- [ ] Personally Known
- [ ] Credible Witness(es)

Ref. #1

Ref. #2

X SIGN HERE

Right Thumbprint

6

- [ ] Driver's License
- [ ] Passport
- [ ] Other ID #1 - describe
- [ ] Other ID #2 - describe
- [ ] Personally Known
- [ ] Credible Witness(es)

Ref. #1

Ref. #2

X SIGN HERE

Right Thumbprint

7

- [ ] Driver's License
- [ ] Passport
- [ ] Other ID #1 - describe
- [ ] Other ID #2 - describe
- [ ] Personally Known
- [ ] Credible Witness(es)

Ref. #1

Ref. #2

X SIGN HERE

Right Thumbprint

8

- [ ] Driver's License
- [ ] Passport
- [ ] Other ID #1 - describe
- [ ] Other ID #2 - describe
- [ ] Personally Known
- [ ] Credible Witness(es)

Ref. #1

Ref. #2

X SIGN HERE

Right Thumbprint

1

Notarization Date and Time

Date on Document(s) Reference #

Fees
$
Paid? ☐

A J Compliance Agmt.   A J E & O   A J Proof of ID Aff.   A J Adv. Health. Dir.   A J SDB Verification
A J Correction Agmt.   A J Occ. Aff.   A J Sig./Name Aff.   A J Trust - Irr. / Living   A J Vehicle - O+VIN / TT
A J DOT / Mortgage   A J Own. Aff.   A J Survey Aff.   A J Will - LWT / Living   A J
A J Deed - G / QC / W   A J POA - L / D   A J   A J   A J C ☐ Other ▼

2

Notarization Date and Time

Date on Document(s) Reference #

Fees
$
Paid? ☐

A J Compliance Agmt.   A J E & O   A J Proof of ID Aff.   A J Adv. Health. Dir.   A J SDB Verification
A J Correction Agmt.   A J Occ. Aff.   A J Sig./Name Aff.   A J Trust - Irr. / Living   A J Vehicle - O+VIN / TT
A J DOT / Mortgage   A J Own. Aff.   A J Survey Aff.   A J Will - LWT / Living   A J
A J Deed - G / QC / W   A J POA - L / D   A J   A J   A J C ☐ Other ▼

3

Notarization Date and Time

Date on Document(s) Reference #

Fees
$
Paid? ☐

A J Compliance Agmt.   A J E & O   A J Proof of ID Aff.   A J Adv. Health. Dir.   A J SDB Verification
A J Correction Agmt.   A J Occ. Aff.   A J Sig./Name Aff.   A J Trust - Irr. / Living   A J Vehicle - O+VIN / TT
A J DOT / Mortgage   A J Own. Aff.   A J Survey Aff.   A J Will - LWT / Living   A J
A J Deed - G / QC / W   A J POA - L / D   A J   A J   A J C ☐ Other ▼

4

Notarization Date and Time

Date on Document(s) Reference #

Fees
$
Paid? ☐

A J Compliance Agmt.   A J E & O   A J Proof of ID Aff.   A J Adv. Health. Dir.   A J SDB Verification
A J Correction Agmt.   A J Occ. Aff.   A J Sig./Name Aff.   A J Trust - Irr. / Living   A J Vehicle - O+VIN / TT
A J DOT / Mortgage   A J Own. Aff.   A J Survey Aff.   A J Will - LWT / Living   A J
A J Deed - G / QC / W   A J POA - L / D   A J   A J   A J C ☐ Other ▼

5

Notarization Date and Time

Date on Document(s) Reference #

Fees
$
Paid? ☐

A J Compliance Agmt.   A J E & O   A J Proof of ID Aff.   A J Adv. Health. Dir.   A J SDB Verification
A J Correction Agmt.   A J Occ. Aff.   A J Sig./Name Aff.   A J Trust - Irr. / Living   A J Vehicle - O+VIN / TT
A J DOT / Mortgage   A J Own. Aff.   A J Survey Aff.   A J Will - LWT / Living   A J
A J Deed - G / QC / W   A J POA - L / D   A J   A J   A J C ☐ Other ▼

6

Notarization Date and Time

Date on Document(s) Reference #

Fees
$
Paid? ☐

A J Compliance Agmt.   A J E & O   A J Proof of ID Aff.   A J Adv. Health. Dir.   A J SDB Verification
A J Correction Agmt.   A J Occ. Aff.   A J Sig./Name Aff.   A J Trust - Irr. / Living   A J Vehicle - O+VIN / TT
A J DOT / Mortgage   A J Own. Aff.   A J Survey Aff.   A J Will - LWT / Living   A J
A J Deed - G / QC / W   A J POA - L / D   A J   A J   A J C ☐ Other ▼

7

Notarization Date and Time

Date on Document(s) Reference #

Fees
$
Paid? ☐

A J Compliance Agmt.   A J E & O   A J Proof of ID Aff.   A J Adv. Health. Dir.   A J SDB Verification
A J Correction Agmt.   A J Occ. Aff.   A J Sig./Name Aff.   A J Trust - Irr. / Living   A J Vehicle - O+VIN / TT
A J DOT / Mortgage   A J Own. Aff.   A J Survey Aff.   A J Will - LWT / Living   A J
A J Deed - G / QC / W   A J POA - L / D   A J   A J   A J C ☐ Other ▼

8

Notarization Date and Time

Date on Document(s) Reference #

Fees
$
Paid? ☐

A J Compliance Agmt.   A J E & O   A J Proof of ID Aff.   A J Adv. Health. Dir.   A J SDB Verification
A J Correction Agmt.   A J Occ. Aff.   A J Sig./Name Aff.   A J Trust - Irr. / Living   A J Vehicle - O+VIN / TT
A J DOT / Mortgage   A J Own. Aff.   A J Survey Aff.   A J Will - LWT / Living   A J
A J Deed - G / QC / W   A J POA - L / D   A J   A J   A J C ☐ Other ▼

1

Signer Name and Address:

Method of Identification:
- [ ] Driver's License
- [ ] Passport
- [ ] Other ID #1 - describe
- [ ] Other ID #2 - describe
- [ ] Personally Known
- [ ] Credible Witness(es)

Ref. #1

Ref. #2

X _____ SIGN HERE

Right Thumbprint

2

Method of Identification:
- [ ] Driver's License
- [ ] Passport
- [ ] Other ID #1 - describe
- [ ] Other ID #2 - describe
- [ ] Personally Known
- [ ] Credible Witness(es)

Ref. #1

Ref. #2

X _____ SIGN HERE

Right Thumbprint

3

Method of Identification:
- [ ] Driver's License
- [ ] Passport
- [ ] Other ID #1 - describe
- [ ] Other ID #2 - describe
- [ ] Personally Known
- [ ] Credible Witness(es)

Ref. #1

Ref. #2

X _____ SIGN HERE

Right Thumbprint

4

Method of Identification:
- [ ] Driver's License
- [ ] Passport
- [ ] Other ID #1 - describe
- [ ] Other ID #2 - describe
- [ ] Personally Known
- [ ] Credible Witness(es)

Ref. #1

Ref. #2

X _____ SIGN HERE

Right Thumbprint

5

Method of Identification:
- [ ] Driver's License
- [ ] Passport
- [ ] Other ID #1 - describe
- [ ] Other ID #2 - describe
- [ ] Personally Known
- [ ] Credible Witness(es)

Ref. #1

Ref. #2

X _____ SIGN HERE

Right Thumbprint

6

Method of Identification:
- [ ] Driver's License
- [ ] Passport
- [ ] Other ID #1 - describe
- [ ] Other ID #2 - describe
- [ ] Personally Known
- [ ] Credible Witness(es)

Ref. #1

Ref. #2

X _____ SIGN HERE

Right Thumbprint

7

Method of Identification:
- [ ] Driver's License
- [ ] Passport
- [ ] Other ID #1 - describe
- [ ] Other ID #2 - describe
- [ ] Personally Known
- [ ] Credible Witness(es)

Ref. #1

Ref. #2

X _____ SIGN HERE

Right Thumbprint

8

Method of Identification:
- [ ] Driver's License
- [ ] Passport
- [ ] Other ID #1 - describe
- [ ] Other ID #2 - describe
- [ ] Personally Known
- [ ] Credible Witness(es)

Ref. #1

Ref. #2

X _____ SIGN HERE

Right Thumbprint

1

Notarization Date and Time

Date on Document(s)   Reference #

Fees $ Paid? ☐

A J	Compliance Agmt.	A J	E & O	A J	Proof of ID Aff.	A J	Adv. Health. Dir.	A J	SDB Verification
A J	Correction Agmt.	A J	Occ. Aff.	A J	Sig./Name Aff.	A J	Trust - Irr. / Living	A J	Vehicle - O+VIN / TT
A J	DOT / Mortgage	A J	Own. Aff.	A J	Survey Aff.	A J	Will - LWT / Living	A J	
A J	Deed - G / QC / W	A J	POA - L / D	A J		A J		A J C ☐	Other ▼

2

Notarization Date and Time

Date on Document(s)   Reference #

Fees $ Paid? ☐

A J	Compliance Agmt.	A J	E & O	A J	Proof of ID Aff.	A J	Adv. Health. Dir.	A J	SDB Verification
A J	Correction Agmt.	A J	Occ. Aff.	A J	Sig./Name Aff.	A J	Trust - Irr. / Living	A J	Vehicle - O+VIN / TT
A J	DOT / Mortgage	A J	Own. Aff.	A J	Survey Aff.	A J	Will - LWT / Living	A J	
A J	Deed - G / QC / W	A J	POA - L / D	A J		A J		A J C ☐	Other ▼

3

Notarization Date and Time

Date on Document(s)   Reference #

Fees $ Paid? ☐

A J	Compliance Agmt.	A J	E & O	A J	Proof of ID Aff.	A J	Adv. Health. Dir.	A J	SDB Verification
A J	Correction Agmt.	A J	Occ. Aff.	A J	Sig./Name Aff.	A J	Trust - Irr. / Living	A J	Vehicle - O+VIN / TT
A J	DOT / Mortgage	A J	Own. Aff.	A J	Survey Aff.	A J	Will - LWT / Living	A J	
A J	Deed - G / QC / W	A J	POA - L / D	A J		A J		A J C ☐	Other ▼

4

Notarization Date and Time

Date on Document(s)   Reference #

Fees $ Paid? ☐

A J	Compliance Agmt.	A J	E & O	A J	Proof of ID Aff.	A J	Adv. Health. Dir.	A J	SDB Verification
A J	Correction Agmt.	A J	Occ. Aff.	A J	Sig./Name Aff.	A J	Trust - Irr. / Living	A J	Vehicle - O+VIN / TT
A J	DOT / Mortgage	A J	Own. Aff.	A J	Survey Aff.	A J	Will - LWT / Living	A J	
A J	Deed - G / QC / W	A J	POA - L / D	A J		A J		A J C ☐	Other ▼

5

Notarization Date and Time

Date on Document(s)   Reference #

Fees $ Paid? ☐

A J	Compliance Agmt.	A J	E & O	A J	Proof of ID Aff.	A J	Adv. Health. Dir.	A J	SDB Verification
A J	Correction Agmt.	A J	Occ. Aff.	A J	Sig./Name Aff.	A J	Trust - Irr. / Living	A J	Vehicle - O+VIN / TT
A J	DOT / Mortgage	A J	Own. Aff.	A J	Survey Aff.	A J	Will - LWT / Living	A J	
A J	Deed - G / QC / W	A J	POA - L / D	A J		A J		A J C ☐	Other ▼

6

Notarization Date and Time

Date on Document(s)   Reference #

Fees $ Paid? ☐

A J	Compliance Agmt.	A J	E & O	A J	Proof of ID Aff.	A J	Adv. Health. Dir.	A J	SDB Verification
A J	Correction Agmt.	A J	Occ. Aff.	A J	Sig./Name Aff.	A J	Trust - Irr. / Living	A J	Vehicle - O+VIN / TT
A J	DOT / Mortgage	A J	Own. Aff.	A J	Survey Aff.	A J	Will - LWT / Living	A J	
A J	Deed - G / QC / W	A J	POA - L / D	A J		A J		A J C ☐	Other ▼

7

Notarization Date and Time

Date on Document(s)   Reference #

Fees $ Paid? ☐

A J	Compliance Agmt.	A J	E & O	A J	Proof of ID Aff.	A J	Adv. Health. Dir.	A J	SDB Verification
A J	Correction Agmt.	A J	Occ. Aff.	A J	Sig./Name Aff.	A J	Trust - Irr. / Living	A J	Vehicle - O+VIN / TT
A J	DOT / Mortgage	A J	Own. Aff.	A J	Survey Aff.	A J	Will - LWT / Living	A J	
A J	Deed - G / QC / W	A J	POA - L / D	A J		A J		A J C ☐	Other ▼

8

Notarization Date and Time

Date on Document(s)   Reference #

Fees $ Paid? ☐

A J	Compliance Agmt.	A J	E & O	A J	Proof of ID Aff.	A J	Adv. Health. Dir.	A J	SDB Verification
A J	Correction Agmt.	A J	Occ. Aff.	A J	Sig./Name Aff.	A J	Trust - Irr. / Living	A J	Vehicle - O+VIN / TT
A J	DOT / Mortgage	A J	Own. Aff.	A J	Survey Aff.	A J	Will - LWT / Living	A J	
A J	Deed - G / QC / W	A J	POA - L / D	A J		A J		A J C ☐	Other ▼

1

- [ ] Driver's License
- [ ] Passport
- [ ] Other ID #1 - describe
- [ ] Other ID #2 - describe
- [ ] Personally Known
- [ ] Credible Witness(es)

Ref. #1

Ref. #2

x SIGN HERE

Right Thumbprint

2

- [ ] Driver's License
- [ ] Passport
- [ ] Other ID #1 - describe
- [ ] Other ID #2 - describe
- [ ] Personally Known
- [ ] Credible Witness(es)

Ref. #1

Ref. #2

x SIGN HERE

Right Thumbprint

3

- [ ] Driver's License
- [ ] Passport
- [ ] Other ID #1 - describe
- [ ] Other ID #2 - describe
- [ ] Personally Known
- [ ] Credible Witness(es)

Ref. #1

Ref. #2

x SIGN HERE

Right Thumbprint

4

- [ ] Driver's License
- [ ] Passport
- [ ] Other ID #1 - describe
- [ ] Other ID #2 - describe
- [ ] Personally Known
- [ ] Credible Witness(es)

Ref. #1

Ref. #2

x SIGN HERE

Right Thumbprint

5

- [ ] Driver's License
- [ ] Passport
- [ ] Other ID #1 - describe
- [ ] Other ID #2 - describe
- [ ] Personally Known
- [ ] Credible Witness(es)

Ref. #1

Ref. #2

x SIGN HERE

Right Thumbprint

6

- [ ] Driver's License
- [ ] Passport
- [ ] Other ID #1 - describe
- [ ] Other ID #2 - describe
- [ ] Personally Known
- [ ] Credible Witness(es)

Ref. #1

Ref. #2

x SIGN HERE

Right Thumbprint

7

- [ ] Driver's License
- [ ] Passport
- [ ] Other ID #1 - describe
- [ ] Other ID #2 - describe
- [ ] Personally Known
- [ ] Credible Witness(es)

Ref. #1

Ref. #2

x SIGN HERE

Right Thumbprint

8

- [ ] Driver's License
- [ ] Passport
- [ ] Other ID #1 - describe
- [ ] Other ID #2 - describe
- [ ] Personally Known
- [ ] Credible Witness(es)

Ref. #1

Ref. #2

x SIGN HERE

Right Thumbprint

1

Notarization Date and Time

Date on Document(s)   Reference #

Fees   Paid?
$

A J	Compliance Agmt.	A J	E & O	A J	Proof of ID Aff.	A J	Adv. Health. Dir.	A J	SDB Verification
A J	Correction Agmt.	A J	Occ. Aff.	A J	Sig./Name Aff.	A J	Trust - Irr. / Living	A J	Vehicle - O+VIN / TT
A J	DOT / Mortgage	A J	Own. Aff.	A J	Survey Aff.	A J	Will - LWT / Living	A J	
A J	Deed - G / QC / W	A J	POA - L / D	A J		A J		A J C	Other ▼

2

Notarization Date and Time

Date on Document(s)   Reference #

Fees   Paid?
$

A J	Compliance Agmt.	A J	E & O	A J	Proof of ID Aff.	A J	Adv. Health. Dir.	A J	SDB Verification
A J	Correction Agmt.	A J	Occ. Aff.	A J	Sig./Name Aff.	A J	Trust - Irr. / Living	A J	Vehicle - O+VIN / TT
A J	DOT / Mortgage	A J	Own. Aff.	A J	Survey Aff.	A J	Will - LWT / Living	A J	
A J	Deed - G / QC / W	A J	POA - L / D	A J		A J		A J C	Other ▼

3

Notarization Date and Time

Date on Document(s)   Reference #

Fees   Paid?
$

A J	Compliance Agmt.	A J	E & O	A J	Proof of ID Aff.	A J	Adv. Health. Dir.	A J	SDB Verification
A J	Correction Agmt.	A J	Occ. Aff.	A J	Sig./Name Aff.	A J	Trust - Irr. / Living	A J	Vehicle - O+VIN / TT
A J	DOT / Mortgage	A J	Own. Aff.	A J	Survey Aff.	A J	Will - LWT / Living	A J	
A J	Deed - G / QC / W	A J	POA - L / D	A J		A J		A J C	Other ▼

4

Notarization Date and Time

Date on Document(s)   Reference #

Fees   Paid?
$

A J	Compliance Agmt.	A J	E & O	A J	Proof of ID Aff.	A J	Adv. Health. Dir.	A J	SDB Verification
A J	Correction Agmt.	A J	Occ. Aff.	A J	Sig./Name Aff.	A J	Trust - Irr. / Living	A J	Vehicle - O+VIN / TT
A J	DOT / Mortgage	A J	Own. Aff.	A J	Survey Aff.	A J	Will - LWT / Living	A J	
A J	Deed - G / QC / W	A J	POA - L / D	A J		A J		A J C	Other ▼

5

Notarization Date and Time

Date on Document(s)   Reference #

Fees   Paid?
$

A J	Compliance Agmt.	A J	E & O	A J	Proof of ID Aff.	A J	Adv. Health. Dir.	A J	SDB Verification
A J	Correction Agmt.	A J	Occ. Aff.	A J	Sig./Name Aff.	A J	Trust - Irr. / Living	A J	Vehicle - O+VIN / TT
A J	DOT / Mortgage	A J	Own. Aff.	A J	Survey Aff.	A J	Will - LWT / Living	A J	
A J	Deed - G / QC / W	A J	POA - L / D	A J		A J		A J C	Other ▼

6

Notarization Date and Time

Date on Document(s)   Reference #

Fees   Paid?
$

A J	Compliance Agmt.	A J	E & O	A J	Proof of ID Aff.	A J	Adv. Health. Dir.	A J	SDB Verification
A J	Correction Agmt.	A J	Occ. Aff.	A J	Sig./Name Aff.	A J	Trust - Irr. / Living	A J	Vehicle - O+VIN / TT
A J	DOT / Mortgage	A J	Own. Aff.	A J	Survey Aff.	A J	Will - LWT / Living	A J	
A J	Deed - G / QC / W	A J	POA - L / D	A J		A J		A J C	Other ▼

7

Notarization Date and Time

Date on Document(s)   Reference #

Fees   Paid?
$

A J	Compliance Agmt.	A J	E & O	A J	Proof of ID Aff.	A J	Adv. Health. Dir.	A J	SDB Verification
A J	Correction Agmt.	A J	Occ. Aff.	A J	Sig./Name Aff.	A J	Trust - Irr. / Living	A J	Vehicle - O+VIN / TT
A J	DOT / Mortgage	A J	Own. Aff.	A J	Survey Aff.	A J	Will - LWT / Living	A J	
A J	Deed - G / QC / W	A J	POA - L / D	A J		A J		A J C	Other ▼

8

Notarization Date and Time

Date on Document(s)   Reference #

Fees   Paid?
$

A J	Compliance Agmt.	A J	E & O	A J	Proof of ID Aff.	A J	Adv. Health. Dir.	A J	SDB Verification
A J	Correction Agmt.	A J	Occ. Aff.	A J	Sig./Name Aff.	A J	Trust - Irr. / Living	A J	Vehicle - O+VIN / TT
A J	DOT / Mortgage	A J	Own. Aff.	A J	Survey Aff.	A J	Will - LWT / Living	A J	
A J	Deed - G / QC / W	A J	POA - L / D	A J		A J		A J C	Other ▼

1

Driver's License ☐   Other ID #1 - describe ☐   Personally Known ☐
Passport ☐   Other ID #2 - describe ☐   Credible Witness(es) ☐

Ref. #1

Ref. #2

Right Thumbprint

X SIGN HERE

2

Driver's License ☐   Other ID #1 - describe ☐   Personally Known ☐
Passport ☐   Other ID #2 - describe ☐   Credible Witness(es) ☐

Ref. #1

Ref. #2

Right Thumbprint

X SIGN HERE

3

Driver's License ☐   Other ID #1 - describe ☐   Personally Known ☐
Passport ☐   Other ID #2 - describe ☐   Credible Witness(es) ☐

Ref. #1

Ref. #2

Right Thumbprint

X SIGN HERE

4

Driver's License ☐   Other ID #1 - describe ☐   Personally Known ☐
Passport ☐   Other ID #2 - describe ☐   Credible Witness(es) ☐

Ref. #1

Ref. #2

Right Thumbprint

X SIGN HERE

5

Driver's License ☐   Other ID #1 - describe ☐   Personally Known ☐
Passport ☐   Other ID #2 - describe ☐   Credible Witness(es) ☐

Ref. #1

Ref. #2

Right Thumbprint

X SIGN HERE

6

Driver's License ☐   Other ID #1 - describe ☐   Personally Known ☐
Passport ☐   Other ID #2 - describe ☐   Credible Witness(es) ☐

Ref. #1

Ref. #2

Right Thumbprint

X SIGN HERE

7

Driver's License ☐   Other ID #1 - describe ☐   Personally Known ☐
Passport ☐   Other ID #2 - describe ☐   Credible Witness(es) ☐

Ref. #1

Ref. #2

Right Thumbprint

X SIGN HERE

8

Driver's License ☐   Other ID #1 - describe ☐   Personally Known ☐
Passport ☐   Other ID #2 - describe ☐   Credible Witness(es) ☐

Ref. #1

Ref. #2

Right Thumbprint

X SIGN HERE

1

Notarization Date and Time

Date on Document(s)   **Reference #**

Fees   **Paid?**
$

A	J	Compliance Agmt.	A	J	E & O	A	J	Proof of ID Aff.	A	J	Adv. Health. Dir.	A	J	SDB Verification
A	J	Correction Agmt.	A	J	Occ. Aff.	A	J	Sig./Name Aff.	A	J	Trust - Irr. / Living	A	J	Vehicle - O+VIN / TT
A	J	DOT / Mortgage	A	J	Own. Aff.	A	J	Survey Aff.	A	J	Will - LWT / Living	A	J	
A	J	Deed - G / QC / W	A	J	POA - L / D	A	J		A	J		A	J	C	Other

2

Notarization Date and Time

Date on Document(s)   **Reference #**

Fees   **Paid?**
$

A	J	Compliance Agmt.	A	J	E & O	A	J	Proof of ID Aff.	A	J	Adv. Health. Dir.	A	J	SDB Verification
A	J	Correction Agmt.	A	J	Occ. Aff.	A	J	Sig./Name Aff.	A	J	Trust - Irr. / Living	A	J	Vehicle - O+VIN / TT
A	J	DOT / Mortgage	A	J	Own. Aff.	A	J	Survey Aff.	A	J	Will - LWT / Living	A	J	
A	J	Deed - G / QC / W	A	J	POA - L / D	A	J		A	J		A	J	C	Other

3

Notarization Date and Time

Date on Document(s)   **Reference #**

Fees   **Paid?**
$

A	J	Compliance Agmt.	A	J	E & O	A	J	Proof of ID Aff.	A	J	Adv. Health. Dir.	A	J	SDB Verification
A	J	Correction Agmt.	A	J	Occ. Aff.	A	J	Sig./Name Aff.	A	J	Trust - Irr. / Living	A	J	Vehicle - O+VIN / TT
A	J	DOT / Mortgage	A	J	Own. Aff.	A	J	Survey Aff.	A	J	Will - LWT / Living	A	J	
A	J	Deed - G / QC / W	A	J	POA - L / D	A	J		A	J		A	J	C	Other

4

Notarization Date and Time

Date on Document(s)   **Reference #**

Fees   **Paid?**
$

A	J	Compliance Agmt.	A	J	E & O	A	J	Proof of ID Aff.	A	J	Adv. Health. Dir.	A	J	SDB Verification
A	J	Correction Agmt.	A	J	Occ. Aff.	A	J	Sig./Name Aff.	A	J	Trust - Irr. / Living	A	J	Vehicle - O+VIN / TT
A	J	DOT / Mortgage	A	J	Own. Aff.	A	J	Survey Aff.	A	J	Will - LWT / Living	A	J	
A	J	Deed - G / QC / W	A	J	POA - L / D	A	J		A	J		A	J	C	Other

5

Notarization Date and Time

Date on Document(s)   **Reference #**

Fees   **Paid?**
$

A	J	Compliance Agmt.	A	J	E & O	A	J	Proof of ID Aff.	A	J	Adv. Health. Dir.	A	J	SDB Verification
A	J	Correction Agmt.	A	J	Occ. Aff.	A	J	Sig./Name Aff.	A	J	Trust - Irr. / Living	A	J	Vehicle - O+VIN / TT
A	J	DOT / Mortgage	A	J	Own. Aff.	A	J	Survey Aff.	A	J	Will - LWT / Living	A	J	
A	J	Deed - G / QC / W	A	J	POA - L / D	A	J		A	J		A	J	C	Other

6

Notarization Date and Time

Date on Document(s)   **Reference #**

Fees   **Paid?**
$

A	J	Compliance Agmt.	A	J	E & O	A	J	Proof of ID Aff.	A	J	Adv. Health. Dir.	A	J	SDB Verification
A	J	Correction Agmt.	A	J	Occ. Aff.	A	J	Sig./Name Aff.	A	J	Trust - Irr. / Living	A	J	Vehicle - O+VIN / TT
A	J	DOT / Mortgage	A	J	Own. Aff.	A	J	Survey Aff.	A	J	Will - LWT / Living	A	J	
A	J	Deed - G / QC / W	A	J	POA - L / D	A	J		A	J		A	J	C	Other

7

Notarization Date and Time

Date on Document(s)   **Reference #**

Fees   **Paid?**
$

A	J	Compliance Agmt.	A	J	E & O	A	J	Proof of ID Aff.	A	J	Adv. Health. Dir.	A	J	SDB Verification
A	J	Correction Agmt.	A	J	Occ. Aff.	A	J	Sig./Name Aff.	A	J	Trust - Irr. / Living	A	J	Vehicle - O+VIN / TT
A	J	DOT / Mortgage	A	J	Own. Aff.	A	J	Survey Aff.	A	J	Will - LWT / Living	A	J	
A	J	Deed - G / QC / W	A	J	POA - L / D	A	J		A	J		A	J	C	Other

8

Notarization Date and Time

Date on Document(s)   **Reference #**

Fees   **Paid?**
$

A	J	Compliance Agmt.	A	J	E & O	A	J	Proof of ID Aff.	A	J	Adv. Health. Dir.	A	J	SDB Verification
A	J	Correction Agmt.	A	J	Occ. Aff.	A	J	Sig./Name Aff.	A	J	Trust - Irr. / Living	A	J	Vehicle - O+VIN / TT
A	J	DOT / Mortgage	A	J	Own. Aff.	A	J	Survey Aff.	A	J	Will - LWT / Living	A	J	
A	J	Deed - G / QC / W	A	J	POA - L / D	A	J		A	J		A	J	C	Other

1

☐ Driver's License ☐ Other ID #1 - describe ☐ Personally Known
☐ Passport ☐ Other ID #2 - describe ☐ Credible Witness(es)

Ref. #1

Ref. #2

X SIGN HERE

Right Thumbprint

2

☐ Driver's License ☐ Other ID #1 - describe ☐ Personally Known
☐ Passport ☐ Other ID #2 - describe ☐ Credible Witness(es)

Ref. #1

Ref. #2

X SIGN HERE

Right Thumbprint

3

☐ Driver's License ☐ Other ID #1 - describe ☐ Personally Known
☐ Passport ☐ Other ID #2 - describe ☐ Credible Witness(es)

Ref. #1

Ref. #2

X SIGN HERE

Right Thumbprint

4

☐ Driver's License ☐ Other ID #1 - describe ☐ Personally Known
☐ Passport ☐ Other ID #2 - describe ☐ Credible Witness(es)

Ref. #1

Ref. #2

X SIGN HERE

Right Thumbprint

5

☐ Driver's License ☐ Other ID #1 - describe ☐ Personally Known
☐ Passport ☐ Other ID #2 - describe ☐ Credible Witness(es)

Ref. #1

Ref. #2

X SIGN HERE

Right Thumbprint

6

☐ Driver's License ☐ Other ID #1 - describe ☐ Personally Known
☐ Passport ☐ Other ID #2 - describe ☐ Credible Witness(es)

Ref. #1

Ref. #2

X SIGN HERE

Right Thumbprint

7

☐ Driver's License ☐ Other ID #1 - describe ☐ Personally Known
☐ Passport ☐ Other ID #2 - describe ☐ Credible Witness(es)

Ref. #1

Ref. #2

X SIGN HERE

Right Thumbprint

8

☐ Driver's License ☐ Other ID #1 - describe ☐ Personally Known
☐ Passport ☐ Other ID #2 - describe ☐ Credible Witness(es)

Ref. #1

Ref. #2

X SIGN HERE

Right Thumbprint

Entry 1

Dates and Fees:
- Notarization Date and Time
- Date on Document(s) — Reference #
- Fees: $ — Paid? ☐

Description of Document(s) or Proceeding:

A J	Compliance Agmt.	A J E & O	A J Proof of ID Aff.	A J Adv. Health. Dir.	A J SDB Verification
A J	Correction Agmt.	A J Occ. Aff.	A J Sig./Name Aff.	A J Trust - Irr. / Living	A J Vehicle - O+VIN / TT
A J	DOT / Mortgage	A J Own. Aff.	A J Survey Aff.	A J Will - LWT / Living	A J
A J	Deed - G / QC / W	A J POA - L / D	A J	A J	A J C☐ Other ▼

Additional Information

Entry 2

Dates and Fees:
- Notarization Date and Time
- Date on Document(s) — Reference #
- Fees: $ — Paid? ☐

A J	Compliance Agmt.	A J E & O	A J Proof of ID Aff.	A J Adv. Health. Dir.	A J SDB Verification
A J	Correction Agmt.	A J Occ. Aff.	A J Sig./Name Aff.	A J Trust - Irr. / Living	A J Vehicle - O+VIN / TT
A J	DOT / Mortgage	A J Own. Aff.	A J Survey Aff.	A J Will - LWT / Living	A J
A J	Deed - G / QC / W	A J POA - L / D	A J	A J	A J C☐ Other ▼

Additional Information

Entry 3

Dates and Fees:
- Notarization Date and Time
- Date on Document(s) — Reference #
- Fees: $ — Paid? ☐

A J	Compliance Agmt.	A J E & O	A J Proof of ID Aff.	A J Adv. Health. Dir.	A J SDB Verification
A J	Correction Agmt.	A J Occ. Aff.	A J Sig./Name Aff.	A J Trust - Irr. / Living	A J Vehicle - O+VIN / TT
A J	DOT / Mortgage	A J Own. Aff.	A J Survey Aff.	A J Will - LWT / Living	A J
A J	Deed - G / QC / W	A J POA - L / D	A J	A J	A J C☐ Other ▼

Additional Information

Entry 4

Dates and Fees:
- Notarization Date and Time
- Date on Document(s) — Reference #
- Fees: $ — Paid? ☐

A J	Compliance Agmt.	A J E & O	A J Proof of ID Aff.	A J Adv. Health. Dir.	A J SDB Verification
A J	Correction Agmt.	A J Occ. Aff.	A J Sig./Name Aff.	A J Trust - Irr. / Living	A J Vehicle - O+VIN / TT
A J	DOT / Mortgage	A J Own. Aff.	A J Survey Aff.	A J Will - LWT / Living	A J
A J	Deed - G / QC / W	A J POA - L / D	A J	A J	A J C☐ Other ▼

Additional Information

Entry 5

Dates and Fees:
- Notarization Date and Time
- Date on Document(s) — Reference #
- Fees: $ — Paid? ☐

A J	Compliance Agmt.	A J E & O	A J Proof of ID Aff.	A J Adv. Health. Dir.	A J SDB Verification
A J	Correction Agmt.	A J Occ. Aff.	A J Sig./Name Aff.	A J Trust - Irr. / Living	A J Vehicle - O+VIN / TT
A J	DOT / Mortgage	A J Own. Aff.	A J Survey Aff.	A J Will - LWT / Living	A J
A J	Deed - G / QC / W	A J POA - L / D	A J	A J	A J C☐ Other ▼

Additional Information

Entry 6

Dates and Fees:
- Notarization Date and Time
- Date on Document(s) — Reference #
- Fees: $ — Paid? ☐

A J	Compliance Agmt.	A J E & O	A J Proof of ID Aff.	A J Adv. Health. Dir.	A J SDB Verification
A J	Correction Agmt.	A J Occ. Aff.	A J Sig./Name Aff.	A J Trust - Irr. / Living	A J Vehicle - O+VIN / TT
A J	DOT / Mortgage	A J Own. Aff.	A J Survey Aff.	A J Will - LWT / Living	A J
A J	Deed - G / QC / W	A J POA - L / D	A J	A J	A J C☐ Other ▼

Additional Information

Entry 7

Dates and Fees:
- Notarization Date and Time
- Date on Document(s) — Reference #
- Fees: $ — Paid? ☐

A J	Compliance Agmt.	A J E & O	A J Proof of ID Aff.	A J Adv. Health. Dir.	A J SDB Verification
A J	Correction Agmt.	A J Occ. Aff.	A J Sig./Name Aff.	A J Trust - Irr. / Living	A J Vehicle - O+VIN / TT
A J	DOT / Mortgage	A J Own. Aff.	A J Survey Aff.	A J Will - LWT / Living	A J
A J	Deed - G / QC / W	A J POA - L / D	A J	A J	A J C☐ Other ▼

Additional Information

Entry 8

Dates and Fees:
- Notarization Date and Time
- Date on Document(s) — Reference #
- Fees: $ — Paid? ☐

A J	Compliance Agmt.	A J E & O	A J Proof of ID Aff.	A J Adv. Health. Dir.	A J SDB Verification
A J	Correction Agmt.	A J Occ. Aff.	A J Sig./Name Aff.	A J Trust - Irr. / Living	A J Vehicle - O+VIN / TT
A J	DOT / Mortgage	A J Own. Aff.	A J Survey Aff.	A J Will - LWT / Living	A J
A J	Deed - G / QC / W	A J POA - L / D	A J	A J	A J C☐ Other ▼

Additional Information

Signer Name and Address	Method of Identification	Signature and Thumbprint	

Signer Name and Address   **Method of Identification**   **Signature and Thumbprint**   46

1
- ☐ Driver's License ☐ Other ID #1 - describe ☐ Personally Known
- ☐ Passport ☐ Other ID #2 - describe ☐ Credible Witness(es)

Ref. #1

Ref. #2

Right Thumbprint

X _SIGN HERE_

2
- ☐ Driver's License ☐ Other ID #1 - describe ☐ Personally Known
- ☐ Passport ☐ Other ID #2 - describe ☐ Credible Witness(es)

Ref. #1

Ref. #2

Right Thumbprint

X _SIGN HERE_

3
- ☐ Driver's License ☐ Other ID #1 - describe ☐ Personally Known
- ☐ Passport ☐ Other ID #2 - describe ☐ Credible Witness(es)

Ref. #1

Ref. #2

Right Thumbprint

X _SIGN HERE_

4
- ☐ Driver's License ☐ Other ID #1 - describe ☐ Personally Known
- ☐ Passport ☐ Other ID #2 - describe ☐ Credible Witness(es)

Ref. #1

Ref. #2

Right Thumbprint

X _SIGN HERE_

5
- ☐ Driver's License ☐ Other ID #1 - describe ☐ Personally Known
- ☐ Passport ☐ Other ID #2 - describe ☐ Credible Witness(es)

Ref. #1

Ref. #2

Right Thumbprint

X _SIGN HERE_

6
- ☐ Driver's License ☐ Other ID #1 - describe ☐ Personally Known
- ☐ Passport ☐ Other ID #2 - describe ☐ Credible Witness(es)

Ref. #1

Ref. #2

Right Thumbprint

X _SIGN HERE_

7
- ☐ Driver's License ☐ Other ID #1 - describe ☐ Personally Known
- ☐ Passport ☐ Other ID #2 - describe ☐ Credible Witness(es)

Ref. #1

Ref. #2

Right Thumbprint

X _SIGN HERE_

8
- ☐ Driver's License ☐ Other ID #1 - describe ☐ Personally Known
- ☐ Passport ☐ Other ID #2 - describe ☐ Credible Witness(es)

Ref. #1

Ref. #2

Right Thumbprint

X _SIGN HERE_

1

Notarization Date and Time

Date on Document(s)   Reference #

Fees $ Paid? ☐

A J Compliance Agmt.   A J E & O   A J Proof of ID Aff.   A J Adv. Health. Dir.   A J SDB Verification
A J Correction Agmt.   A J Occ. Aff.   A J Sig./Name Aff.   A J Trust - Irr. / Living   A J Vehicle - O+VIN / TT
A J DOT / Mortgage   A J Own. Aff.   A J Survey Aff.   A J Will - LWT / Living   A J
A J Deed - G / QC / W   A J POA - L / D   A J   A J   A J C ☐ Other ▼

2

Notarization Date and Time

Date on Document(s)   Reference #

Fees $ Paid? ☐

A J Compliance Agmt.   A J E & O   A J Proof of ID Aff.   A J Adv. Health. Dir.   A J SDB Verification
A J Correction Agmt.   A J Occ. Aff.   A J Sig./Name Aff.   A J Trust - Irr. / Living   A J Vehicle - O+VIN / TT
A J DOT / Mortgage   A J Own. Aff.   A J Survey Aff.   A J Will - LWT / Living   A J
A J Deed - G / QC / W   A J POA - L / D   A J   A J   A J C ☐ Other ▼

3

Notarization Date and Time

Date on Document(s)   Reference #

Fees $ Paid? ☐

A J Compliance Agmt.   A J E & O   A J Proof of ID Aff.   A J Adv. Health. Dir.   A J SDB Verification
A J Correction Agmt.   A J Occ. Aff.   A J Sig./Name Aff.   A J Trust - Irr. / Living   A J Vehicle - O+VIN / TT
A J DOT / Mortgage   A J Own. Aff.   A J Survey Aff.   A J Will - LWT / Living   A J
A J Deed - G / QC / W   A J POA - L / D   A J   A J   A J C ☐ Other ▼

4

Notarization Date and Time

Date on Document(s)   Reference #

Fees $ Paid? ☐

A J Compliance Agmt.   A J E & O   A J Proof of ID Aff.   A J Adv. Health. Dir.   A J SDB Verification
A J Correction Agmt.   A J Occ. Aff.   A J Sig./Name Aff.   A J Trust - Irr. / Living   A J Vehicle - O+VIN / TT
A J DOT / Mortgage   A J Own. Aff.   A J Survey Aff.   A J Will - LWT / Living   A J
A J Deed - G / QC / W   A J POA - L / D   A J   A J   A J C ☐ Other ▼

5

Notarization Date and Time

Date on Document(s)   Reference #

Fees $ Paid? ☐

A J Compliance Agmt.   A J E & O   A J Proof of ID Aff.   A J Adv. Health. Dir.   A J SDB Verification
A J Correction Agmt.   A J Occ. Aff.   A J Sig./Name Aff.   A J Trust - Irr. / Living   A J Vehicle - O+VIN / TT
A J DOT / Mortgage   A J Own. Aff.   A J Survey Aff.   A J Will - LWT / Living   A J
A J Deed - G / QC / W   A J POA - L / D   A J   A J   A J C ☐ Other ▼

6

Notarization Date and Time

Date on Document(s)   Reference #

Fees $ Paid? ☐

A J Compliance Agmt.   A J E & O   A J Proof of ID Aff.   A J Adv. Health. Dir.   A J SDB Verification
A J Correction Agmt.   A J Occ. Aff.   A J Sig./Name Aff.   A J Trust - Irr. / Living   A J Vehicle - O+VIN / TT
A J DOT / Mortgage   A J Own. Aff.   A J Survey Aff.   A J Will - LWT / Living   A J
A J Deed - G / QC / W   A J POA - L / D   A J   A J   A J C ☐ Other ▼

7

Notarization Date and Time

Date on Document(s)   Reference #

Fees $ Paid? ☐

A J Compliance Agmt.   A J E & O   A J Proof of ID Aff.   A J Adv. Health. Dir.   A J SDB Verification
A J Correction Agmt.   A J Occ. Aff.   A J Sig./Name Aff.   A J Trust - Irr. / Living   A J Vehicle - O+VIN / TT
A J DOT / Mortgage   A J Own. Aff.   A J Survey Aff.   A J Will - LWT / Living   A J
A J Deed - G / QC / W   A J POA - L / D   A J   A J   A J C ☐ Other ▼

8

Notarization Date and Time

Date on Document(s)   Reference #

Fees $ Paid? ☐

A J Compliance Agmt.   A J E & O   A J Proof of ID Aff.   A J Adv. Health. Dir.   A J SDB Verification
A J Correction Agmt.   A J Occ. Aff.   A J Sig./Name Aff.   A J Trust - Irr. / Living   A J Vehicle - O+VIN / TT
A J DOT / Mortgage   A J Own. Aff.   A J Survey Aff.   A J Will - LWT / Living   A J
A J Deed - G / QC / W   A J POA - L / D   A J   A J   A J C ☐ Other ▼

1

☐ Driver's License ☐ Other ID #1 - describe ☐ Personally Known
☐ Passport ☐ Other ID #2 - describe ☐ Credible Witness(es)

Ref. #1

Ref. #2

x SIGN HERE

Right Thumbprint

2

☐ Driver's License ☐ Other ID #1 - describe ☐ Personally Known
☐ Passport ☐ Other ID #2 - describe ☐ Credible Witness(es)

Ref. #1

Ref. #2

x SIGN HERE

Right Thumbprint

3

☐ Driver's License ☐ Other ID #1 - describe ☐ Personally Known
☐ Passport ☐ Other ID #2 - describe ☐ Credible Witness(es)

Ref. #1

Ref. #2

x SIGN HERE

Right Thumbprint

4

☐ Driver's License ☐ Other ID #1 - describe ☐ Personally Known
☐ Passport ☐ Other ID #2 - describe ☐ Credible Witness(es)

Ref. #1

Ref. #2

x SIGN HERE

Right Thumbprint

5

☐ Driver's License ☐ Other ID #1 - describe ☐ Personally Known
☐ Passport ☐ Other ID #2 - describe ☐ Credible Witness(es)

Ref. #1

Ref. #2

x SIGN HERE

Right Thumbprint

6

☐ Driver's License ☐ Other ID #1 - describe ☐ Personally Known
☐ Passport ☐ Other ID #2 - describe ☐ Credible Witness(es)

Ref. #1

Ref. #2

x SIGN HERE

Right Thumbprint

7

☐ Driver's License ☐ Other ID #1 - describe ☐ Personally Known
☐ Passport ☐ Other ID #2 - describe ☐ Credible Witness(es)

Ref. #1

Ref. #2

x SIGN HERE

Right Thumbprint

8

☐ Driver's License ☐ Other ID #1 - describe ☐ Personally Known
☐ Passport ☐ Other ID #2 - describe ☐ Credible Witness(es)

Ref. #1

Ref. #2

x SIGN HERE

Right Thumbprint

1

Notarization Date and Time

Date on Document(s) Reference #

Fees Paid?
$

- [A] [J] Compliance Agmt. [A] [J] E & O [A] [J] Proof of ID Aff. [A] [J] Adv. Health. Dir. [A] [J] SDB Verification
- [A] [J] Correction Agmt. [A] [J] Occ. Aff. [A] [J] Sig./Name Aff. [A] [J] Trust - Irr./Living [A] [J] Vehicle - O+VIN / TT
- [A] [J] DOT / Mortgage [A] [J] Own. Aff. [A] [J] Survey Aff. [A] [J] Will - LWT / Living [A] [J]
- [A] [J] Deed - G / QC / W [A] [J] POA - L / D [A] [J] [A] [J] [A] [J] [C] [ ] Other ▼

2

Notarization Date and Time

Date on Document(s) Reference #

Fees Paid?
$

- [A] [J] Compliance Agmt. [A] [J] E & O [A] [J] Proof of ID Aff. [A] [J] Adv. Health. Dir. [A] [J] SDB Verification
- [A] [J] Correction Agmt. [A] [J] Occ. Aff. [A] [J] Sig./Name Aff. [A] [J] Trust - Irr./Living [A] [J] Vehicle - O+VIN / TT
- [A] [J] DOT / Mortgage [A] [J] Own. Aff. [A] [J] Survey Aff. [A] [J] Will - LWT / Living [A] [J]
- [A] [J] Deed - G / QC / W [A] [J] POA - L / D [A] [J] [A] [J] [A] [J] [C] [ ] Other ▼

3

Notarization Date and Time

Date on Document(s) Reference #

Fees Paid?
$

- [A] [J] Compliance Agmt. [A] [J] E & O [A] [J] Proof of ID Aff. [A] [J] Adv. Health. Dir. [A] [J] SDB Verification
- [A] [J] Correction Agmt. [A] [J] Occ. Aff. [A] [J] Sig./Name Aff. [A] [J] Trust - Irr./Living [A] [J] Vehicle - O+VIN / TT
- [A] [J] DOT / Mortgage [A] [J] Own. Aff. [A] [J] Survey Aff. [A] [J] Will - LWT / Living [A] [J]
- [A] [J] Deed - G / QC / W [A] [J] POA - L / D [A] [J] [A] [J] [A] [J] [C] [ ] Other ▼

4

Notarization Date and Time

Date on Document(s) Reference #

Fees Paid?
$

- [A] [J] Compliance Agmt. [A] [J] E & O [A] [J] Proof of ID Aff. [A] [J] Adv. Health. Dir. [A] [J] SDB Verification
- [A] [J] Correction Agmt. [A] [J] Occ. Aff. [A] [J] Sig./Name Aff. [A] [J] Trust - Irr./Living [A] [J] Vehicle - O+VIN / TT
- [A] [J] DOT / Mortgage [A] [J] Own. Aff. [A] [J] Survey Aff. [A] [J] Will - LWT / Living [A] [J]
- [A] [J] Deed - G / QC / W [A] [J] POA - L / D [A] [J] [A] [J] [A] [J] [C] [ ] Other ▼

5

Notarization Date and Time

Date on Document(s) Reference #

Fees Paid?
$

- [A] [J] Compliance Agmt. [A] [J] E & O [A] [J] Proof of ID Aff. [A] [J] Adv. Health. Dir. [A] [J] SDB Verification
- [A] [J] Correction Agmt. [A] [J] Occ. Aff. [A] [J] Sig./Name Aff. [A] [J] Trust - Irr./Living [A] [J] Vehicle - O+VIN / TT
- [A] [J] DOT / Mortgage [A] [J] Own. Aff. [A] [J] Survey Aff. [A] [J] Will - LWT / Living [A] [J]
- [A] [J] Deed - G / QC / W [A] [J] POA - L / D [A] [J] [A] [J] [A] [J] [C] [ ] Other ▼

6

Notarization Date and Time

Date on Document(s) Reference #

Fees Paid?
$

- [A] [J] Compliance Agmt. [A] [J] E & O [A] [J] Proof of ID Aff. [A] [J] Adv. Health. Dir. [A] [J] SDB Verification
- [A] [J] Correction Agmt. [A] [J] Occ. Aff. [A] [J] Sig./Name Aff. [A] [J] Trust - Irr./Living [A] [J] Vehicle - O+VIN / TT
- [A] [J] DOT / Mortgage [A] [J] Own. Aff. [A] [J] Survey Aff. [A] [J] Will - LWT / Living [A] [J]
- [A] [J] Deed - G / QC / W [A] [J] POA - L / D [A] [J] [A] [J] [A] [J] [C] [ ] Other ▼

7

Notarization Date and Time

Date on Document(s) Reference #

Fees Paid?
$

- [A] [J] Compliance Agmt. [A] [J] E & O [A] [J] Proof of ID Aff. [A] [J] Adv. Health. Dir. [A] [J] SDB Verification
- [A] [J] Correction Agmt. [A] [J] Occ. Aff. [A] [J] Sig./Name Aff. [A] [J] Trust - Irr./Living [A] [J] Vehicle - O+VIN / TT
- [A] [J] DOT / Mortgage [A] [J] Own. Aff. [A] [J] Survey Aff. [A] [J] Will - LWT / Living [A] [J]
- [A] [J] Deed - G / QC / W [A] [J] POA - L / D [A] [J] [A] [J] [A] [J] [C] [ ] Other ▼

8

Notarization Date and Time

Date on Document(s) Reference #

Fees Paid?
$

- [A] [J] Compliance Agmt. [A] [J] E & O [A] [J] Proof of ID Aff. [A] [J] Adv. Health. Dir. [A] [J] SDB Verification
- [A] [J] Correction Agmt. [A] [J] Occ. Aff. [A] [J] Sig./Name Aff. [A] [J] Trust - Irr./Living [A] [J] Vehicle - O+VIN / TT
- [A] [J] DOT / Mortgage [A] [J] Own. Aff. [A] [J] Survey Aff. [A] [J] Will - LWT / Living [A] [J]
- [A] [J] Deed - G / QC / W [A] [J] POA - L / D [A] [J] [A] [J] [A] [J] [C] [ ] Other ▼

Signer Name and Address	Method of Identification	Signature and Thumbprint	50

1

☐ Driver's License ☐ Other ID #1 - describe ☐ Personally Known
☐ Passport ☐ Other ID #2 - describe ☐ Credible Witness(es)

Ref. #1

Ref. #2

x **SIGN HERE**

Right Thumbprint

2

☐ Driver's License ☐ Other ID #1 - describe ☐ Personally Known
☐ Passport ☐ Other ID #2 - describe ☐ Credible Witness(es)

Ref. #1

Ref. #2

x **SIGN HERE**

Right Thumbprint

3

☐ Driver's License ☐ Other ID #1 - describe ☐ Personally Known
☐ Passport ☐ Other ID #2 - describe ☐ Credible Witness(es)

Ref. #1

Ref. #2

x **SIGN HERE**

Right Thumbprint

4

☐ Driver's License ☐ Other ID #1 - describe ☐ Personally Known
☐ Passport ☐ Other ID #2 - describe ☐ Credible Witness(es)

Ref. #1

Ref. #2

x **SIGN HERE**

Right Thumbprint

5

☐ Driver's License ☐ Other ID #1 - describe ☐ Personally Known
☐ Passport ☐ Other ID #2 - describe ☐ Credible Witness(es)

Ref. #1

Ref. #2

x **SIGN HERE**

Right Thumbprint

6

☐ Driver's License ☐ Other ID #1 - describe ☐ Personally Known
☐ Passport ☐ Other ID #2 - describe ☐ Credible Witness(es)

Ref. #1

Ref. #2

x **SIGN HERE**

Right Thumbprint

7

☐ Driver's License ☐ Other ID #1 - describe ☐ Personally Known
☐ Passport ☐ Other ID #2 - describe ☐ Credible Witness(es)

Ref. #1

Ref. #2

x **SIGN HERE**

Right Thumbprint

8

☐ Driver's License ☐ Other ID #1 - describe ☐ Personally Known
☐ Passport ☐ Other ID #2 - describe ☐ Credible Witness(es)

Ref. #1

Ref. #2

x **SIGN HERE**

Right Thumbprint

1

Notarization Date and Time

Date on Document(s) **Reference #**

Fees $ **Paid?** ☐

A J Compliance Agmt.	A J E & O	A J Proof of ID Aff.	A J Adv. Health. Dir.	A J SDB Verification
A J Correction Agmt.	A J Occ. Aff.	A J Sig./Name Aff.	A J Trust - Irr. / Living	A J Vehicle - O+VIN / TT
A J DOT / Mortgage	A J Own. Aff.	A J Survey Aff.	A J Will - LWT / Living	A J
A J Deed - G / QC / W	A J POA - L / D	A J	A J	A J C ☐ Other ▼

2

Notarization Date and Time

Date on Document(s) **Reference #**

Fees $ **Paid?** ☐

A J Compliance Agmt.	A J E & O	A J Proof of ID Aff.	A J Adv. Health. Dir.	A J SDB Verification
A J Correction Agmt.	A J Occ. Aff.	A J Sig./Name Aff.	A J Trust - Irr. / Living	A J Vehicle - O+VIN / TT
A J DOT / Mortgage	A J Own. Aff.	A J Survey Aff.	A J Will - LWT / Living	A J
A J Deed - G / QC / W	A J POA - L / D	A J	A J	A J C ☐ Other ▼

3

Notarization Date and Time

Date on Document(s) **Reference #**

Fees $ **Paid?** ☐

A J Compliance Agmt.	A J E & O	A J Proof of ID Aff.	A J Adv. Health. Dir.	A J SDB Verification
A J Correction Agmt.	A J Occ. Aff.	A J Sig./Name Aff.	A J Trust - Irr. / Living	A J Vehicle - O+VIN / TT
A J DOT / Mortgage	A J Own. Aff.	A J Survey Aff.	A J Will - LWT / Living	A J
A J Deed - G / QC / W	A J POA - L / D	A J	A J	A J C ☐ Other ▼

4

Notarization Date and Time

Date on Document(s) **Reference #**

Fees $ **Paid?** ☐

A J Compliance Agmt.	A J E & O	A J Proof of ID Aff.	A J Adv. Health. Dir.	A J SDB Verification
A J Correction Agmt.	A J Occ. Aff.	A J Sig./Name Aff.	A J Trust - Irr. / Living	A J Vehicle - O+VIN / TT
A J DOT / Mortgage	A J Own. Aff.	A J Survey Aff.	A J Will - LWT / Living	A J
A J Deed - G / QC / W	A J POA - L / D	A J	A J	A J C ☐ Other ▼

5

Notarization Date and Time

Date on Document(s) **Reference #**

Fees $ **Paid?** ☐

A J Compliance Agmt.	A J E & O	A J Proof of ID Aff.	A J Adv. Health. Dir.	A J SDB Verification
A J Correction Agmt.	A J Occ. Aff.	A J Sig./Name Aff.	A J Trust - Irr. / Living	A J Vehicle - O+VIN / TT
A J DOT / Mortgage	A J Own. Aff.	A J Survey Aff.	A J Will - LWT / Living	A J
A J Deed - G / QC / W	A J POA - L / D	A J	A J	A J C ☐ Other ▼

6

Notarization Date and Time

Date on Document(s) **Reference #**

Fees $ **Paid?** ☐

A J Compliance Agmt.	A J E & O	A J Proof of ID Aff.	A J Adv. Health. Dir.	A J SDB Verification
A J Correction Agmt.	A J Occ. Aff.	A J Sig./Name Aff.	A J Trust - Irr. / Living	A J Vehicle - O+VIN / TT
A J DOT / Mortgage	A J Own. Aff.	A J Survey Aff.	A J Will - LWT / Living	A J
A J Deed - G / QC / W	A J POA - L / D	A J	A J	A J C ☐ Other ▼

7

Notarization Date and Time

Date on Document(s) **Reference #**

Fees $ **Paid?** ☐

A J Compliance Agmt.	A J E & O	A J Proof of ID Aff.	A J Adv. Health. Dir.	A J SDB Verification
A J Correction Agmt.	A J Occ. Aff.	A J Sig./Name Aff.	A J Trust - Irr. / Living	A J Vehicle - O+VIN / TT
A J DOT / Mortgage	A J Own. Aff.	A J Survey Aff.	A J Will - LWT / Living	A J
A J Deed - G / QC / W	A J POA - L / D	A J	A J	A J C ☐ Other ▼

8

Notarization Date and Time

Date on Document(s) **Reference #**

Fees $ **Paid?** ☐

A J Compliance Agmt.	A J E & O	A J Proof of ID Aff.	A J Adv. Health. Dir.	A J SDB Verification
A J Correction Agmt.	A J Occ. Aff.	A J Sig./Name Aff.	A J Trust - Irr. / Living	A J Vehicle - O+VIN / TT
A J DOT / Mortgage	A J Own. Aff.	A J Survey Aff.	A J Will - LWT / Living	A J
A J Deed - G / QC / W	A J POA - L / D	A J	A J	A J C ☐ Other ▼

1

Signer Name and Address

Method of Identification:
- [ ] Driver's License
- [ ] Passport
- [ ] Other ID #1 - describe
- [ ] Other ID #2 - describe
- [ ] Personally Known
- [ ] Credible Witness(es)

Ref. #1

Ref. #2

x _SIGN HERE_

Right Thumbprint

2

Method of Identification:
- [ ] Driver's License
- [ ] Passport
- [ ] Other ID #1 - describe
- [ ] Other ID #2 - describe
- [ ] Personally Known
- [ ] Credible Witness(es)

Ref. #1

Ref. #2

x _SIGN HERE_

Right Thumbprint

3

Method of Identification:
- [ ] Driver's License
- [ ] Passport
- [ ] Other ID #1 - describe
- [ ] Other ID #2 - describe
- [ ] Personally Known
- [ ] Credible Witness(es)

Ref. #1

Ref. #2

x _SIGN HERE_

Right Thumbprint

4

Method of Identification:
- [ ] Driver's License
- [ ] Passport
- [ ] Other ID #1 - describe
- [ ] Other ID #2 - describe
- [ ] Personally Known
- [ ] Credible Witness(es)

Ref. #1

Ref. #2

x _SIGN HERE_

Right Thumbprint

5

Method of Identification:
- [ ] Driver's License
- [ ] Passport
- [ ] Other ID #1 - describe
- [ ] Other ID #2 - describe
- [ ] Personally Known
- [ ] Credible Witness(es)

Ref. #1

Ref. #2

x _SIGN HERE_

Right Thumbprint

6

Method of Identification:
- [ ] Driver's License
- [ ] Passport
- [ ] Other ID #1 - describe
- [ ] Other ID #2 - describe
- [ ] Personally Known
- [ ] Credible Witness(es)

Ref. #1

Ref. #2

x _SIGN HERE_

Right Thumbprint

7

Method of Identification:
- [ ] Driver's License
- [ ] Passport
- [ ] Other ID #1 - describe
- [ ] Other ID #2 - describe
- [ ] Personally Known
- [ ] Credible Witness(es)

Ref. #1

Ref. #2

x _SIGN HERE_

Right Thumbprint

8

Method of Identification:
- [ ] Driver's License
- [ ] Passport
- [ ] Other ID #1 - describe
- [ ] Other ID #2 - describe
- [ ] Personally Known
- [ ] Credible Witness(es)

Ref. #1

Ref. #2

x _SIGN HERE_

Right Thumbprint

1

Notarization Date and Time

Date on Document(s) | Reference #

Fees $ | Paid? ☐

- A J Compliance Agmt.
- A J Correction Agmt.
- A J DOT / Mortgage
- A J Deed - G / QC / W
- A J E & O
- A J Occ. Aff.
- A J Own. Aff.
- A J POA - L / D
- A J Proof of ID Aff.
- A J Sig./Name Aff.
- A J Survey Aff.
- A J Adv. Health. Dir.
- A J Trust - Irr. / Living
- A J Will - LWT / Living
- A J SDB Verification
- A J Vehicle - O+VIN / TT
- A J C ☐ Other ▼

Additional Information

2

Notarization Date and Time

Date on Document(s) | Reference #

Fees $ | Paid? ☐

- A J Compliance Agmt.
- A J Correction Agmt.
- A J DOT / Mortgage
- A J Deed - G / QC / W
- A J E & O
- A J Occ. Aff.
- A J Own. Aff.
- A J POA - L / D
- A J Proof of ID Aff.
- A J Sig./Name Aff.
- A J Survey Aff.
- A J Adv. Health. Dir.
- A J Trust - Irr. / Living
- A J Will - LWT / Living
- A J SDB Verification
- A J Vehicle - O+VIN / TT
- A J C ☐ Other ▼

Additional Information

3

Notarization Date and Time

Date on Document(s) | Reference #

Fees $ | Paid? ☐

- A J Compliance Agmt.
- A J Correction Agmt.
- A J DOT / Mortgage
- A J Deed - G / QC / W
- A J E & O
- A J Occ. Aff.
- A J Own. Aff.
- A J POA - L / D
- A J Proof of ID Aff.
- A J Sig./Name Aff.
- A J Survey Aff.
- A J Adv. Health. Dir.
- A J Trust - Irr. / Living
- A J Will - LWT / Living
- A J SDB Verification
- A J Vehicle - O+VIN / TT
- A J C ☐ Other ▼

Additional Information

4

Notarization Date and Time

Date on Document(s) | Reference #

Fees $ | Paid? ☐

- A J Compliance Agmt.
- A J Correction Agmt.
- A J DOT / Mortgage
- A J Deed - G / QC / W
- A J E & O
- A J Occ. Aff.
- A J Own. Aff.
- A J POA - L / D
- A J Proof of ID Aff.
- A J Sig./Name Aff.
- A J Survey Aff.
- A J Adv. Health. Dir.
- A J Trust - Irr. / Living
- A J Will - LWT / Living
- A J SDB Verification
- A J Vehicle - O+VIN / TT
- A J C ☐ Other ▼

Additional Information

5

Notarization Date and Time

Date on Document(s) | Reference #

Fees $ | Paid? ☐

- A J Compliance Agmt.
- A J Correction Agmt.
- A J DOT / Mortgage
- A J Deed - G / QC / W
- A J E & O
- A J Occ. Aff.
- A J Own. Aff.
- A J POA - L / D
- A J Proof of ID Aff.
- A J Sig./Name Aff.
- A J Survey Aff.
- A J Adv. Health. Dir.
- A J Trust - Irr. / Living
- A J Will - LWT / Living
- A J SDB Verification
- A J Vehicle - O+VIN / TT
- A J C ☐ Other ▼

Additional Information

6

Notarization Date and Time

Date on Document(s) | Reference #

Fees $ | Paid? ☐

- A J Compliance Agmt.
- A J Correction Agmt.
- A J DOT / Mortgage
- A J Deed - G / QC / W
- A J E & O
- A J Occ. Aff.
- A J Own. Aff.
- A J POA - L / D
- A J Proof of ID Aff.
- A J Sig./Name Aff.
- A J Survey Aff.
- A J Adv. Health. Dir.
- A J Trust - Irr. / Living
- A J Will - LWT / Living
- A J SDB Verification
- A J Vehicle - O+VIN / TT
- A J C ☐ Other ▼

Additional Information

7

Notarization Date and Time

Date on Document(s) | Reference #

Fees $ | Paid? ☐

- A J Compliance Agmt.
- A J Correction Agmt.
- A J DOT / Mortgage
- A J Deed - G / QC / W
- A J E & O
- A J Occ. Aff.
- A J Own. Aff.
- A J POA - L / D
- A J Proof of ID Aff.
- A J Sig./Name Aff.
- A J Survey Aff.
- A J Adv. Health. Dir.
- A J Trust - Irr. / Living
- A J Will - LWT / Living
- A J SDB Verification
- A J Vehicle - O+VIN / TT
- A J C ☐ Other ▼

Additional Information

8

Notarization Date and Time

Date on Document(s) | Reference #

Fees $ | Paid? ☐

- A J Compliance Agmt.
- A J Correction Agmt.
- A J DOT / Mortgage
- A J Deed - G / QC / W
- A J E & O
- A J Occ. Aff.
- A J Own. Aff.
- A J POA - L / D
- A J Proof of ID Aff.
- A J Sig./Name Aff.
- A J Survey Aff.
- A J Adv. Health. Dir.
- A J Trust - Irr. / Living
- A J Will - LWT / Living
- A J SDB Verification
- A J Vehicle - O+VIN / TT
- A J C ☐ Other ▼

Additional Information

Entry 1
- ☐ Driver's License ☐ Other ID #1 - describe ☐ Personally Known
- ☐ Passport ☐ Other ID #2 - describe ☐ Credible Witness(es)
- Ref. #1
- Ref. #2
- X SIGN HERE
- Right Thumbprint

Entry 2
- ☐ Driver's License ☐ Other ID #1 - describe ☐ Personally Known
- ☐ Passport ☐ Other ID #2 - describe ☐ Credible Witness(es)
- Ref. #1
- Ref. #2
- X SIGN HERE
- Right Thumbprint

Entry 3
- ☐ Driver's License ☐ Other ID #1 - describe ☐ Personally Known
- ☐ Passport ☐ Other ID #2 - describe ☐ Credible Witness(es)
- Ref. #1
- Ref. #2
- X SIGN HERE
- Right Thumbprint

Entry 4
- ☐ Driver's License ☐ Other ID #1 - describe ☐ Personally Known
- ☐ Passport ☐ Other ID #2 - describe ☐ Credible Witness(es)
- Ref. #1
- Ref. #2
- X SIGN HERE
- Right Thumbprint

Entry 5
- ☐ Driver's License ☐ Other ID #1 - describe ☐ Personally Known
- ☐ Passport ☐ Other ID #2 - describe ☐ Credible Witness(es)
- Ref. #1
- Ref. #2
- X SIGN HERE
- Right Thumbprint

Entry 6
- ☐ Driver's License ☐ Other ID #1 - describe ☐ Personally Known
- ☐ Passport ☐ Other ID #2 - describe ☐ Credible Witness(es)
- Ref. #1
- Ref. #2
- X SIGN HERE
- Right Thumbprint

Entry 7
- ☐ Driver's License ☐ Other ID #1 - describe ☐ Personally Known
- ☐ Passport ☐ Other ID #2 - describe ☐ Credible Witness(es)
- Ref. #1
- Ref. #2
- X SIGN HERE
- Right Thumbprint

Entry 8
- ☐ Driver's License ☐ Other ID #1 - describe ☐ Personally Known
- ☐ Passport ☐ Other ID #2 - describe ☐ Credible Witness(es)
- Ref. #1
- Ref. #2
- X SIGN HERE
- Right Thumbprint

1

Notarization Date and Time

Date on Document(s) Reference #

Fees $ Paid? ☐

A J Compliance Agmt.	A J E & O	A J Proof of ID Aff.	A J Adv. Health. Dir.	A J SDB Verification
A J Correction Agmt.	A J Occ. Aff.	A J Sig./Name Aff.	A J Trust - Irr. / Living	A J Vehicle - O+VIN / TT
A J DOT / Mortgage	A J Own. Aff.	A J Survey Aff.	A J Will - LWT / Living	A J
A J Deed - G / QC / W	A J POA - L / D	A J	A J	A J C ☐ Other ▼

2

Notarization Date and Time

Date on Document(s) Reference #

Fees $ Paid? ☐

A J Compliance Agmt.	A J E & O	A J Proof of ID Aff.	A J Adv. Health. Dir.	A J SDB Verification
A J Correction Agmt.	A J Occ. Aff.	A J Sig./Name Aff.	A J Trust - Irr. / Living	A J Vehicle - O+VIN / TT
A J DOT / Mortgage	A J Own. Aff.	A J Survey Aff.	A J Will - LWT / Living	A J
A J Deed - G / QC / W	A J POA - L / D	A J	A J	A J C ☐ Other ▼

3

Notarization Date and Time

Date on Document(s) Reference #

Fees $ Paid? ☐

A J Compliance Agmt.	A J E & O	A J Proof of ID Aff.	A J Adv. Health. Dir.	A J SDB Verification
A J Correction Agmt.	A J Occ. Aff.	A J Sig./Name Aff.	A J Trust - Irr. / Living	A J Vehicle - O+VIN / TT
A J DOT / Mortgage	A J Own. Aff.	A J Survey Aff.	A J Will - LWT / Living	A J
A J Deed - G / QC / W	A J POA - L / D	A J	A J	A J C ☐ Other ▼

4

Notarization Date and Time

Date on Document(s) Reference #

Fees $ Paid? ☐

A J Compliance Agmt.	A J E & O	A J Proof of ID Aff.	A J Adv. Health. Dir.	A J SDB Verification
A J Correction Agmt.	A J Occ. Aff.	A J Sig./Name Aff.	A J Trust - Irr. / Living	A J Vehicle - O+VIN / TT
A J DOT / Mortgage	A J Own. Aff.	A J Survey Aff.	A J Will - LWT / Living	A J
A J Deed - G / QC / W	A J POA - L / D	A J	A J	A J C ☐ Other ▼

5

Notarization Date and Time

Date on Document(s) Reference #

Fees $ Paid? ☐

A J Compliance Agmt.	A J E & O	A J Proof of ID Aff.	A J Adv. Health. Dir.	A J SDB Verification
A J Correction Agmt.	A J Occ. Aff.	A J Sig./Name Aff.	A J Trust - Irr. / Living	A J Vehicle - O+VIN / TT
A J DOT / Mortgage	A J Own. Aff.	A J Survey Aff.	A J Will - LWT / Living	A J
A J Deed - G / QC / W	A J POA - L / D	A J	A J	A J C ☐ Other ▼

6

Notarization Date and Time

Date on Document(s) Reference #

Fees $ Paid? ☐

A J Compliance Agmt.	A J E & O	A J Proof of ID Aff.	A J Adv. Health. Dir.	A J SDB Verification
A J Correction Agmt.	A J Occ. Aff.	A J Sig./Name Aff.	A J Trust - Irr. / Living	A J Vehicle - O+VIN / TT
A J DOT / Mortgage	A J Own. Aff.	A J Survey Aff.	A J Will - LWT / Living	A J
A J Deed - G / QC / W	A J POA - L / D	A J	A J	A J C ☐ Other ▼

7

Notarization Date and Time

Date on Document(s) Reference #

Fees $ Paid? ☐

A J Compliance Agmt.	A J E & O	A J Proof of ID Aff.	A J Adv. Health. Dir.	A J SDB Verification
A J Correction Agmt.	A J Occ. Aff.	A J Sig./Name Aff.	A J Trust - Irr. / Living	A J Vehicle - O+VIN / TT
A J DOT / Mortgage	A J Own. Aff.	A J Survey Aff.	A J Will - LWT / Living	A J
A J Deed - G / QC / W	A J POA - L / D	A J	A J	A J C ☐ Other ▼

8

Notarization Date and Time

Date on Document(s) Reference #

Fees $ Paid? ☐

A J Compliance Agmt.	A J E & O	A J Proof of ID Aff.	A J Adv. Health. Dir.	A J SDB Verification
A J Correction Agmt.	A J Occ. Aff.	A J Sig./Name Aff.	A J Trust - Irr. / Living	A J Vehicle - O+VIN / TT
A J DOT / Mortgage	A J Own. Aff.	A J Survey Aff.	A J Will - LWT / Living	A J
A J Deed - G / QC / W	A J POA - L / D	A J	A J	A J C ☐ Other ▼

Signer Name and Address	Method of Identification	Signature and Thumbprint	

56

1
☐ Driver's License ☐ Other ID #1 - describe ☐ Personally Known
☐ Passport ☐ Other ID #2 - describe ☐ Credible Witness(es)

Ref. #1

Ref. #2

X SIGN HERE

Right Thumbprint

2
☐ Driver's License ☐ Other ID #1 - describe ☐ Personally Known
☐ Passport ☐ Other ID #2 - describe ☐ Credible Witness(es)

Ref. #1

Ref. #2

X SIGN HERE

Right Thumbprint

3
☐ Driver's License ☐ Other ID #1 - describe ☐ Personally Known
☐ Passport ☐ Other ID #2 - describe ☐ Credible Witness(es)

Ref. #1

Ref. #2

X SIGN HERE

Right Thumbprint

4
☐ Driver's License ☐ Other ID #1 - describe ☐ Personally Known
☐ Passport ☐ Other ID #2 - describe ☐ Credible Witness(es)

Ref. #1

Ref. #2

X SIGN HERE

Right Thumbprint

5
☐ Driver's License ☐ Other ID #1 - describe ☐ Personally Known
☐ Passport ☐ Other ID #2 - describe ☐ Credible Witness(es)

Ref. #1

Ref. #2

X SIGN HERE

Right Thumbprint

6
☐ Driver's License ☐ Other ID #1 - describe ☐ Personally Known
☐ Passport ☐ Other ID #2 - describe ☐ Credible Witness(es)

Ref. #1

Ref. #2

X SIGN HERE

Right Thumbprint

7
☐ Driver's License ☐ Other ID #1 - describe ☐ Personally Known
☐ Passport ☐ Other ID #2 - describe ☐ Credible Witness(es)

Ref. #1

Ref. #2

X SIGN HERE

Right Thumbprint

8
☐ Driver's License ☐ Other ID #1 - describe ☐ Personally Known
☐ Passport ☐ Other ID #2 - describe ☐ Credible Witness(es)

Ref. #1

Ref. #2

X SIGN HERE

Right Thumbprint

1

Notarization Date and Time

Date on Document(s) | Reference #

Fees $ | Paid? ☐

A J Compliance Agmt.	A J E & O	A J Proof of ID Aff.	A J Adv. Health. Dir.	A J SDB Verification
A J Correction Agmt.	A J Occ. Aff.	A J Sig./Name Aff.	A J Trust - Irr. / Living	A J Vehicle - O+VIN / TT
A J DOT / Mortgage	A J Own. Aff.	A J Survey Aff.	A J Will - LWT / Living	A J
A J Deed - G / QC / W	A J POA - L / D	A J	A J	A J C ☐ Other ▼

2

Notarization Date and Time

Date on Document(s) | Reference #

Fees $ | Paid? ☐

A J Compliance Agmt.	A J E & O	A J Proof of ID Aff.	A J Adv. Health. Dir.	A J SDB Verification
A J Correction Agmt.	A J Occ. Aff.	A J Sig./Name Aff.	A J Trust - Irr. / Living	A J Vehicle - O+VIN / TT
A J DOT / Mortgage	A J Own. Aff.	A J Survey Aff.	A J Will - LWT / Living	A J
A J Deed - G / QC / W	A J POA - L / D	A J	A J	A J C ☐ Other ▼

3

Notarization Date and Time

Date on Document(s) | Reference #

Fees $ | Paid? ☐

A J Compliance Agmt.	A J E & O	A J Proof of ID Aff.	A J Adv. Health. Dir.	A J SDB Verification
A J Correction Agmt.	A J Occ. Aff.	A J Sig./Name Aff.	A J Trust - Irr. / Living	A J Vehicle - O+VIN / TT
A J DOT / Mortgage	A J Own. Aff.	A J Survey Aff.	A J Will - LWT / Living	A J
A J Deed - G / QC / W	A J POA - L / D	A J	A J	A J C ☐ Other ▼

4

Notarization Date and Time

Date on Document(s) | Reference #

Fees $ | Paid? ☐

A J Compliance Agmt.	A J E & O	A J Proof of ID Aff.	A J Adv. Health. Dir.	A J SDB Verification
A J Correction Agmt.	A J Occ. Aff.	A J Sig./Name Aff.	A J Trust - Irr. / Living	A J Vehicle - O+VIN / TT
A J DOT / Mortgage	A J Own. Aff.	A J Survey Aff.	A J Will - LWT / Living	A J
A J Deed - G / QC / W	A J POA - L / D	A J	A J	A J C ☐ Other ▼

5

Notarization Date and Time

Date on Document(s) | Reference #

Fees $ | Paid? ☐

A J Compliance Agmt.	A J E & O	A J Proof of ID Aff.	A J Adv. Health. Dir.	A J SDB Verification
A J Correction Agmt.	A J Occ. Aff.	A J Sig./Name Aff.	A J Trust - Irr. / Living	A J Vehicle - O+VIN / TT
A J DOT / Mortgage	A J Own. Aff.	A J Survey Aff.	A J Will - LWT / Living	A J
A J Deed - G / QC / W	A J POA - L / D	A J	A J	A J C ☐ Other ▼

6

Notarization Date and Time

Date on Document(s) | Reference #

Fees $ | Paid? ☐

A J Compliance Agmt.	A J E & O	A J Proof of ID Aff.	A J Adv. Health. Dir.	A J SDB Verification
A J Correction Agmt.	A J Occ. Aff.	A J Sig./Name Aff.	A J Trust - Irr. / Living	A J Vehicle - O+VIN / TT
A J DOT / Mortgage	A J Own. Aff.	A J Survey Aff.	A J Will - LWT / Living	A J
A J Deed - G / QC / W	A J POA - L / D	A J	A J	A J C ☐ Other ▼

7

Notarization Date and Time

Date on Document(s) | Reference #

Fees $ | Paid? ☐

A J Compliance Agmt.	A J E & O	A J Proof of ID Aff.	A J Adv. Health. Dir.	A J SDB Verification
A J Correction Agmt.	A J Occ. Aff.	A J Sig./Name Aff.	A J Trust - Irr. / Living	A J Vehicle - O+VIN / TT
A J DOT / Mortgage	A J Own. Aff.	A J Survey Aff.	A J Will - LWT / Living	A J
A J Deed - G / QC / W	A J POA - L / D	A J	A J	A J C ☐ Other ▼

8

Notarization Date and Time

Date on Document(s) | Reference #

Fees $ | Paid? ☐

A J Compliance Agmt.	A J E & O	A J Proof of ID Aff.	A J Adv. Health. Dir.	A J SDB Verification
A J Correction Agmt.	A J Occ. Aff.	A J Sig./Name Aff.	A J Trust - Irr. / Living	A J Vehicle - O+VIN / TT
A J DOT / Mortgage	A J Own. Aff.	A J Survey Aff.	A J Will - LWT / Living	A J
A J Deed - G / QC / W	A J POA - L / D	A J	A J	A J C ☐ Other ▼

Signer Name and Address	Method of Identification	Signature and Thumbprint	

58

1
- ☐ Driver's License   ☐ Other ID #1 - describe   ☐ Personally Known
- ☐ Passport   ☐ Other ID #2 - describe   ☐ Credible Witness(es)
- Ref. #1
- Ref. #2
- X **SIGN HERE**
- Right Thumbprint

2
- ☐ Driver's License   ☐ Other ID #1 - describe   ☐ Personally Known
- ☐ Passport   ☐ Other ID #2 - describe   ☐ Credible Witness(es)
- Ref. #1
- Ref. #2
- X **SIGN HERE**
- Right Thumbprint

3
- ☐ Driver's License   ☐ Other ID #1 - describe   ☐ Personally Known
- ☐ Passport   ☐ Other ID #2 - describe   ☐ Credible Witness(es)
- Ref. #1
- Ref. #2
- X **SIGN HERE**
- Right Thumbprint

4
- ☐ Driver's License   ☐ Other ID #1 - describe   ☐ Personally Known
- ☐ Passport   ☐ Other ID #2 - describe   ☐ Credible Witness(es)
- Ref. #1
- Ref. #2
- X **SIGN HERE**
- Right Thumbprint

5
- ☐ Driver's License   ☐ Other ID #1 - describe   ☐ Personally Known
- ☐ Passport   ☐ Other ID #2 - describe   ☐ Credible Witness(es)
- Ref. #1
- Ref. #2
- X **SIGN HERE**
- Right Thumbprint

6
- ☐ Driver's License   ☐ Other ID #1 - describe   ☐ Personally Known
- ☐ Passport   ☐ Other ID #2 - describe   ☐ Credible Witness(es)
- Ref. #1
- Ref. #2
- X **SIGN HERE**
- Right Thumbprint

7
- ☐ Driver's License   ☐ Other ID #1 - describe   ☐ Personally Known
- ☐ Passport   ☐ Other ID #2 - describe   ☐ Credible Witness(es)
- Ref. #1
- Ref. #2
- X **SIGN HERE**
- Right Thumbprint

8
- ☐ Driver's License   ☐ Other ID #1 - describe   ☐ Personally Known
- ☐ Passport   ☐ Other ID #2 - describe   ☐ Credible Witness(es)
- Ref. #1
- Ref. #2
- X **SIGN HERE**
- Right Thumbprint

1

Notarization Date and Time

Date on Document(s) Reference #

Fees $ Paid? ☐

- [A] [J] Compliance Agmt. [A] [J] E & O [A] [J] Proof of ID Aff. [A] [J] Adv. Health. Dir. [A] [J] SDB Verification
- [A] [J] Correction Agmt. [A] [J] Occ. Aff. [A] [J] Sig./Name Aff. [A] [J] Trust - Irr./Living [A] [J] Vehicle - O+VIN / TT
- [A] [J] DOT / Mortgage [A] [J] Own. Aff. [A] [J] Survey Aff. [A] [J] Will - LWT / Living [A] [J]
- [A] [J] Deed - G / QC / W [A] [J] POA - L / D [A] [J] [A] [J] [A] [J] [C] ☐ Other ▼

2

Notarization Date and Time

Date on Document(s) Reference #

Fees $ Paid? ☐

- [A] [J] Compliance Agmt. [A] [J] E & O [A] [J] Proof of ID Aff. [A] [J] Adv. Health. Dir. [A] [J] SDB Verification
- [A] [J] Correction Agmt. [A] [J] Occ. Aff. [A] [J] Sig./Name Aff. [A] [J] Trust - Irr./Living [A] [J] Vehicle - O+VIN / TT
- [A] [J] DOT / Mortgage [A] [J] Own. Aff. [A] [J] Survey Aff. [A] [J] Will - LWT / Living [A] [J]
- [A] [J] Deed - G / QC / W [A] [J] POA - L / D [A] [J] [A] [J] [A] [J] [C] ☐ Other ▼

3

Notarization Date and Time

Date on Document(s) Reference #

Fees $ Paid? ☐

- [A] [J] Compliance Agmt. [A] [J] E & O [A] [J] Proof of ID Aff. [A] [J] Adv. Health. Dir. [A] [J] SDB Verification
- [A] [J] Correction Agmt. [A] [J] Occ. Aff. [A] [J] Sig./Name Aff. [A] [J] Trust - Irr./Living [A] [J] Vehicle - O+VIN / TT
- [A] [J] DOT / Mortgage [A] [J] Own. Aff. [A] [J] Survey Aff. [A] [J] Will - LWT / Living [A] [J]
- [A] [J] Deed - G / QC / W [A] [J] POA - L / D [A] [J] [A] [J] [A] [J] [C] ☐ Other ▼

4

Notarization Date and Time

Date on Document(s) Reference #

Fees $ Paid? ☐

- [A] [J] Compliance Agmt. [A] [J] E & O [A] [J] Proof of ID Aff. [A] [J] Adv. Health. Dir. [A] [J] SDB Verification
- [A] [J] Correction Agmt. [A] [J] Occ. Aff. [A] [J] Sig./Name Aff. [A] [J] Trust - Irr./Living [A] [J] Vehicle - O+VIN / TT
- [A] [J] DOT / Mortgage [A] [J] Own. Aff. [A] [J] Survey Aff. [A] [J] Will - LWT / Living [A] [J]
- [A] [J] Deed - G / QC / W [A] [J] POA - L / D [A] [J] [A] [J] [A] [J] [C] ☐ Other ▼

5

Notarization Date and Time

Date on Document(s) Reference #

Fees $ Paid? ☐

- [A] [J] Compliance Agmt. [A] [J] E & O [A] [J] Proof of ID Aff. [A] [J] Adv. Health. Dir. [A] [J] SDB Verification
- [A] [J] Correction Agmt. [A] [J] Occ. Aff. [A] [J] Sig./Name Aff. [A] [J] Trust - Irr./Living [A] [J] Vehicle - O+VIN / TT
- [A] [J] DOT / Mortgage [A] [J] Own. Aff. [A] [J] Survey Aff. [A] [J] Will - LWT / Living [A] [J]
- [A] [J] Deed - G / QC / W [A] [J] POA - L / D [A] [J] [A] [J] [A] [J] [C] ☐ Other ▼

6

Notarization Date and Time

Date on Document(s) Reference #

Fees $ Paid? ☐

- [A] [J] Compliance Agmt. [A] [J] E & O [A] [J] Proof of ID Aff. [A] [J] Adv. Health. Dir. [A] [J] SDB Verification
- [A] [J] Correction Agmt. [A] [J] Occ. Aff. [A] [J] Sig./Name Aff. [A] [J] Trust - Irr./Living [A] [J] Vehicle - O+VIN / TT
- [A] [J] DOT / Mortgage [A] [J] Own. Aff. [A] [J] Survey Aff. [A] [J] Will - LWT / Living [A] [J]
- [A] [J] Deed - G / QC / W [A] [J] POA - L / D [A] [J] [A] [J] [A] [J] [C] ☐ Other ▼

7

Notarization Date and Time

Date on Document(s) Reference #

Fees $ Paid? ☐

- [A] [J] Compliance Agmt. [A] [J] E & O [A] [J] Proof of ID Aff. [A] [J] Adv. Health. Dir. [A] [J] SDB Verification
- [A] [J] Correction Agmt. [A] [J] Occ. Aff. [A] [J] Sig./Name Aff. [A] [J] Trust - Irr./Living [A] [J] Vehicle - O+VIN / TT
- [A] [J] DOT / Mortgage [A] [J] Own. Aff. [A] [J] Survey Aff. [A] [J] Will - LWT / Living [A] [J]
- [A] [J] Deed - G / QC / W [A] [J] POA - L / D [A] [J] [A] [J] [A] [J] [C] ☐ Other ▼

8

Notarization Date and Time

Date on Document(s) Reference #

Fees $ Paid? ☐

- [A] [J] Compliance Agmt. [A] [J] E & O [A] [J] Proof of ID Aff. [A] [J] Adv. Health. Dir. [A] [J] SDB Verification
- [A] [J] Correction Agmt. [A] [J] Occ. Aff. [A] [J] Sig./Name Aff. [A] [J] Trust - Irr./Living [A] [J] Vehicle - O+VIN / TT
- [A] [J] DOT / Mortgage [A] [J] Own. Aff. [A] [J] Survey Aff. [A] [J] Will - LWT / Living [A] [J]
- [A] [J] Deed - G / QC / W [A] [J] POA - L / D [A] [J] [A] [J] [A] [J] [C] ☐ Other ▼

1

Driver's License ☐   Other ID #1 - describe ☐   Personally Known ☐
Passport ☐   Other ID #2 - describe ☐   Credible Witness(es) ☐

Ref. #1

Ref. #2

X **SIGN HERE**

Right Thumbprint

2

Driver's License ☐   Other ID #1 - describe ☐   Personally Known ☐
Passport ☐   Other ID #2 - describe ☐   Credible Witness(es) ☐

Ref. #1

Ref. #2

X **SIGN HERE**

Right Thumbprint

3

Driver's License ☐   Other ID #1 - describe ☐   Personally Known ☐
Passport ☐   Other ID #2 - describe ☐   Credible Witness(es) ☐

Ref. #1

Ref. #2

X **SIGN HERE**

Right Thumbprint

4

Driver's License ☐   Other ID #1 - describe ☐   Personally Known ☐
Passport ☐   Other ID #2 - describe ☐   Credible Witness(es) ☐

Ref. #1

Ref. #2

X **SIGN HERE**

Right Thumbprint

5

Driver's License ☐   Other ID #1 - describe ☐   Personally Known ☐
Passport ☐   Other ID #2 - describe ☐   Credible Witness(es) ☐

Ref. #1

Ref. #2

X **SIGN HERE**

Right Thumbprint

6

Driver's License ☐   Other ID #1 - describe ☐   Personally Known ☐
Passport ☐   Other ID #2 - describe ☐   Credible Witness(es) ☐

Ref. #1

Ref. #2

X **SIGN HERE**

Right Thumbprint

7

Driver's License ☐   Other ID #1 - describe ☐   Personally Known ☐
Passport ☐   Other ID #2 - describe ☐   Credible Witness(es) ☐

Ref. #1

Ref. #2

X **SIGN HERE**

Right Thumbprint

8

Driver's License ☐   Other ID #1 - describe ☐   Personally Known ☐
Passport ☐   Other ID #2 - describe ☐   Credible Witness(es) ☐

Ref. #1

Ref. #2

X **SIGN HERE**

Right Thumbprint

1

Notarization Date and Time

Date on Document(s) | **Reference #**

Fees $ **Paid?** ☐

- [A][J] Compliance Agmt.   [A][J] E & O   [A][J] Proof of ID Aff.   [A][J] Adv. Health. Dir.   [A][J] SDB Verification
- [A][J] Correction Agmt.   [A][J] Occ. Aff.   [A][J] Sig./Name Aff.   [A][J] Trust - Irr. / Living   [A][J] Vehicle - O+VIN / TT
- [A][J] DOT / Mortgage   [A][J] Own. Aff.   [A][J] Survey Aff.   [A][J] Will - LWT / Living   [A][J]
- [A][J] Deed - G / QC / W   [A][J] POA - L / D   [A][J]   [A][J]   [A][J][C] Other ▼

2

Notarization Date and Time

Date on Document(s) | **Reference #**

Fees $ **Paid?** ☐

- [A][J] Compliance Agmt.   [A][J] E & O   [A][J] Proof of ID Aff.   [A][J] Adv. Health. Dir.   [A][J] SDB Verification
- [A][J] Correction Agmt.   [A][J] Occ. Aff.   [A][J] Sig./Name Aff.   [A][J] Trust - Irr. / Living   [A][J] Vehicle - O+VIN / TT
- [A][J] DOT / Mortgage   [A][J] Own. Aff.   [A][J] Survey Aff.   [A][J] Will - LWT / Living   [A][J]
- [A][J] Deed - G / QC / W   [A][J] POA - L / D   [A][J]   [A][J]   [A][J][C] Other ▼

3

Notarization Date and Time

Date on Document(s) | **Reference #**

Fees $ **Paid?** ☐

- [A][J] Compliance Agmt.   [A][J] E & O   [A][J] Proof of ID Aff.   [A][J] Adv. Health. Dir.   [A][J] SDB Verification
- [A][J] Correction Agmt.   [A][J] Occ. Aff.   [A][J] Sig./Name Aff.   [A][J] Trust - Irr. / Living   [A][J] Vehicle - O+VIN / TT
- [A][J] DOT / Mortgage   [A][J] Own. Aff.   [A][J] Survey Aff.   [A][J] Will - LWT / Living   [A][J]
- [A][J] Deed - G / QC / W   [A][J] POA - L / D   [A][J]   [A][J]   [A][J][C] Other ▼

4

Notarization Date and Time

Date on Document(s) | **Reference #**

Fees $ **Paid?** ☐

- [A][J] Compliance Agmt.   [A][J] E & O   [A][J] Proof of ID Aff.   [A][J] Adv. Health. Dir.   [A][J] SDB Verification
- [A][J] Correction Agmt.   [A][J] Occ. Aff.   [A][J] Sig./Name Aff.   [A][J] Trust - Irr. / Living   [A][J] Vehicle - O+VIN / TT
- [A][J] DOT / Mortgage   [A][J] Own. Aff.   [A][J] Survey Aff.   [A][J] Will - LWT / Living   [A][J]
- [A][J] Deed - G / QC / W   [A][J] POA - L / D   [A][J]   [A][J]   [A][J][C] Other ▼

5

Notarization Date and Time

Date on Document(s) | **Reference #**

Fees $ **Paid?** ☐

- [A][J] Compliance Agmt.   [A][J] E & O   [A][J] Proof of ID Aff.   [A][J] Adv. Health. Dir.   [A][J] SDB Verification
- [A][J] Correction Agmt.   [A][J] Occ. Aff.   [A][J] Sig./Name Aff.   [A][J] Trust - Irr. / Living   [A][J] Vehicle - O+VIN / TT
- [A][J] DOT / Mortgage   [A][J] Own. Aff.   [A][J] Survey Aff.   [A][J] Will - LWT / Living   [A][J]
- [A][J] Deed - G / QC / W   [A][J] POA - L / D   [A][J]   [A][J]   [A][J][C] Other ▼

6

Notarization Date and Time

Date on Document(s) | **Reference #**

Fees $ **Paid?** ☐

- [A][J] Compliance Agmt.   [A][J] E & O   [A][J] Proof of ID Aff.   [A][J] Adv. Health. Dir.   [A][J] SDB Verification
- [A][J] Correction Agmt.   [A][J] Occ. Aff.   [A][J] Sig./Name Aff.   [A][J] Trust - Irr. / Living   [A][J] Vehicle - O+VIN / TT
- [A][J] DOT / Mortgage   [A][J] Own. Aff.   [A][J] Survey Aff.   [A][J] Will - LWT / Living   [A][J]
- [A][J] Deed - G / QC / W   [A][J] POA - L / D   [A][J]   [A][J]   [A][J][C] Other ▼

7

Notarization Date and Time

Date on Document(s) | **Reference #**

Fees $ **Paid?** ☐

- [A][J] Compliance Agmt.   [A][J] E & O   [A][J] Proof of ID Aff.   [A][J] Adv. Health. Dir.   [A][J] SDB Verification
- [A][J] Correction Agmt.   [A][J] Occ. Aff.   [A][J] Sig./Name Aff.   [A][J] Trust - Irr. / Living   [A][J] Vehicle - O+VIN / TT
- [A][J] DOT / Mortgage   [A][J] Own. Aff.   [A][J] Survey Aff.   [A][J] Will - LWT / Living   [A][J]
- [A][J] Deed - G / QC / W   [A][J] POA - L / D   [A][J]   [A][J]   [A][J][C] Other ▼

8

Notarization Date and Time

Date on Document(s) | **Reference #**

Fees $ **Paid?** ☐

- [A][J] Compliance Agmt.   [A][J] E & O   [A][J] Proof of ID Aff.   [A][J] Adv. Health. Dir.   [A][J] SDB Verification
- [A][J] Correction Agmt.   [A][J] Occ. Aff.   [A][J] Sig./Name Aff.   [A][J] Trust - Irr. / Living   [A][J] Vehicle - O+VIN / TT
- [A][J] DOT / Mortgage   [A][J] Own. Aff.   [A][J] Survey Aff.   [A][J] Will - LWT / Living   [A][J]
- [A][J] Deed - G / QC / W   [A][J] POA - L / D   [A][J]   [A][J]   [A][J][C] Other ▼

Signer Name and Address	Method of Identification	Signature and Thumbprint	62

Row 1

Method of Identification:
- ☐ Driver's License
- ☐ Passport
- ☐ Other ID #1 - describe
- ☐ Other ID #2 - describe
- ☐ Personally Known
- ☐ Credible Witness(es)

Ref. #1

Ref. #2

x SIGN HERE

Right Thumbprint

1

Row 2

Method of Identification:
- ☐ Driver's License
- ☐ Passport
- ☐ Other ID #1 - describe
- ☐ Other ID #2 - describe
- ☐ Personally Known
- ☐ Credible Witness(es)

Ref. #1

Ref. #2

x SIGN HERE

Right Thumbprint

2

Row 3

Method of Identification:
- ☐ Driver's License
- ☐ Passport
- ☐ Other ID #1 - describe
- ☐ Other ID #2 - describe
- ☐ Personally Known
- ☐ Credible Witness(es)

Ref. #1

Ref. #2

x SIGN HERE

Right Thumbprint

3

Row 4

Method of Identification:
- ☐ Driver's License
- ☐ Passport
- ☐ Other ID #1 - describe
- ☐ Other ID #2 - describe
- ☐ Personally Known
- ☐ Credible Witness(es)

Ref. #1

Ref. #2

x SIGN HERE

Right Thumbprint

4

Row 5

Method of Identification:
- ☐ Driver's License
- ☐ Passport
- ☐ Other ID #1 - describe
- ☐ Other ID #2 - describe
- ☐ Personally Known
- ☐ Credible Witness(es)

Ref. #1

Ref. #2

x SIGN HERE

Right Thumbprint

5

Row 6

Method of Identification:
- ☐ Driver's License
- ☐ Passport
- ☐ Other ID #1 - describe
- ☐ Other ID #2 - describe
- ☐ Personally Known
- ☐ Credible Witness(es)

Ref. #1

Ref. #2

x SIGN HERE

Right Thumbprint

6

Row 7

Method of Identification:
- ☐ Driver's License
- ☐ Passport
- ☐ Other ID #1 - describe
- ☐ Other ID #2 - describe
- ☐ Personally Known
- ☐ Credible Witness(es)

Ref. #1

Ref. #2

x SIGN HERE

Right Thumbprint

7

Row 8

Method of Identification:
- ☐ Driver's License
- ☐ Passport
- ☐ Other ID #1 - describe
- ☐ Other ID #2 - describe
- ☐ Personally Known
- ☐ Credible Witness(es)

Ref. #1

Ref. #2

x SIGN HERE

Right Thumbprint

8

1

Notarization Date and Time

Date on Document(s)   Reference #

Fees $ Paid? ☐

A J Compliance Agmt.	A J E & O	A J Proof of ID Aff.	A J Adv. Health. Dir.	A J SDB Verification
A J Correction Agmt.	A J Occ. Aff.	A J Sig./Name Aff.	A J Trust - Irr. / Living	A J Vehicle - O+VIN / TT
A J DOT / Mortgage	A J Own. Aff.	A J Survey Aff.	A J Will - LWT / Living	A J
A J Deed - G / QC / W	A J POA - L / D	A J	A J	A J C ☐ Other ▼

2

Notarization Date and Time

Date on Document(s)   Reference #

Fees $ Paid? ☐

A J Compliance Agmt.	A J E & O	A J Proof of ID Aff.	A J Adv. Health. Dir.	A J SDB Verification
A J Correction Agmt.	A J Occ. Aff.	A J Sig./Name Aff.	A J Trust - Irr. / Living	A J Vehicle - O+VIN / TT
A J DOT / Mortgage	A J Own. Aff.	A J Survey Aff.	A J Will - LWT / Living	A J
A J Deed - G / QC / W	A J POA - L / D	A J	A J	A J C ☐ Other ▼

3

Notarization Date and Time

Date on Document(s)   Reference #

Fees $ Paid? ☐

A J Compliance Agmt.	A J E & O	A J Proof of ID Aff.	A J Adv. Health. Dir.	A J SDB Verification
A J Correction Agmt.	A J Occ. Aff.	A J Sig./Name Aff.	A J Trust - Irr. / Living	A J Vehicle - O+VIN / TT
A J DOT / Mortgage	A J Own. Aff.	A J Survey Aff.	A J Will - LWT / Living	A J
A J Deed - G / QC / W	A J POA - L / D	A J	A J	A J C ☐ Other ▼

4

Notarization Date and Time

Date on Document(s)   Reference #

Fees $ Paid? ☐

A J Compliance Agmt.	A J E & O	A J Proof of ID Aff.	A J Adv. Health. Dir.	A J SDB Verification
A J Correction Agmt.	A J Occ. Aff.	A J Sig./Name Aff.	A J Trust - Irr. / Living	A J Vehicle - O+VIN / TT
A J DOT / Mortgage	A J Own. Aff.	A J Survey Aff.	A J Will - LWT / Living	A J
A J Deed - G / QC / W	A J POA - L / D	A J	A J	A J C ☐ Other ▼

5

Notarization Date and Time

Date on Document(s)   Reference #

Fees $ Paid? ☐

A J Compliance Agmt.	A J E & O	A J Proof of ID Aff.	A J Adv. Health. Dir.	A J SDB Verification
A J Correction Agmt.	A J Occ. Aff.	A J Sig./Name Aff.	A J Trust - Irr. / Living	A J Vehicle - O+VIN / TT
A J DOT / Mortgage	A J Own. Aff.	A J Survey Aff.	A J Will - LWT / Living	A J
A J Deed - G / QC / W	A J POA - L / D	A J	A J	A J C ☐ Other ▼

6

Notarization Date and Time

Date on Document(s)   Reference #

Fees $ Paid? ☐

A J Compliance Agmt.	A J E & O	A J Proof of ID Aff.	A J Adv. Health. Dir.	A J SDB Verification
A J Correction Agmt.	A J Occ. Aff.	A J Sig./Name Aff.	A J Trust - Irr. / Living	A J Vehicle - O+VIN / TT
A J DOT / Mortgage	A J Own. Aff.	A J Survey Aff.	A J Will - LWT / Living	A J
A J Deed - G / QC / W	A J POA - L / D	A J	A J	A J C ☐ Other ▼

7

Notarization Date and Time

Date on Document(s)   Reference #

Fees $ Paid? ☐

A J Compliance Agmt.	A J E & O	A J Proof of ID Aff.	A J Adv. Health. Dir.	A J SDB Verification
A J Correction Agmt.	A J Occ. Aff.	A J Sig./Name Aff.	A J Trust - Irr. / Living	A J Vehicle - O+VIN / TT
A J DOT / Mortgage	A J Own. Aff.	A J Survey Aff.	A J Will - LWT / Living	A J
A J Deed - G / QC / W	A J POA - L / D	A J	A J	A J C ☐ Other ▼

8

Notarization Date and Time

Date on Document(s)   Reference #

Fees $ Paid? ☐

A J Compliance Agmt.	A J E & O	A J Proof of ID Aff.	A J Adv. Health. Dir.	A J SDB Verification
A J Correction Agmt.	A J Occ. Aff.	A J Sig./Name Aff.	A J Trust - Irr. / Living	A J Vehicle - O+VIN / TT
A J DOT / Mortgage	A J Own. Aff.	A J Survey Aff.	A J Will - LWT / Living	A J
A J Deed - G / QC / W	A J POA - L / D	A J	A J	A J C ☐ Other ▼

Signer Name and Address	Method of Identification	Signature and Thumbprint	

64

1
- ☐ Driver's License ☐ Other ID #1 - describe ☐ Personally Known
- ☐ Passport ☐ Other ID #2 - describe ☐ Credible Witness(es)

Ref. #1

Ref. #2

X *SIGN HERE*

Right Thumbprint

2
- ☐ Driver's License ☐ Other ID #1 - describe ☐ Personally Known
- ☐ Passport ☐ Other ID #2 - describe ☐ Credible Witness(es)

Ref. #1

Ref. #2

X *SIGN HERE*

Right Thumbprint

3
- ☐ Driver's License ☐ Other ID #1 - describe ☐ Personally Known
- ☐ Passport ☐ Other ID #2 - describe ☐ Credible Witness(es)

Ref. #1

Ref. #2

X *SIGN HERE*

Right Thumbprint

4
- ☐ Driver's License ☐ Other ID #1 - describe ☐ Personally Known
- ☐ Passport ☐ Other ID #2 - describe ☐ Credible Witness(es)

Ref. #1

Ref. #2

X *SIGN HERE*

Right Thumbprint

5
- ☐ Driver's License ☐ Other ID #1 - describe ☐ Personally Known
- ☐ Passport ☐ Other ID #2 - describe ☐ Credible Witness(es)

Ref. #1

Ref. #2

X *SIGN HERE*

Right Thumbprint

6
- ☐ Driver's License ☐ Other ID #1 - describe ☐ Personally Known
- ☐ Passport ☐ Other ID #2 - describe ☐ Credible Witness(es)

Ref. #1

Ref. #2

X *SIGN HERE*

Right Thumbprint

7
- ☐ Driver's License ☐ Other ID #1 - describe ☐ Personally Known
- ☐ Passport ☐ Other ID #2 - describe ☐ Credible Witness(es)

Ref. #1

Ref. #2

X *SIGN HERE*

Right Thumbprint

8
- ☐ Driver's License ☐ Other ID #1 - describe ☐ Personally Known
- ☐ Passport ☐ Other ID #2 - describe ☐ Credible Witness(es)

Ref. #1

Ref. #2

X *SIGN HERE*

Right Thumbprint

1

Notarization Date and Time

Date on Document(s)   Reference #

Fees $

Paid?

A J	Compliance Agmt.	A J	E & O	A J	Proof of ID Aff.	A J	Adv. Health. Dir.	A J	SDB Verification
A J	Correction Agmt.	A J	Occ. Aff.	A J	Sig./Name Aff.	A J	Trust - Irr. / Living	A J	Vehicle - O+VIN / TT
A J	DOT / Mortgage	A J	Own. Aff.	A J	Survey Aff.	A J	Will - LWT / Living	A J	
A J	Deed - G / QC / W	A J	POA - L / D	A J		A J		A J C	Other ▼

2

Notarization Date and Time

Date on Document(s)   Reference #

Fees $

Paid?

A J	Compliance Agmt.	A J	E & O	A J	Proof of ID Aff.	A J	Adv. Health. Dir.	A J	SDB Verification
A J	Correction Agmt.	A J	Occ. Aff.	A J	Sig./Name Aff.	A J	Trust - Irr. / Living	A J	Vehicle - O+VIN / TT
A J	DOT / Mortgage	A J	Own. Aff.	A J	Survey Aff.	A J	Will - LWT / Living	A J	
A J	Deed - G / QC / W	A J	POA - L / D	A J		A J		A J C	Other ▼

3

Notarization Date and Time

Date on Document(s)   Reference #

Fees $

Paid?

A J	Compliance Agmt.	A J	E & O	A J	Proof of ID Aff.	A J	Adv. Health. Dir.	A J	SDB Verification
A J	Correction Agmt.	A J	Occ. Aff.	A J	Sig./Name Aff.	A J	Trust - Irr. / Living	A J	Vehicle - O+VIN / TT
A J	DOT / Mortgage	A J	Own. Aff.	A J	Survey Aff.	A J	Will - LWT / Living	A J	
A J	Deed - G / QC / W	A J	POA - L / D	A J		A J		A J C	Other ▼

4

Notarization Date and Time

Date on Document(s)   Reference #

Fees $

Paid?

A J	Compliance Agmt.	A J	E & O	A J	Proof of ID Aff.	A J	Adv. Health. Dir.	A J	SDB Verification
A J	Correction Agmt.	A J	Occ. Aff.	A J	Sig./Name Aff.	A J	Trust - Irr. / Living	A J	Vehicle - O+VIN / TT
A J	DOT / Mortgage	A J	Own. Aff.	A J	Survey Aff.	A J	Will - LWT / Living	A J	
A J	Deed - G / QC / W	A J	POA - L / D	A J		A J		A J C	Other ▼

5

Notarization Date and Time

Date on Document(s)   Reference #

Fees $

Paid?

A J	Compliance Agmt.	A J	E & O	A J	Proof of ID Aff.	A J	Adv. Health. Dir.	A J	SDB Verification
A J	Correction Agmt.	A J	Occ. Aff.	A J	Sig./Name Aff.	A J	Trust - Irr. / Living	A J	Vehicle - O+VIN / TT
A J	DOT / Mortgage	A J	Own. Aff.	A J	Survey Aff.	A J	Will - LWT / Living	A J	
A J	Deed - G / QC / W	A J	POA - L / D	A J		A J		A J C	Other ▼

6

Notarization Date and Time

Date on Document(s)   Reference #

Fees $

Paid?

A J	Compliance Agmt.	A J	E & O	A J	Proof of ID Aff.	A J	Adv. Health. Dir.	A J	SDB Verification
A J	Correction Agmt.	A J	Occ. Aff.	A J	Sig./Name Aff.	A J	Trust - Irr. / Living	A J	Vehicle - O+VIN / TT
A J	DOT / Mortgage	A J	Own. Aff.	A J	Survey Aff.	A J	Will - LWT / Living	A J	
A J	Deed - G / QC / W	A J	POA - L / D	A J		A J		A J C	Other ▼

7

Notarization Date and Time

Date on Document(s)   Reference #

Fees $

Paid?

A J	Compliance Agmt.	A J	E & O	A J	Proof of ID Aff.	A J	Adv. Health. Dir.	A J	SDB Verification
A J	Correction Agmt.	A J	Occ. Aff.	A J	Sig./Name Aff.	A J	Trust - Irr. / Living	A J	Vehicle - O+VIN / TT
A J	DOT / Mortgage	A J	Own. Aff.	A J	Survey Aff.	A J	Will - LWT / Living	A J	
A J	Deed - G / QC / W	A J	POA - L / D	A J		A J		A J C	Other ▼

8

Notarization Date and Time

Date on Document(s)   Reference #

Fees $

Paid?

A J	Compliance Agmt.	A J	E & O	A J	Proof of ID Aff.	A J	Adv. Health. Dir.	A J	SDB Verification
A J	Correction Agmt.	A J	Occ. Aff.	A J	Sig./Name Aff.	A J	Trust - Irr. / Living	A J	Vehicle - O+VIN / TT
A J	DOT / Mortgage	A J	Own. Aff.	A J	Survey Aff.	A J	Will - LWT / Living	A J	
A J	Deed - G / QC / W	A J	POA - L / D	A J		A J		A J C	Other ▼

Signer Name and Address	Method of Identification	Signature and Thumbprint	

66

1
Driver's License Other ID #1 - describe Personally Known
Passport Other ID #2 - describe Credible Witness(es)
Ref. #1
Ref. #2
X _SIGN HERE_
Right Thumbprint

2
Driver's License Other ID #1 - describe Personally Known
Passport Other ID #2 - describe Credible Witness(es)
Ref. #1
Ref. #2
X _SIGN HERE_
Right Thumbprint

3
Driver's License Other ID #1 - describe Personally Known
Passport Other ID #2 - describe Credible Witness(es)
Ref. #1
Ref. #2
X _SIGN HERE_
Right Thumbprint

4
Driver's License Other ID #1 - describe Personally Known
Passport Other ID #2 - describe Credible Witness(es)
Ref. #1
Ref. #2
X _SIGN HERE_
Right Thumbprint

5
Driver's License Other ID #1 - describe Personally Known
Passport Other ID #2 - describe Credible Witness(es)
Ref. #1
Ref. #2
X _SIGN HERE_
Right Thumbprint

6
Driver's License Other ID #1 - describe Personally Known
Passport Other ID #2 - describe Credible Witness(es)
Ref. #1
Ref. #2
X _SIGN HERE_
Right Thumbprint

7
Driver's License Other ID #1 - describe Personally Known
Passport Other ID #2 - describe Credible Witness(es)
Ref. #1
Ref. #2
X _SIGN HERE_
Right Thumbprint

8
Driver's License Other ID #1 - describe Personally Known
Passport Other ID #2 - describe Credible Witness(es)
Ref. #1
Ref. #2
X _SIGN HERE_
Right Thumbprint

1

Notarization Date and Time

Date on Document(s)   Reference #

Fees $ Paid? ☐

A J Compliance Agmt.	A J E & O	A J Proof of ID Aff.	A J Adv. Health. Dir.	A J SDB Verification
A J Correction Agmt.	A J Occ. Aff.	A J Sig./Name Aff.	A J Trust - Irr./ Living	A J Vehicle - O+VIN / TT
A J DOT / Mortgage	A J Own. Aff.	A J Survey Aff.	A J Will - LWT / Living	A J
A J Deed - G / QC / W	A J POA - L / D	A J	A J	A J C ☐ Other ▼

2

Notarization Date and Time

Date on Document(s)   Reference #

Fees $ Paid? ☐

A J Compliance Agmt.	A J E & O	A J Proof of ID Aff.	A J Adv. Health. Dir.	A J SDB Verification
A J Correction Agmt.	A J Occ. Aff.	A J Sig./Name Aff.	A J Trust - Irr./ Living	A J Vehicle - O+VIN / TT
A J DOT / Mortgage	A J Own. Aff.	A J Survey Aff.	A J Will - LWT / Living	A J
A J Deed - G / QC / W	A J POA - L / D	A J	A J	A J C ☐ Other ▼

3

Notarization Date and Time

Date on Document(s)   Reference #

Fees $ Paid? ☐

A J Compliance Agmt.	A J E & O	A J Proof of ID Aff.	A J Adv. Health. Dir.	A J SDB Verification
A J Correction Agmt.	A J Occ. Aff.	A J Sig./Name Aff.	A J Trust - Irr./ Living	A J Vehicle - O+VIN / TT
A J DOT / Mortgage	A J Own. Aff.	A J Survey Aff.	A J Will - LWT / Living	A J
A J Deed - G / QC / W	A J POA - L / D	A J	A J	A J C ☐ Other ▼

4

Notarization Date and Time

Date on Document(s)   Reference #

Fees $ Paid? ☐

A J Compliance Agmt.	A J E & O	A J Proof of ID Aff.	A J Adv. Health. Dir.	A J SDB Verification
A J Correction Agmt.	A J Occ. Aff.	A J Sig./Name Aff.	A J Trust - Irr./ Living	A J Vehicle - O+VIN / TT
A J DOT / Mortgage	A J Own. Aff.	A J Survey Aff.	A J Will - LWT / Living	A J
A J Deed - G / QC / W	A J POA - L / D	A J	A J	A J C ☐ Other ▼

5

Notarization Date and Time

Date on Document(s)   Reference #

Fees $ Paid? ☐

A J Compliance Agmt.	A J E & O	A J Proof of ID Aff.	A J Adv. Health. Dir.	A J SDB Verification
A J Correction Agmt.	A J Occ. Aff.	A J Sig./Name Aff.	A J Trust - Irr./ Living	A J Vehicle - O+VIN / TT
A J DOT / Mortgage	A J Own. Aff.	A J Survey Aff.	A J Will - LWT / Living	A J
A J Deed - G / QC / W	A J POA - L / D	A J	A J	A J C ☐ Other ▼

6

Notarization Date and Time

Date on Document(s)   Reference #

Fees $ Paid? ☐

A J Compliance Agmt.	A J E & O	A J Proof of ID Aff.	A J Adv. Health. Dir.	A J SDB Verification
A J Correction Agmt.	A J Occ. Aff.	A J Sig./Name Aff.	A J Trust - Irr./ Living	A J Vehicle - O+VIN / TT
A J DOT / Mortgage	A J Own. Aff.	A J Survey Aff.	A J Will - LWT / Living	A J
A J Deed - G / QC / W	A J POA - L / D	A J	A J	A J C ☐ Other ▼

7

Notarization Date and Time

Date on Document(s)   Reference #

Fees $ Paid? ☐

A J Compliance Agmt.	A J E & O	A J Proof of ID Aff.	A J Adv. Health. Dir.	A J SDB Verification
A J Correction Agmt.	A J Occ. Aff.	A J Sig./Name Aff.	A J Trust - Irr./ Living	A J Vehicle - O+VIN / TT
A J DOT / Mortgage	A J Own. Aff.	A J Survey Aff.	A J Will - LWT / Living	A J
A J Deed - G / QC / W	A J POA - L / D	A J	A J	A J C ☐ Other ▼

8

Notarization Date and Time

Date on Document(s)   Reference #

Fees $ Paid? ☐

A J Compliance Agmt.	A J E & O	A J Proof of ID Aff.	A J Adv. Health. Dir.	A J SDB Verification
A J Correction Agmt.	A J Occ. Aff.	A J Sig./Name Aff.	A J Trust - Irr./ Living	A J Vehicle - O+VIN / TT
A J DOT / Mortgage	A J Own. Aff.	A J Survey Aff.	A J Will - LWT / Living	A J
A J Deed - G / QC / W	A J POA - L / D	A J	A J	A J C ☐ Other ▼

1

Signer Name and Address

Method of Identification

☐ Driver's License ☐ Other ID #1 - describe ☐ Personally Known
☐ Passport ☐ Other ID #2 - describe ☐ Credible Witness(es)

Ref. #1

Ref. #2

X _____ SIGN HERE

Right Thumbprint

2

☐ Driver's License ☐ Other ID #1 - describe ☐ Personally Known
☐ Passport ☐ Other ID #2 - describe ☐ Credible Witness(es)

Ref. #1

Ref. #2

X _____ SIGN HERE

Right Thumbprint

3

☐ Driver's License ☐ Other ID #1 - describe ☐ Personally Known
☐ Passport ☐ Other ID #2 - describe ☐ Credible Witness(es)

Ref. #1

Ref. #2

X _____ SIGN HERE

Right Thumbprint

4

☐ Driver's License ☐ Other ID #1 - describe ☐ Personally Known
☐ Passport ☐ Other ID #2 - describe ☐ Credible Witness(es)

Ref. #1

Ref. #2

X _____ SIGN HERE

Right Thumbprint

5

☐ Driver's License ☐ Other ID #1 - describe ☐ Personally Known
☐ Passport ☐ Other ID #2 - describe ☐ Credible Witness(es)

Ref. #1

Ref. #2

X _____ SIGN HERE

Right Thumbprint

6

☐ Driver's License ☐ Other ID #1 - describe ☐ Personally Known
☐ Passport ☐ Other ID #2 - describe ☐ Credible Witness(es)

Ref. #1

Ref. #2

X _____ SIGN HERE

Right Thumbprint

7

☐ Driver's License ☐ Other ID #1 - describe ☐ Personally Known
☐ Passport ☐ Other ID #2 - describe ☐ Credible Witness(es)

Ref. #1

Ref. #2

X _____ SIGN HERE

Right Thumbprint

8

☐ Driver's License ☐ Other ID #1 - describe ☐ Personally Known
☐ Passport ☐ Other ID #2 - describe ☐ Credible Witness(es)

Ref. #1

Ref. #2

X _____ SIGN HERE

Right Thumbprint

Entry 1

Notarization Date and Time

Date on Document(s)   **Reference #**

Fees   **Paid?**
$

A J	Compliance Agmt.	A J	E & O	A J	Proof of ID Aff.	A J	Adv. Health. Dir.	A J	SDB Verification
A J	Correction Agmt.	A J	Occ. Aff.	A J	Sig./Name Aff.	A J	Trust - Irr. / Living	A J	Vehicle - O+VIN / TT
A J	DOT / Mortgage	A J	Own. Aff.	A J	Survey Aff.	A J	Will - LWT / Living	A J	
A J	Deed - G / QC / W	A J	POA - L / D	A J		A J		A J C	Other ▼

Entry 2

Notarization Date and Time

Date on Document(s)   **Reference #**

Fees   **Paid?**
$

A J	Compliance Agmt.	A J	E & O	A J	Proof of ID Aff.	A J	Adv. Health. Dir.	A J	SDB Verification
A J	Correction Agmt.	A J	Occ. Aff.	A J	Sig./Name Aff.	A J	Trust - Irr. / Living	A J	Vehicle - O+VIN / TT
A J	DOT / Mortgage	A J	Own. Aff.	A J	Survey Aff.	A J	Will - LWT / Living	A J	
A J	Deed - G / QC / W	A J	POA - L / D	A J		A J		A J C	Other ▼

Entry 3

Notarization Date and Time

Date on Document(s)   **Reference #**

Fees   **Paid?**
$

A J	Compliance Agmt.	A J	E & O	A J	Proof of ID Aff.	A J	Adv. Health. Dir.	A J	SDB Verification
A J	Correction Agmt.	A J	Occ. Aff.	A J	Sig./Name Aff.	A J	Trust - Irr. / Living	A J	Vehicle - O+VIN / TT
A J	DOT / Mortgage	A J	Own. Aff.	A J	Survey Aff.	A J	Will - LWT / Living	A J	
A J	Deed - G / QC / W	A J	POA - L / D	A J		A J		A J C	Other ▼

Entry 4

Notarization Date and Time

Date on Document(s)   **Reference #**

Fees   **Paid?**
$

A J	Compliance Agmt.	A J	E & O	A J	Proof of ID Aff.	A J	Adv. Health. Dir.	A J	SDB Verification
A J	Correction Agmt.	A J	Occ. Aff.	A J	Sig./Name Aff.	A J	Trust - Irr. / Living	A J	Vehicle - O+VIN / TT
A J	DOT / Mortgage	A J	Own. Aff.	A J	Survey Aff.	A J	Will - LWT / Living	A J	
A J	Deed - G / QC / W	A J	POA - L / D	A J		A J		A J C	Other ▼

Entry 5

Notarization Date and Time

Date on Document(s)   **Reference #**

Fees   **Paid?**
$

A J	Compliance Agmt.	A J	E & O	A J	Proof of ID Aff.	A J	Adv. Health. Dir.	A J	SDB Verification
A J	Correction Agmt.	A J	Occ. Aff.	A J	Sig./Name Aff.	A J	Trust - Irr. / Living	A J	Vehicle - O+VIN / TT
A J	DOT / Mortgage	A J	Own. Aff.	A J	Survey Aff.	A J	Will - LWT / Living	A J	
A J	Deed - G / QC / W	A J	POA - L / D	A J		A J		A J C	Other ▼

Entry 6

Notarization Date and Time

Date on Document(s)   **Reference #**

Fees   **Paid?**
$

A J	Compliance Agmt.	A J	E & O	A J	Proof of ID Aff.	A J	Adv. Health. Dir.	A J	SDB Verification
A J	Correction Agmt.	A J	Occ. Aff.	A J	Sig./Name Aff.	A J	Trust - Irr. / Living	A J	Vehicle - O+VIN / TT
A J	DOT / Mortgage	A J	Own. Aff.	A J	Survey Aff.	A J	Will - LWT / Living	A J	
A J	Deed - G / QC / W	A J	POA - L / D	A J		A J		A J C	Other ▼

Entry 7

Notarization Date and Time

Date on Document(s)   **Reference #**

Fees   **Paid?**
$

A J	Compliance Agmt.	A J	E & O	A J	Proof of ID Aff.	A J	Adv. Health. Dir.	A J	SDB Verification
A J	Correction Agmt.	A J	Occ. Aff.	A J	Sig./Name Aff.	A J	Trust - Irr. / Living	A J	Vehicle - O+VIN / TT
A J	DOT / Mortgage	A J	Own. Aff.	A J	Survey Aff.	A J	Will - LWT / Living	A J	
A J	Deed - G / QC / W	A J	POA - L / D	A J		A J		A J C	Other ▼

Entry 8

Notarization Date and Time

Date on Document(s)   **Reference #**

Fees   **Paid?**
$

A J	Compliance Agmt.	A J	E & O	A J	Proof of ID Aff.	A J	Adv. Health. Dir.	A J	SDB Verification
A J	Correction Agmt.	A J	Occ. Aff.	A J	Sig./Name Aff.	A J	Trust - Irr. / Living	A J	Vehicle - O+VIN / TT
A J	DOT / Mortgage	A J	Own. Aff.	A J	Survey Aff.	A J	Will - LWT / Living	A J	
A J	Deed - G / QC / W	A J	POA - L / D	A J		A J		A J C	Other ▼

Signer Name and Address	Method of Identification	Signature and Thumbprint	

Signer Name and Address — **Method of Identification** — **Signature and Thumbprint** — **70**

1
- ☐ Driver's License ☐ Other ID #1 - describe ☐ Personally Known
- ☐ Passport ☐ Other ID #2 - describe ☐ Credible Witness(es)

Ref. #1

Ref. #2

X _SIGN HERE_

Right Thumbprint

2
- ☐ Driver's License ☐ Other ID #1 - describe ☐ Personally Known
- ☐ Passport ☐ Other ID #2 - describe ☐ Credible Witness(es)

Ref. #1

Ref. #2

X _SIGN HERE_

Right Thumbprint

3
- ☐ Driver's License ☐ Other ID #1 - describe ☐ Personally Known
- ☐ Passport ☐ Other ID #2 - describe ☐ Credible Witness(es)

Ref. #1

Ref. #2

X _SIGN HERE_

Right Thumbprint

4
- ☐ Driver's License ☐ Other ID #1 - describe ☐ Personally Known
- ☐ Passport ☐ Other ID #2 - describe ☐ Credible Witness(es)

Ref. #1

Ref. #2

X _SIGN HERE_

Right Thumbprint

5
- ☐ Driver's License ☐ Other ID #1 - describe ☐ Personally Known
- ☐ Passport ☐ Other ID #2 - describe ☐ Credible Witness(es)

Ref. #1

Ref. #2

X _SIGN HERE_

Right Thumbprint

6
- ☐ Driver's License ☐ Other ID #1 - describe ☐ Personally Known
- ☐ Passport ☐ Other ID #2 - describe ☐ Credible Witness(es)

Ref. #1

Ref. #2

X _SIGN HERE_

Right Thumbprint

7
- ☐ Driver's License ☐ Other ID #1 - describe ☐ Personally Known
- ☐ Passport ☐ Other ID #2 - describe ☐ Credible Witness(es)

Ref. #1

Ref. #2

X _SIGN HERE_

Right Thumbprint

8
- ☐ Driver's License ☐ Other ID #1 - describe ☐ Personally Known
- ☐ Passport ☐ Other ID #2 - describe ☐ Credible Witness(es)

Ref. #1

Ref. #2

X _SIGN HERE_

Right Thumbprint

1

Notarization Date and Time

Date on Document(s) | Reference #

Fees $ | Paid? ☐

A J	Compliance Agmt.	A J	E & O	A J	Proof of ID Aff.	A J	Adv. Health. Dir.	A J	SDB Verification
A J	Correction Agmt.	A J	Occ. Aff.	A J	Sig./Name Aff.	A J	Trust - Irr./Living	A J	Vehicle - O+VIN/TT
A J	DOT / Mortgage	A J	Own. Aff.	A J	Survey Aff.	A J	Will - LWT/Living	A J	
A J	Deed - G/QC/W	A J	POA - L/D	A J		A J		A J C ☐	Other ▼

2

Notarization Date and Time

Date on Document(s) | Reference #

Fees $ | Paid? ☐

A J	Compliance Agmt.	A J	E & O	A J	Proof of ID Aff.	A J	Adv. Health. Dir.	A J	SDB Verification
A J	Correction Agmt.	A J	Occ. Aff.	A J	Sig./Name Aff.	A J	Trust - Irr./Living	A J	Vehicle - O+VIN/TT
A J	DOT / Mortgage	A J	Own. Aff.	A J	Survey Aff.	A J	Will - LWT/Living	A J	
A J	Deed - G/QC/W	A J	POA - L/D	A J		A J		A J C ☐	Other ▼

3

Notarization Date and Time

Date on Document(s) | Reference #

Fees $ | Paid? ☐

A J	Compliance Agmt.	A J	E & O	A J	Proof of ID Aff.	A J	Adv. Health. Dir.	A J	SDB Verification
A J	Correction Agmt.	A J	Occ. Aff.	A J	Sig./Name Aff.	A J	Trust - Irr./Living	A J	Vehicle - O+VIN/TT
A J	DOT / Mortgage	A J	Own. Aff.	A J	Survey Aff.	A J	Will - LWT/Living	A J	
A J	Deed - G/QC/W	A J	POA - L/D	A J		A J		A J C ☐	Other ▼

4

Notarization Date and Time

Date on Document(s) | Reference #

Fees $ | Paid? ☐

A J	Compliance Agmt.	A J	E & O	A J	Proof of ID Aff.	A J	Adv. Health. Dir.	A J	SDB Verification
A J	Correction Agmt.	A J	Occ. Aff.	A J	Sig./Name Aff.	A J	Trust - Irr./Living	A J	Vehicle - O+VIN/TT
A J	DOT / Mortgage	A J	Own. Aff.	A J	Survey Aff.	A J	Will - LWT/Living	A J	
A J	Deed - G/QC/W	A J	POA - L/D	A J		A J		A J C ☐	Other ▼

5

Notarization Date and Time

Date on Document(s) | Reference #

Fees $ | Paid? ☐

A J	Compliance Agmt.	A J	E & O	A J	Proof of ID Aff.	A J	Adv. Health. Dir.	A J	SDB Verification
A J	Correction Agmt.	A J	Occ. Aff.	A J	Sig./Name Aff.	A J	Trust - Irr./Living	A J	Vehicle - O+VIN/TT
A J	DOT / Mortgage	A J	Own. Aff.	A J	Survey Aff.	A J	Will - LWT/Living	A J	
A J	Deed - G/QC/W	A J	POA - L/D	A J		A J		A J C ☐	Other ▼

6

Notarization Date and Time

Date on Document(s) | Reference #

Fees $ | Paid? ☐

A J	Compliance Agmt.	A J	E & O	A J	Proof of ID Aff.	A J	Adv. Health. Dir.	A J	SDB Verification
A J	Correction Agmt.	A J	Occ. Aff.	A J	Sig./Name Aff.	A J	Trust - Irr./Living	A J	Vehicle - O+VIN/TT
A J	DOT / Mortgage	A J	Own. Aff.	A J	Survey Aff.	A J	Will - LWT/Living	A J	
A J	Deed - G/QC/W	A J	POA - L/D	A J		A J		A J C ☐	Other ▼

7

Notarization Date and Time

Date on Document(s) | Reference #

Fees $ | Paid? ☐

A J	Compliance Agmt.	A J	E & O	A J	Proof of ID Aff.	A J	Adv. Health. Dir.	A J	SDB Verification
A J	Correction Agmt.	A J	Occ. Aff.	A J	Sig./Name Aff.	A J	Trust - Irr./Living	A J	Vehicle - O+VIN/TT
A J	DOT / Mortgage	A J	Own. Aff.	A J	Survey Aff.	A J	Will - LWT/Living	A J	
A J	Deed - G/QC/W	A J	POA - L/D	A J		A J		A J C ☐	Other ▼

8

Notarization Date and Time

Date on Document(s) | Reference #

Fees $ | Paid? ☐

A J	Compliance Agmt.	A J	E & O	A J	Proof of ID Aff.	A J	Adv. Health. Dir.	A J	SDB Verification
A J	Correction Agmt.	A J	Occ. Aff.	A J	Sig./Name Aff.	A J	Trust - Irr./Living	A J	Vehicle - O+VIN/TT
A J	DOT / Mortgage	A J	Own. Aff.	A J	Survey Aff.	A J	Will - LWT/Living	A J	
A J	Deed - G/QC/W	A J	POA - L/D	A J		A J		A J C ☐	Other ▼

1

- ☐ Driver's License ☐ Other ID #1 - describe ☐ Personally Known
- ☐ Passport ☐ Other ID #2 - describe ☐ Credible Witness(es)

Ref. #1

Ref. #2

X SIGN HERE

Right Thumbprint

2

- ☐ Driver's License ☐ Other ID #1 - describe ☐ Personally Known
- ☐ Passport ☐ Other ID #2 - describe ☐ Credible Witness(es)

Ref. #1

Ref. #2

X SIGN HERE

Right Thumbprint

3

- ☐ Driver's License ☐ Other ID #1 - describe ☐ Personally Known
- ☐ Passport ☐ Other ID #2 - describe ☐ Credible Witness(es)

Ref. #1

Ref. #2

X SIGN HERE

Right Thumbprint

4

- ☐ Driver's License ☐ Other ID #1 - describe ☐ Personally Known
- ☐ Passport ☐ Other ID #2 - describe ☐ Credible Witness(es)

Ref. #1

Ref. #2

X SIGN HERE

Right Thumbprint

5

- ☐ Driver's License ☐ Other ID #1 - describe ☐ Personally Known
- ☐ Passport ☐ Other ID #2 - describe ☐ Credible Witness(es)

Ref. #1

Ref. #2

X SIGN HERE

Right Thumbprint

6

- ☐ Driver's License ☐ Other ID #1 - describe ☐ Personally Known
- ☐ Passport ☐ Other ID #2 - describe ☐ Credible Witness(es)

Ref. #1

Ref. #2

X SIGN HERE

Right Thumbprint

7

- ☐ Driver's License ☐ Other ID #1 - describe ☐ Personally Known
- ☐ Passport ☐ Other ID #2 - describe ☐ Credible Witness(es)

Ref. #1

Ref. #2

X SIGN HERE

Right Thumbprint

8

- ☐ Driver's License ☐ Other ID #1 - describe ☐ Personally Known
- ☐ Passport ☐ Other ID #2 - describe ☐ Credible Witness(es)

Ref. #1

Ref. #2

X SIGN HERE

Right Thumbprint

1

Notarization Date and Time

Date on Document(s)   Reference #

Fees   Paid?
$

A J Compliance Agmt.   A J E & O   A J Proof of ID Aff.   A J Adv. Health. Dir.   A J SDB Verification
A J Correction Agmt.   A J Occ. Aff.   A J Sig./Name Aff.   A J Trust - Irr. / Living   A J Vehicle - O+VIN / TT
A J DOT / Mortgage   A J Own. Aff.   A J Survey Aff.   A J Will - LWT / Living   A J
A J Deed - G / QC / W   A J POA - L / D   A J   A J   A J C ☐ Other ▼

2

Notarization Date and Time

Date on Document(s)   Reference #

Fees   Paid?
$

A J Compliance Agmt.   A J E & O   A J Proof of ID Aff.   A J Adv. Health. Dir.   A J SDB Verification
A J Correction Agmt.   A J Occ. Aff.   A J Sig./Name Aff.   A J Trust - Irr. / Living   A J Vehicle - O+VIN / TT
A J DOT / Mortgage   A J Own. Aff.   A J Survey Aff.   A J Will - LWT / Living   A J
A J Deed - G / QC / W   A J POA - L / D   A J   A J   A J C ☐ Other ▼

3

Notarization Date and Time

Date on Document(s)   Reference #

Fees   Paid?
$

A J Compliance Agmt.   A J E & O   A J Proof of ID Aff.   A J Adv. Health. Dir.   A J SDB Verification
A J Correction Agmt.   A J Occ. Aff.   A J Sig./Name Aff.   A J Trust - Irr. / Living   A J Vehicle - O+VIN / TT
A J DOT / Mortgage   A J Own. Aff.   A J Survey Aff.   A J Will - LWT / Living   A J
A J Deed - G / QC / W   A J POA - L / D   A J   A J   A J C ☐ Other ▼

4

Notarization Date and Time

Date on Document(s)   Reference #

Fees   Paid?
$

A J Compliance Agmt.   A J E & O   A J Proof of ID Aff.   A J Adv. Health. Dir.   A J SDB Verification
A J Correction Agmt.   A J Occ. Aff.   A J Sig./Name Aff.   A J Trust - Irr. / Living   A J Vehicle - O+VIN / TT
A J DOT / Mortgage   A J Own. Aff.   A J Survey Aff.   A J Will - LWT / Living   A J
A J Deed - G / QC / W   A J POA - L / D   A J   A J   A J C ☐ Other ▼

5

Notarization Date and Time

Date on Document(s)   Reference #

Fees   Paid?
$

A J Compliance Agmt.   A J E & O   A J Proof of ID Aff.   A J Adv. Health. Dir.   A J SDB Verification
A J Correction Agmt.   A J Occ. Aff.   A J Sig./Name Aff.   A J Trust - Irr. / Living   A J Vehicle - O+VIN / TT
A J DOT / Mortgage   A J Own. Aff.   A J Survey Aff.   A J Will - LWT / Living   A J
A J Deed - G / QC / W   A J POA - L / D   A J   A J   A J C ☐ Other ▼

6

Notarization Date and Time

Date on Document(s)   Reference #

Fees   Paid?
$

A J Compliance Agmt.   A J E & O   A J Proof of ID Aff.   A J Adv. Health. Dir.   A J SDB Verification
A J Correction Agmt.   A J Occ. Aff.   A J Sig./Name Aff.   A J Trust - Irr. / Living   A J Vehicle - O+VIN / TT
A J DOT / Mortgage   A J Own. Aff.   A J Survey Aff.   A J Will - LWT / Living   A J
A J Deed - G / QC / W   A J POA - L / D   A J   A J   A J C ☐ Other ▼

7

Notarization Date and Time

Date on Document(s)   Reference #

Fees   Paid?
$

A J Compliance Agmt.   A J E & O   A J Proof of ID Aff.   A J Adv. Health. Dir.   A J SDB Verification
A J Correction Agmt.   A J Occ. Aff.   A J Sig./Name Aff.   A J Trust - Irr. / Living   A J Vehicle - O+VIN / TT
A J DOT / Mortgage   A J Own. Aff.   A J Survey Aff.   A J Will - LWT / Living   A J
A J Deed - G / QC / W   A J POA - L / D   A J   A J   A J C ☐ Other ▼

8

Notarization Date and Time

Date on Document(s)   Reference #

Fees   Paid?
$

A J Compliance Agmt.   A J E & O   A J Proof of ID Aff.   A J Adv. Health. Dir.   A J SDB Verification
A J Correction Agmt.   A J Occ. Aff.   A J Sig./Name Aff.   A J Trust - Irr. / Living   A J Vehicle - O+VIN / TT
A J DOT / Mortgage   A J Own. Aff.   A J Survey Aff.   A J Will - LWT / Living   A J
A J Deed - G / QC / W   A J POA - L / D   A J   A J   A J C ☐ Other ▼

	Method of Identification		
	☐ Driver's License ☐ Other ID #1 - describe ☐ Personally Known ☐ Passport ☐ Other ID #2 - describe ☐ Credible Witness(es) Ref. #1 Ref. #2	X **SIGN HERE**	Right Thumbprint **1**
	☐ Driver's License ☐ Other ID #1 - describe ☐ Personally Known ☐ Passport ☐ Other ID #2 - describe ☐ Credible Witness(es) Ref. #1 Ref. #2	X **SIGN HERE**	Right Thumbprint **2**
	☐ Driver's License ☐ Other ID #1 - describe ☐ Personally Known ☐ Passport ☐ Other ID #2 - describe ☐ Credible Witness(es) Ref. #1 Ref. #2	X **SIGN HERE**	Right Thumbprint **3**
	☐ Driver's License ☐ Other ID #1 - describe ☐ Personally Known ☐ Passport ☐ Other ID #2 - describe ☐ Credible Witness(es) Ref. #1 Ref. #2	X **SIGN HERE**	Right Thumbprint **4**
	☐ Driver's License ☐ Other ID #1 - describe ☐ Personally Known ☐ Passport ☐ Other ID #2 - describe ☐ Credible Witness(es) Ref. #1 Ref. #2	X **SIGN HERE**	Right Thumbprint **5**
	☐ Driver's License ☐ Other ID #1 - describe ☐ Personally Known ☐ Passport ☐ Other ID #2 - describe ☐ Credible Witness(es) Ref. #1 Ref. #2	X **SIGN HERE**	Right Thumbprint **6**
	☐ Driver's License ☐ Other ID #1 - describe ☐ Personally Known ☐ Passport ☐ Other ID #2 - describe ☐ Credible Witness(es) Ref. #1 Ref. #2	X **SIGN HERE**	Right Thumbprint **7**
	☐ Driver's License ☐ Other ID #1 - describe ☐ Personally Known ☐ Passport ☐ Other ID #2 - describe ☐ Credible Witness(es) Ref. #1 Ref. #2	X **SIGN HERE**	Right Thumbprint **8**

1

Notarization Date and Time

Date on Document(s)　Reference #

Fees　$　Paid? ☐

- A J Compliance Agmt.　A J E & O　A J Proof of ID Aff.　A J Adv. Health. Dir.　A J SDB Verification
- A J Correction Agmt.　A J Occ. Aff.　A J Sig./Name Aff.　A J Trust - Irr. / Living　A J Vehicle - O+VIN / TT
- A J DOT / Mortgage　A J Own. Aff.　A J Survey Aff.　A J Will - LWT / Living　A J
- A J Deed - G / QC / W　A J POA - L / D　A J　A J　A J C ☐ Other ▼

2

Notarization Date and Time

Date on Document(s)　Reference #

Fees　$　Paid? ☐

- A J Compliance Agmt.　A J E & O　A J Proof of ID Aff.　A J Adv. Health. Dir.　A J SDB Verification
- A J Correction Agmt.　A J Occ. Aff.　A J Sig./Name Aff.　A J Trust - Irr. / Living　A J Vehicle - O+VIN / TT
- A J DOT / Mortgage　A J Own. Aff.　A J Survey Aff.　A J Will - LWT / Living　A J
- A J Deed - G / QC / W　A J POA - L / D　A J　A J　A J C ☐ Other ▼

3

Notarization Date and Time

Date on Document(s)　Reference #

Fees　$　Paid? ☐

- A J Compliance Agmt.　A J E & O　A J Proof of ID Aff.　A J Adv. Health. Dir.　A J SDB Verification
- A J Correction Agmt.　A J Occ. Aff.　A J Sig./Name Aff.　A J Trust - Irr. / Living　A J Vehicle - O+VIN / TT
- A J DOT / Mortgage　A J Own. Aff.　A J Survey Aff.　A J Will - LWT / Living　A J
- A J Deed - G / QC / W　A J POA - L / D　A J　A J　A J C ☐ Other ▼

4

Notarization Date and Time

Date on Document(s)　Reference #

Fees　$　Paid? ☐

- A J Compliance Agmt.　A J E & O　A J Proof of ID Aff.　A J Adv. Health. Dir.　A J SDB Verification
- A J Correction Agmt.　A J Occ. Aff.　A J Sig./Name Aff.　A J Trust - Irr. / Living　A J Vehicle - O+VIN / TT
- A J DOT / Mortgage　A J Own. Aff.　A J Survey Aff.　A J Will - LWT / Living　A J
- A J Deed - G / QC / W　A J POA - L / D　A J　A J　A J C ☐ Other ▼

5

Notarization Date and Time

Date on Document(s)　Reference #

Fees　$　Paid? ☐

- A J Compliance Agmt.　A J E & O　A J Proof of ID Aff.　A J Adv. Health. Dir.　A J SDB Verification
- A J Correction Agmt.　A J Occ. Aff.　A J Sig./Name Aff.　A J Trust - Irr. / Living　A J Vehicle - O+VIN / TT
- A J DOT / Mortgage　A J Own. Aff.　A J Survey Aff.　A J Will - LWT / Living　A J
- A J Deed - G / QC / W　A J POA - L / D　A J　A J　A J C ☐ Other ▼

6

Notarization Date and Time

Date on Document(s)　Reference #

Fees　$　Paid? ☐

- A J Compliance Agmt.　A J E & O　A J Proof of ID Aff.　A J Adv. Health. Dir.　A J SDB Verification
- A J Correction Agmt.　A J Occ. Aff.　A J Sig./Name Aff.　A J Trust - Irr. / Living　A J Vehicle - O+VIN / TT
- A J DOT / Mortgage　A J Own. Aff.　A J Survey Aff.　A J Will - LWT / Living　A J
- A J Deed - G / QC / W　A J POA - L / D　A J　A J　A J C ☐ Other ▼

7

Notarization Date and Time

Date on Document(s)　Reference #

Fees　$　Paid? ☐

- A J Compliance Agmt.　A J E & O　A J Proof of ID Aff.　A J Adv. Health. Dir.　A J SDB Verification
- A J Correction Agmt.　A J Occ. Aff.　A J Sig./Name Aff.　A J Trust - Irr. / Living　A J Vehicle - O+VIN / TT
- A J DOT / Mortgage　A J Own. Aff.　A J Survey Aff.　A J Will - LWT / Living　A J
- A J Deed - G / QC / W　A J POA - L / D　A J　A J　A J C ☐ Other ▼

8

Notarization Date and Time

Date on Document(s)　Reference #

Fees　$　Paid? ☐

- A J Compliance Agmt.　A J E & O　A J Proof of ID Aff.　A J Adv. Health. Dir.　A J SDB Verification
- A J Correction Agmt.　A J Occ. Aff.　A J Sig./Name Aff.　A J Trust - Irr. / Living　A J Vehicle - O+VIN / TT
- A J DOT / Mortgage　A J Own. Aff.　A J Survey Aff.　A J Will - LWT / Living　A J
- A J Deed - G / QC / W　A J POA - L / D　A J　A J　A J C ☐ Other ▼

Row 1

☐ Driver's License ☐ Other ID #1 - describe ☐ Personally Known
☐ Passport ☐ Other ID #2 - describe ☐ Credible Witness(es)

Ref. #1

Ref. #2

x SIGN HERE

Right Thumbprint

1

Row 2

☐ Driver's License ☐ Other ID #1 - describe ☐ Personally Known
☐ Passport ☐ Other ID #2 - describe ☐ Credible Witness(es)

Ref. #1

Ref. #2

x SIGN HERE

Right Thumbprint

2

Row 3

☐ Driver's License ☐ Other ID #1 - describe ☐ Personally Known
☐ Passport ☐ Other ID #2 - describe ☐ Credible Witness(es)

Ref. #1

Ref. #2

x SIGN HERE

Right Thumbprint

3

Row 4

☐ Driver's License ☐ Other ID #1 - describe ☐ Personally Known
☐ Passport ☐ Other ID #2 - describe ☐ Credible Witness(es)

Ref. #1

Ref. #2

x SIGN HERE

Right Thumbprint

4

Row 5

☐ Driver's License ☐ Other ID #1 - describe ☐ Personally Known
☐ Passport ☐ Other ID #2 - describe ☐ Credible Witness(es)

Ref. #1

Ref. #2

x SIGN HERE

Right Thumbprint

5

Row 6

☐ Driver's License ☐ Other ID #1 - describe ☐ Personally Known
☐ Passport ☐ Other ID #2 - describe ☐ Credible Witness(es)

Ref. #1

Ref. #2

x SIGN HERE

Right Thumbprint

6

Row 7

☐ Driver's License ☐ Other ID #1 - describe ☐ Personally Known
☐ Passport ☐ Other ID #2 - describe ☐ Credible Witness(es)

Ref. #1

Ref. #2

x SIGN HERE

Right Thumbprint

7

Row 8

☐ Driver's License ☐ Other ID #1 - describe ☐ Personally Known
☐ Passport ☐ Other ID #2 - describe ☐ Credible Witness(es)

Ref. #1

Ref. #2

x SIGN HERE

Right Thumbprint

8

1

Notarization Date and Time

Date on Document(s) | Reference #

Fees $ | Paid? ☐

A J Compliance Agmt.	A J E & O	A J Proof of ID Aff.	A J Adv. Health. Dir.	A J SDB Verification
A J Correction Agmt.	A J Occ. Aff.	A J Sig./Name Aff.	A J Trust - Irr./Living	A J Vehicle - O+VIN/TT
A J DOT / Mortgage	A J Own. Aff.	A J Survey Aff.	A J Will - LWT/Living	A J
A J Deed - G/QC/W	A J POA - L/D	A J	A J	A J C☐ Other ▼

2

Notarization Date and Time

Date on Document(s) | Reference #

Fees $ | Paid? ☐

A J Compliance Agmt.	A J E & O	A J Proof of ID Aff.	A J Adv. Health. Dir.	A J SDB Verification
A J Correction Agmt.	A J Occ. Aff.	A J Sig./Name Aff.	A J Trust - Irr./Living	A J Vehicle - O+VIN/TT
A J DOT / Mortgage	A J Own. Aff.	A J Survey Aff.	A J Will - LWT/Living	A J
A J Deed - G/QC/W	A J POA - L/D	A J	A J	A J C☐ Other ▼

3

Notarization Date and Time

Date on Document(s) | Reference #

Fees $ | Paid? ☐

A J Compliance Agmt.	A J E & O	A J Proof of ID Aff.	A J Adv. Health. Dir.	A J SDB Verification
A J Correction Agmt.	A J Occ. Aff.	A J Sig./Name Aff.	A J Trust - Irr./Living	A J Vehicle - O+VIN/TT
A J DOT / Mortgage	A J Own. Aff.	A J Survey Aff.	A J Will - LWT/Living	A J
A J Deed - G/QC/W	A J POA - L/D	A J	A J	A J C☐ Other ▼

4

Notarization Date and Time

Date on Document(s) | Reference #

Fees $ | Paid? ☐

A J Compliance Agmt.	A J E & O	A J Proof of ID Aff.	A J Adv. Health. Dir.	A J SDB Verification
A J Correction Agmt.	A J Occ. Aff.	A J Sig./Name Aff.	A J Trust - Irr./Living	A J Vehicle - O+VIN/TT
A J DOT / Mortgage	A J Own. Aff.	A J Survey Aff.	A J Will - LWT/Living	A J
A J Deed - G/QC/W	A J POA - L/D	A J	A J	A J C☐ Other ▼

5

Notarization Date and Time

Date on Document(s) | Reference #

Fees $ | Paid? ☐

A J Compliance Agmt.	A J E & O	A J Proof of ID Aff.	A J Adv. Health. Dir.	A J SDB Verification
A J Correction Agmt.	A J Occ. Aff.	A J Sig./Name Aff.	A J Trust - Irr./Living	A J Vehicle - O+VIN/TT
A J DOT / Mortgage	A J Own. Aff.	A J Survey Aff.	A J Will - LWT/Living	A J
A J Deed - G/QC/W	A J POA - L/D	A J	A J	A J C☐ Other ▼

6

Notarization Date and Time

Date on Document(s) | Reference #

Fees $ | Paid? ☐

A J Compliance Agmt.	A J E & O	A J Proof of ID Aff.	A J Adv. Health. Dir.	A J SDB Verification
A J Correction Agmt.	A J Occ. Aff.	A J Sig./Name Aff.	A J Trust - Irr./Living	A J Vehicle - O+VIN/TT
A J DOT / Mortgage	A J Own. Aff.	A J Survey Aff.	A J Will - LWT/Living	A J
A J Deed - G/QC/W	A J POA - L/D	A J	A J	A J C☐ Other ▼

7

Notarization Date and Time

Date on Document(s) | Reference #

Fees $ | Paid? ☐

A J Compliance Agmt.	A J E & O	A J Proof of ID Aff.	A J Adv. Health. Dir.	A J SDB Verification
A J Correction Agmt.	A J Occ. Aff.	A J Sig./Name Aff.	A J Trust - Irr./Living	A J Vehicle - O+VIN/TT
A J DOT / Mortgage	A J Own. Aff.	A J Survey Aff.	A J Will - LWT/Living	A J
A J Deed - G/QC/W	A J POA - L/D	A J	A J	A J C☐ Other ▼

8

Notarization Date and Time

Date on Document(s) | Reference #

Fees $ | Paid? ☐

A J Compliance Agmt.	A J E & O	A J Proof of ID Aff.	A J Adv. Health. Dir.	A J SDB Verification
A J Correction Agmt.	A J Occ. Aff.	A J Sig./Name Aff.	A J Trust - Irr./Living	A J Vehicle - O+VIN/TT
A J DOT / Mortgage	A J Own. Aff.	A J Survey Aff.	A J Will - LWT/Living	A J
A J Deed - G/QC/W	A J POA - L/D	A J	A J	A J C☐ Other ▼

1

☐ Driver's License ☐ Other ID #1 - describe ☐ Personally Known
☐ Passport ☐ Other ID #2 - describe ☐ Credible Witness(es)

Ref. #1

Ref. #2

Right Thumbprint

X SIGN HERE

2

☐ Driver's License ☐ Other ID #1 - describe ☐ Personally Known
☐ Passport ☐ Other ID #2 - describe ☐ Credible Witness(es)

Ref. #1

Ref. #2

Right Thumbprint

X SIGN HERE

3

☐ Driver's License ☐ Other ID #1 - describe ☐ Personally Known
☐ Passport ☐ Other ID #2 - describe ☐ Credible Witness(es)

Ref. #1

Ref. #2

Right Thumbprint

X SIGN HERE

4

☐ Driver's License ☐ Other ID #1 - describe ☐ Personally Known
☐ Passport ☐ Other ID #2 - describe ☐ Credible Witness(es)

Ref. #1

Ref. #2

Right Thumbprint

X SIGN HERE

5

☐ Driver's License ☐ Other ID #1 - describe ☐ Personally Known
☐ Passport ☐ Other ID #2 - describe ☐ Credible Witness(es)

Ref. #1

Ref. #2

Right Thumbprint

X SIGN HERE

6

☐ Driver's License ☐ Other ID #1 - describe ☐ Personally Known
☐ Passport ☐ Other ID #2 - describe ☐ Credible Witness(es)

Ref. #1

Ref. #2

Right Thumbprint

X SIGN HERE

7

☐ Driver's License ☐ Other ID #1 - describe ☐ Personally Known
☐ Passport ☐ Other ID #2 - describe ☐ Credible Witness(es)

Ref. #1

Ref. #2

Right Thumbprint

X SIGN HERE

8

☐ Driver's License ☐ Other ID #1 - describe ☐ Personally Known
☐ Passport ☐ Other ID #2 - describe ☐ Credible Witness(es)

Ref. #1

Ref. #2

Right Thumbprint

X SIGN HERE

1

Notarization Date and Time

Date on Document(s) | **Reference #**

Fees $ | **Paid?** ☐

A J Compliance Agmt.	A J E & O	A J Proof of ID Aff.	A J Adv. Health. Dir.	A J SDB Verification
A J Correction Agmt.	A J Occ. Aff.	A J Sig./Name Aff.	A J Trust - Irr. / Living	A J Vehicle - O+VIN / TT
A J DOT / Mortgage	A J Own. Aff.	A J Survey Aff.	A J Will - LWT / Living	A J
A J Deed - G / QC / W	A J POA - L / D	A J	A J	A J C ☐ Other ▼

2

Notarization Date and Time

Date on Document(s) | **Reference #**

Fees $ | **Paid?** ☐

A J Compliance Agmt.	A J E & O	A J Proof of ID Aff.	A J Adv. Health. Dir.	A J SDB Verification
A J Correction Agmt.	A J Occ. Aff.	A J Sig./Name Aff.	A J Trust - Irr. / Living	A J Vehicle - O+VIN / TT
A J DOT / Mortgage	A J Own. Aff.	A J Survey Aff.	A J Will - LWT / Living	A J
A J Deed - G / QC / W	A J POA - L / D	A J	A J	A J C ☐ Other ▼

3

Notarization Date and Time

Date on Document(s) | **Reference #**

Fees $ | **Paid?** ☐

A J Compliance Agmt.	A J E & O	A J Proof of ID Aff.	A J Adv. Health. Dir.	A J SDB Verification
A J Correction Agmt.	A J Occ. Aff.	A J Sig./Name Aff.	A J Trust - Irr. / Living	A J Vehicle - O+VIN / TT
A J DOT / Mortgage	A J Own. Aff.	A J Survey Aff.	A J Will - LWT / Living	A J
A J Deed - G / QC / W	A J POA - L / D	A J	A J	A J C ☐ Other ▼

4

Notarization Date and Time

Date on Document(s) | **Reference #**

Fees $ | **Paid?** ☐

A J Compliance Agmt.	A J E & O	A J Proof of ID Aff.	A J Adv. Health. Dir.	A J SDB Verification
A J Correction Agmt.	A J Occ. Aff.	A J Sig./Name Aff.	A J Trust - Irr. / Living	A J Vehicle - O+VIN / TT
A J DOT / Mortgage	A J Own. Aff.	A J Survey Aff.	A J Will - LWT / Living	A J
A J Deed - G / QC / W	A J POA - L / D	A J	A J	A J C ☐ Other ▼

5

Notarization Date and Time

Date on Document(s) | **Reference #**

Fees $ | **Paid?** ☐

A J Compliance Agmt.	A J E & O	A J Proof of ID Aff.	A J Adv. Health. Dir.	A J SDB Verification
A J Correction Agmt.	A J Occ. Aff.	A J Sig./Name Aff.	A J Trust - Irr. / Living	A J Vehicle - O+VIN / TT
A J DOT / Mortgage	A J Own. Aff.	A J Survey Aff.	A J Will - LWT / Living	A J
A J Deed - G / QC / W	A J POA - L / D	A J	A J	A J C ☐ Other ▼

6

Notarization Date and Time

Date on Document(s) | **Reference #**

Fees $ | **Paid?** ☐

A J Compliance Agmt.	A J E & O	A J Proof of ID Aff.	A J Adv. Health. Dir.	A J SDB Verification
A J Correction Agmt.	A J Occ. Aff.	A J Sig./Name Aff.	A J Trust - Irr. / Living	A J Vehicle - O+VIN / TT
A J DOT / Mortgage	A J Own. Aff.	A J Survey Aff.	A J Will - LWT / Living	A J
A J Deed - G / QC / W	A J POA - L / D	A J	A J	A J C ☐ Other ▼

7

Notarization Date and Time

Date on Document(s) | **Reference #**

Fees $ | **Paid?** ☐

A J Compliance Agmt.	A J E & O	A J Proof of ID Aff.	A J Adv. Health. Dir.	A J SDB Verification
A J Correction Agmt.	A J Occ. Aff.	A J Sig./Name Aff.	A J Trust - Irr. / Living	A J Vehicle - O+VIN / TT
A J DOT / Mortgage	A J Own. Aff.	A J Survey Aff.	A J Will - LWT / Living	A J
A J Deed - G / QC / W	A J POA - L / D	A J	A J	A J C ☐ Other ▼

8

Notarization Date and Time

Date on Document(s) | **Reference #**

Fees $ | **Paid?** ☐

A J Compliance Agmt.	A J E & O	A J Proof of ID Aff.	A J Adv. Health. Dir.	A J SDB Verification
A J Correction Agmt.	A J Occ. Aff.	A J Sig./Name Aff.	A J Trust - Irr. / Living	A J Vehicle - O+VIN / TT
A J DOT / Mortgage	A J Own. Aff.	A J Survey Aff.	A J Will - LWT / Living	A J
A J Deed - G / QC / W	A J POA - L / D	A J	A J	A J C ☐ Other ▼

1

Signer Name and Address

Method of Identification

☐ Driver's License ☐ Other ID #1 - describe ☐ Personally Known
☐ Passport ☐ Other ID #2 - describe ☐ Credible Witness(es)

Ref. #1

Ref. #2

Signature and Thumbprint

X *SIGN HERE*

Right Thumbprint

2

☐ Driver's License ☐ Other ID #1 - describe ☐ Personally Known
☐ Passport ☐ Other ID #2 - describe ☐ Credible Witness(es)

Ref. #1

Ref. #2

X *SIGN HERE*

Right Thumbprint

3

☐ Driver's License ☐ Other ID #1 - describe ☐ Personally Known
☐ Passport ☐ Other ID #2 - describe ☐ Credible Witness(es)

Ref. #1

Ref. #2

X *SIGN HERE*

Right Thumbprint

4

☐ Driver's License ☐ Other ID #1 - describe ☐ Personally Known
☐ Passport ☐ Other ID #2 - describe ☐ Credible Witness(es)

Ref. #1

Ref. #2

X *SIGN HERE*

Right Thumbprint

5

☐ Driver's License ☐ Other ID #1 - describe ☐ Personally Known
☐ Passport ☐ Other ID #2 - describe ☐ Credible Witness(es)

Ref. #1

Ref. #2

X *SIGN HERE*

Right Thumbprint

6

☐ Driver's License ☐ Other ID #1 - describe ☐ Personally Known
☐ Passport ☐ Other ID #2 - describe ☐ Credible Witness(es)

Ref. #1

Ref. #2

X *SIGN HERE*

Right Thumbprint

7

☐ Driver's License ☐ Other ID #1 - describe ☐ Personally Known
☐ Passport ☐ Other ID #2 - describe ☐ Credible Witness(es)

Ref. #1

Ref. #2

X *SIGN HERE*

Right Thumbprint

8

☐ Driver's License ☐ Other ID #1 - describe ☐ Personally Known
☐ Passport ☐ Other ID #2 - describe ☐ Credible Witness(es)

Ref. #1

Ref. #2

X *SIGN HERE*

Right Thumbprint

1

Notarization Date and Time

Date on Document(s)   Reference #

Fees $ Paid? ☐

A J Compliance Agmt.	A J E & O	A J Proof of ID Aff.	A J Adv. Health. Dir.	A J SDB Verification
A J Correction Agmt.	A J Occ. Aff.	A J Sig./Name Aff.	A J Trust - Irr. / Living	A J Vehicle - O+VIN / TT
A J DOT / Mortgage	A J Own. Aff.	A J Survey Aff.	A J Will - LWT / Living	A J
A J Deed - G / QC / W	A J POA - L / D	A J	A J	A J C ☐ Other ▼

2

Notarization Date and Time

Date on Document(s)   Reference #

Fees $ Paid? ☐

A J Compliance Agmt.	A J E & O	A J Proof of ID Aff.	A J Adv. Health. Dir.	A J SDB Verification
A J Correction Agmt.	A J Occ. Aff.	A J Sig./Name Aff.	A J Trust - Irr. / Living	A J Vehicle - O+VIN / TT
A J DOT / Mortgage	A J Own. Aff.	A J Survey Aff.	A J Will - LWT / Living	A J
A J Deed - G / QC / W	A J POA - L / D	A J	A J	A J C ☐ Other ▼

3

Notarization Date and Time

Date on Document(s)   Reference #

Fees $ Paid? ☐

A J Compliance Agmt.	A J E & O	A J Proof of ID Aff.	A J Adv. Health. Dir.	A J SDB Verification
A J Correction Agmt.	A J Occ. Aff.	A J Sig./Name Aff.	A J Trust - Irr. / Living	A J Vehicle - O+VIN / TT
A J DOT / Mortgage	A J Own. Aff.	A J Survey Aff.	A J Will - LWT / Living	A J
A J Deed - G / QC / W	A J POA - L / D	A J	A J	A J C ☐ Other ▼

4

Notarization Date and Time

Date on Document(s)   Reference #

Fees $ Paid? ☐

A J Compliance Agmt.	A J E & O	A J Proof of ID Aff.	A J Adv. Health. Dir.	A J SDB Verification
A J Correction Agmt.	A J Occ. Aff.	A J Sig./Name Aff.	A J Trust - Irr. / Living	A J Vehicle - O+VIN / TT
A J DOT / Mortgage	A J Own. Aff.	A J Survey Aff.	A J Will - LWT / Living	A J
A J Deed - G / QC / W	A J POA - L / D	A J	A J	A J C ☐ Other ▼

5

Notarization Date and Time

Date on Document(s)   Reference #

Fees $ Paid? ☐

A J Compliance Agmt.	A J E & O	A J Proof of ID Aff.	A J Adv. Health. Dir.	A J SDB Verification
A J Correction Agmt.	A J Occ. Aff.	A J Sig./Name Aff.	A J Trust - Irr. / Living	A J Vehicle - O+VIN / TT
A J DOT / Mortgage	A J Own. Aff.	A J Survey Aff.	A J Will - LWT / Living	A J
A J Deed - G / QC / W	A J POA - L / D	A J	A J	A J C ☐ Other ▼

6

Notarization Date and Time

Date on Document(s)   Reference #

Fees $ Paid? ☐

A J Compliance Agmt.	A J E & O	A J Proof of ID Aff.	A J Adv. Health. Dir.	A J SDB Verification
A J Correction Agmt.	A J Occ. Aff.	A J Sig./Name Aff.	A J Trust - Irr. / Living	A J Vehicle - O+VIN / TT
A J DOT / Mortgage	A J Own. Aff.	A J Survey Aff.	A J Will - LWT / Living	A J
A J Deed - G / QC / W	A J POA - L / D	A J	A J	A J C ☐ Other ▼

7

Notarization Date and Time

Date on Document(s)   Reference #

Fees $ Paid? ☐

A J Compliance Agmt.	A J E & O	A J Proof of ID Aff.	A J Adv. Health. Dir.	A J SDB Verification
A J Correction Agmt.	A J Occ. Aff.	A J Sig./Name Aff.	A J Trust - Irr. / Living	A J Vehicle - O+VIN / TT
A J DOT / Mortgage	A J Own. Aff.	A J Survey Aff.	A J Will - LWT / Living	A J
A J Deed - G / QC / W	A J POA - L / D	A J	A J	A J C ☐ Other ▼

8

Notarization Date and Time

Date on Document(s)   Reference #

Fees $ Paid? ☐

A J Compliance Agmt.	A J E & O	A J Proof of ID Aff.	A J Adv. Health. Dir.	A J SDB Verification
A J Correction Agmt.	A J Occ. Aff.	A J Sig./Name Aff.	A J Trust - Irr. / Living	A J Vehicle - O+VIN / TT
A J DOT / Mortgage	A J Own. Aff.	A J Survey Aff.	A J Will - LWT / Living	A J
A J Deed - G / QC / W	A J POA - L / D	A J	A J	A J C ☐ Other ▼

1

☐ Driver's License ☐ Other ID #1 - describe ☐ Personally Known
☐ Passport ☐ Other ID #2 - describe ☐ Credible Witness(es)

Ref. #1

Ref. #2

X **SIGN HERE**

Right Thumbprint

2

☐ Driver's License ☐ Other ID #1 - describe ☐ Personally Known
☐ Passport ☐ Other ID #2 - describe ☐ Credible Witness(es)

Ref. #1

Ref. #2

X **SIGN HERE**

Right Thumbprint

3

☐ Driver's License ☐ Other ID #1 - describe ☐ Personally Known
☐ Passport ☐ Other ID #2 - describe ☐ Credible Witness(es)

Ref. #1

Ref. #2

X **SIGN HERE**

Right Thumbprint

4

☐ Driver's License ☐ Other ID #1 - describe ☐ Personally Known
☐ Passport ☐ Other ID #2 - describe ☐ Credible Witness(es)

Ref. #1

Ref. #2

X **SIGN HERE**

Right Thumbprint

5

☐ Driver's License ☐ Other ID #1 - describe ☐ Personally Known
☐ Passport ☐ Other ID #2 - describe ☐ Credible Witness(es)

Ref. #1

Ref. #2

X **SIGN HERE**

Right Thumbprint

6

☐ Driver's License ☐ Other ID #1 - describe ☐ Personally Known
☐ Passport ☐ Other ID #2 - describe ☐ Credible Witness(es)

Ref. #1

Ref. #2

X **SIGN HERE**

Right Thumbprint

7

☐ Driver's License ☐ Other ID #1 - describe ☐ Personally Known
☐ Passport ☐ Other ID #2 - describe ☐ Credible Witness(es)

Ref. #1

Ref. #2

X **SIGN HERE**

Right Thumbprint

8

☐ Driver's License ☐ Other ID #1 - describe ☐ Personally Known
☐ Passport ☐ Other ID #2 - describe ☐ Credible Witness(es)

Ref. #1

Ref. #2

X **SIGN HERE**

Right Thumbprint

1

Notarization Date and Time

Date on Document(s)   Reference #

Fees   Paid?
$ ☐

A J Compliance Agmt.	A J E & O	A J Proof of ID Aff.	A J Adv. Health. Dir.	A J SDB Verification
A J Correction Agmt.	A J Occ. Aff.	A J Sig./Name Aff.	A J Trust - Irr. / Living	A J Vehicle - O+VIN / TT
A J DOT / Mortgage	A J Own. Aff.	A J Survey Aff.	A J Will - LWT / Living	A J
A J Deed - G / QC / W	A J POA - L / D	A J	A J	A J C ☐ Other ▼

2

Notarization Date and Time

Date on Document(s)   Reference #

Fees   Paid?
$ ☐

A J Compliance Agmt.	A J E & O	A J Proof of ID Aff.	A J Adv. Health. Dir.	A J SDB Verification
A J Correction Agmt.	A J Occ. Aff.	A J Sig./Name Aff.	A J Trust - Irr. / Living	A J Vehicle - O+VIN / TT
A J DOT / Mortgage	A J Own. Aff.	A J Survey Aff.	A J Will - LWT / Living	A J
A J Deed - G / QC / W	A J POA - L / D	A J	A J	A J C ☐ Other ▼

3

Notarization Date and Time

Date on Document(s)   Reference #

Fees   Paid?
$ ☐

A J Compliance Agmt.	A J E & O	A J Proof of ID Aff.	A J Adv. Health. Dir.	A J SDB Verification
A J Correction Agmt.	A J Occ. Aff.	A J Sig./Name Aff.	A J Trust - Irr. / Living	A J Vehicle - O+VIN / TT
A J DOT / Mortgage	A J Own. Aff.	A J Survey Aff.	A J Will - LWT / Living	A J
A J Deed - G / QC / W	A J POA - L / D	A J	A J	A J C ☐ Other ▼

4

Notarization Date and Time

Date on Document(s)   Reference #

Fees   Paid?
$ ☐

A J Compliance Agmt.	A J E & O	A J Proof of ID Aff.	A J Adv. Health. Dir.	A J SDB Verification
A J Correction Agmt.	A J Occ. Aff.	A J Sig./Name Aff.	A J Trust - Irr. / Living	A J Vehicle - O+VIN / TT
A J DOT / Mortgage	A J Own. Aff.	A J Survey Aff.	A J Will - LWT / Living	A J
A J Deed - G / QC / W	A J POA - L / D	A J	A J	A J C ☐ Other ▼

5

Notarization Date and Time

Date on Document(s)   Reference #

Fees   Paid?
$ ☐

A J Compliance Agmt.	A J E & O	A J Proof of ID Aff.	A J Adv. Health. Dir.	A J SDB Verification
A J Correction Agmt.	A J Occ. Aff.	A J Sig./Name Aff.	A J Trust - Irr. / Living	A J Vehicle - O+VIN / TT
A J DOT / Mortgage	A J Own. Aff.	A J Survey Aff.	A J Will - LWT / Living	A J
A J Deed - G / QC / W	A J POA - L / D	A J	A J	A J C ☐ Other ▼

6

Notarization Date and Time

Date on Document(s)   Reference #

Fees   Paid?
$ ☐

A J Compliance Agmt.	A J E & O	A J Proof of ID Aff.	A J Adv. Health. Dir.	A J SDB Verification
A J Correction Agmt.	A J Occ. Aff.	A J Sig./Name Aff.	A J Trust - Irr. / Living	A J Vehicle - O+VIN / TT
A J DOT / Mortgage	A J Own. Aff.	A J Survey Aff.	A J Will - LWT / Living	A J
A J Deed - G / QC / W	A J POA - L / D	A J	A J	A J C ☐ Other ▼

7

Notarization Date and Time

Date on Document(s)   Reference #

Fees   Paid?
$ ☐

A J Compliance Agmt.	A J E & O	A J Proof of ID Aff.	A J Adv. Health. Dir.	A J SDB Verification
A J Correction Agmt.	A J Occ. Aff.	A J Sig./Name Aff.	A J Trust - Irr. / Living	A J Vehicle - O+VIN / TT
A J DOT / Mortgage	A J Own. Aff.	A J Survey Aff.	A J Will - LWT / Living	A J
A J Deed - G / QC / W	A J POA - L / D	A J	A J	A J C ☐ Other ▼

8

Notarization Date and Time

Date on Document(s)   Reference #

Fees   Paid?
$ ☐

A J Compliance Agmt.	A J E & O	A J Proof of ID Aff.	A J Adv. Health. Dir.	A J SDB Verification
A J Correction Agmt.	A J Occ. Aff.	A J Sig./Name Aff.	A J Trust - Irr. / Living	A J Vehicle - O+VIN / TT
A J DOT / Mortgage	A J Own. Aff.	A J Survey Aff.	A J Will - LWT / Living	A J
A J Deed - G / QC / W	A J POA - L / D	A J	A J	A J C ☐ Other ▼

1

- ☐ Driver's License   ☐ Other ID #1 - describe   ☐ Personally Known
- ☐ Passport   ☐ Other ID #2 - describe   ☐ Credible Witness(es)

Ref. #1

Ref. #2

x SIGN HERE

Right Thumbprint

2

- ☐ Driver's License   ☐ Other ID #1 - describe   ☐ Personally Known
- ☐ Passport   ☐ Other ID #2 - describe   ☐ Credible Witness(es)

Ref. #1

Ref. #2

x SIGN HERE

Right Thumbprint

3

- ☐ Driver's License   ☐ Other ID #1 - describe   ☐ Personally Known
- ☐ Passport   ☐ Other ID #2 - describe   ☐ Credible Witness(es)

Ref. #1

Ref. #2

x SIGN HERE

Right Thumbprint

4

- ☐ Driver's License   ☐ Other ID #1 - describe   ☐ Personally Known
- ☐ Passport   ☐ Other ID #2 - describe   ☐ Credible Witness(es)

Ref. #1

Ref. #2

x SIGN HERE

Right Thumbprint

5

- ☐ Driver's License   ☐ Other ID #1 - describe   ☐ Personally Known
- ☐ Passport   ☐ Other ID #2 - describe   ☐ Credible Witness(es)

Ref. #1

Ref. #2

x SIGN HERE

Right Thumbprint

6

- ☐ Driver's License   ☐ Other ID #1 - describe   ☐ Personally Known
- ☐ Passport   ☐ Other ID #2 - describe   ☐ Credible Witness(es)

Ref. #1

Ref. #2

x SIGN HERE

Right Thumbprint

7

- ☐ Driver's License   ☐ Other ID #1 - describe   ☐ Personally Known
- ☐ Passport   ☐ Other ID #2 - describe   ☐ Credible Witness(es)

Ref. #1

Ref. #2

x SIGN HERE

Right Thumbprint

8

- ☐ Driver's License   ☐ Other ID #1 - describe   ☐ Personally Known
- ☐ Passport   ☐ Other ID #2 - describe   ☐ Credible Witness(es)

Ref. #1

Ref. #2

x SIGN HERE

Right Thumbprint

1

Notarization Date and Time

Date on Document(s)   **Reference #**

Fees   **Paid?**
$

- A J Compliance Agmt.
- A J Correction Agmt.
- A J DOT / Mortgage
- A J Deed - G / QC / W
- A J E & O
- A J Occ. Aff.
- A J Own. Aff.
- A J POA - L / D
- A J Proof of ID Aff.
- A J Sig./Name Aff.
- A J Survey Aff.
- A J Adv. Health. Dir.
- A J Trust - Irr. / Living
- A J Will - LWT / Living
- A J
- A J SDB Verification
- A J Vehicle - O+VIN / TT
- A J
- A J C Other ▼

2

Notarization Date and Time

Date on Document(s)   **Reference #**

Fees   **Paid?**
$

- A J Compliance Agmt.
- A J Correction Agmt.
- A J DOT / Mortgage
- A J Deed - G / QC / W
- A J E & O
- A J Occ. Aff.
- A J Own. Aff.
- A J POA - L / D
- A J Proof of ID Aff.
- A J Sig./Name Aff.
- A J Survey Aff.
- A J Adv. Health. Dir.
- A J Trust - Irr. / Living
- A J Will - LWT / Living
- A J
- A J SDB Verification
- A J Vehicle - O+VIN / TT
- A J
- A J C Other ▼

3

Notarization Date and Time

Date on Document(s)   **Reference #**

Fees   **Paid?**
$

- A J Compliance Agmt.
- A J Correction Agmt.
- A J DOT / Mortgage
- A J Deed - G / QC / W
- A J E & O
- A J Occ. Aff.
- A J Own. Aff.
- A J POA - L / D
- A J Proof of ID Aff.
- A J Sig./Name Aff.
- A J Survey Aff.
- A J Adv. Health. Dir.
- A J Trust - Irr. / Living
- A J Will - LWT / Living
- A J
- A J SDB Verification
- A J Vehicle - O+VIN / TT
- A J
- A J C Other ▼

4

Notarization Date and Time

Date on Document(s)   **Reference #**

Fees   **Paid?**
$

- A J Compliance Agmt.
- A J Correction Agmt.
- A J DOT / Mortgage
- A J Deed - G / QC / W
- A J E & O
- A J Occ. Aff.
- A J Own. Aff.
- A J POA - L / D
- A J Proof of ID Aff.
- A J Sig./Name Aff.
- A J Survey Aff.
- A J Adv. Health. Dir.
- A J Trust - Irr. / Living
- A J Will - LWT / Living
- A J
- A J SDB Verification
- A J Vehicle - O+VIN / TT
- A J
- A J C Other ▼

5

Notarization Date and Time

Date on Document(s)   **Reference #**

Fees   **Paid?**
$

- A J Compliance Agmt.
- A J Correction Agmt.
- A J DOT / Mortgage
- A J Deed - G / QC / W
- A J E & O
- A J Occ. Aff.
- A J Own. Aff.
- A J POA - L / D
- A J Proof of ID Aff.
- A J Sig./Name Aff.
- A J Survey Aff.
- A J Adv. Health. Dir.
- A J Trust - Irr. / Living
- A J Will - LWT / Living
- A J
- A J SDB Verification
- A J Vehicle - O+VIN / TT
- A J
- A J C Other ▼

6

Notarization Date and Time

Date on Document(s)   **Reference #**

Fees   **Paid?**
$

- A J Compliance Agmt.
- A J Correction Agmt.
- A J DOT / Mortgage
- A J Deed - G / QC / W
- A J E & O
- A J Occ. Aff.
- A J Own. Aff.
- A J POA - L / D
- A J Proof of ID Aff.
- A J Sig./Name Aff.
- A J Survey Aff.
- A J Adv. Health. Dir.
- A J Trust - Irr. / Living
- A J Will - LWT / Living
- A J
- A J SDB Verification
- A J Vehicle - O+VIN / TT
- A J
- A J C Other ▼

7

Notarization Date and Time

Date on Document(s)   **Reference #**

Fees   **Paid?**
$

- A J Compliance Agmt.
- A J Correction Agmt.
- A J DOT / Mortgage
- A J Deed - G / QC / W
- A J E & O
- A J Occ. Aff.
- A J Own. Aff.
- A J POA - L / D
- A J Proof of ID Aff.
- A J Sig./Name Aff.
- A J Survey Aff.
- A J Adv. Health. Dir.
- A J Trust - Irr. / Living
- A J Will - LWT / Living
- A J
- A J SDB Verification
- A J Vehicle - O+VIN / TT
- A J
- A J C Other ▼

8

Notarization Date and Time

Date on Document(s)   **Reference #**

Fees   **Paid?**
$

- A J Compliance Agmt.
- A J Correction Agmt.
- A J DOT / Mortgage
- A J Deed - G / QC / W
- A J E & O
- A J Occ. Aff.
- A J Own. Aff.
- A J POA - L / D
- A J Proof of ID Aff.
- A J Sig./Name Aff.
- A J Survey Aff.
- A J Adv. Health. Dir.
- A J Trust - Irr. / Living
- A J Will - LWT / Living
- A J
- A J SDB Verification
- A J Vehicle - O+VIN / TT
- A J
- A J C Other ▼

1

Method of Identification:
- ☐ Driver's License
- ☐ Passport
- ☐ Other ID #1 - describe
- ☐ Other ID #2 - describe
- ☐ Personally Known
- ☐ Credible Witness(es)

Ref. #1

Ref. #2

x _SIGN HERE_____

Right Thumbprint

2

Method of Identification:
- ☐ Driver's License
- ☐ Passport
- ☐ Other ID #1 - describe
- ☐ Other ID #2 - describe
- ☐ Personally Known
- ☐ Credible Witness(es)

Ref. #1

Ref. #2

x _SIGN HERE_____

Right Thumbprint

3

Method of Identification:
- ☐ Driver's License
- ☐ Passport
- ☐ Other ID #1 - describe
- ☐ Other ID #2 - describe
- ☐ Personally Known
- ☐ Credible Witness(es)

Ref. #1

Ref. #2

x _SIGN HERE_____

Right Thumbprint

4

Method of Identification:
- ☐ Driver's License
- ☐ Passport
- ☐ Other ID #1 - describe
- ☐ Other ID #2 - describe
- ☐ Personally Known
- ☐ Credible Witness(es)

Ref. #1

Ref. #2

x _SIGN HERE_____

Right Thumbprint

5

Method of Identification:
- ☐ Driver's License
- ☐ Passport
- ☐ Other ID #1 - describe
- ☐ Other ID #2 - describe
- ☐ Personally Known
- ☐ Credible Witness(es)

Ref. #1

Ref. #2

x _SIGN HERE_____

Right Thumbprint

6

Method of Identification:
- ☐ Driver's License
- ☐ Passport
- ☐ Other ID #1 - describe
- ☐ Other ID #2 - describe
- ☐ Personally Known
- ☐ Credible Witness(es)

Ref. #1

Ref. #2

x _SIGN HERE_____

Right Thumbprint

7

Method of Identification:
- ☐ Driver's License
- ☐ Passport
- ☐ Other ID #1 - describe
- ☐ Other ID #2 - describe
- ☐ Personally Known
- ☐ Credible Witness(es)

Ref. #1

Ref. #2

x _SIGN HERE_____

Right Thumbprint

8

Method of Identification:
- ☐ Driver's License
- ☐ Passport
- ☐ Other ID #1 - describe
- ☐ Other ID #2 - describe
- ☐ Personally Known
- ☐ Credible Witness(es)

Ref. #1

Ref. #2

x _SIGN HERE_____

Right Thumbprint

1

Notarization Date and Time

Date on Document(s)   Reference #

Fees   Paid?
$

A J Compliance Agmt.   A J E & O   A J Proof of ID Aff.   A J Adv. Health. Dir.   A J SDB Verification
A J Correction Agmt.   A J Occ. Aff.   A J Sig./Name Aff.   A J Trust - Irr. / Living   A J Vehicle - O+VIN / TT
A J DOT / Mortgage   A J Own. Aff.   A J Survey Aff.   A J Will - LWT / Living   A J
A J Deed - G / QC / W   A J POA - L / D   A J   A J   A J C Other ▼

2

Notarization Date and Time

Date on Document(s)   Reference #

Fees   Paid?
$

A J Compliance Agmt.   A J E & O   A J Proof of ID Aff.   A J Adv. Health. Dir.   A J SDB Verification
A J Correction Agmt.   A J Occ. Aff.   A J Sig./Name Aff.   A J Trust - Irr. / Living   A J Vehicle - O+VIN / TT
A J DOT / Mortgage   A J Own. Aff.   A J Survey Aff.   A J Will - LWT / Living   A J
A J Deed - G / QC / W   A J POA - L / D   A J   A J   A J C Other ▼

3

Notarization Date and Time

Date on Document(s)   Reference #

Fees   Paid?
$

A J Compliance Agmt.   A J E & O   A J Proof of ID Aff.   A J Adv. Health. Dir.   A J SDB Verification
A J Correction Agmt.   A J Occ. Aff.   A J Sig./Name Aff.   A J Trust - Irr. / Living   A J Vehicle - O+VIN / TT
A J DOT / Mortgage   A J Own. Aff.   A J Survey Aff.   A J Will - LWT / Living   A J
A J Deed - G / QC / W   A J POA - L / D   A J   A J   A J C Other ▼

4

Notarization Date and Time

Date on Document(s)   Reference #

Fees   Paid?
$

A J Compliance Agmt.   A J E & O   A J Proof of ID Aff.   A J Adv. Health. Dir.   A J SDB Verification
A J Correction Agmt.   A J Occ. Aff.   A J Sig./Name Aff.   A J Trust - Irr. / Living   A J Vehicle - O+VIN / TT
A J DOT / Mortgage   A J Own. Aff.   A J Survey Aff.   A J Will - LWT / Living   A J
A J Deed - G / QC / W   A J POA - L / D   A J   A J   A J C Other ▼

5

Notarization Date and Time

Date on Document(s)   Reference #

Fees   Paid?
$

A J Compliance Agmt.   A J E & O   A J Proof of ID Aff.   A J Adv. Health. Dir.   A J SDB Verification
A J Correction Agmt.   A J Occ. Aff.   A J Sig./Name Aff.   A J Trust - Irr. / Living   A J Vehicle - O+VIN / TT
A J DOT / Mortgage   A J Own. Aff.   A J Survey Aff.   A J Will - LWT / Living   A J
A J Deed - G / QC / W   A J POA - L / D   A J   A J   A J C Other ▼

6

Notarization Date and Time

Date on Document(s)   Reference #

Fees   Paid?
$

A J Compliance Agmt.   A J E & O   A J Proof of ID Aff.   A J Adv. Health. Dir.   A J SDB Verification
A J Correction Agmt.   A J Occ. Aff.   A J Sig./Name Aff.   A J Trust - Irr. / Living   A J Vehicle - O+VIN / TT
A J DOT / Mortgage   A J Own. Aff.   A J Survey Aff.   A J Will - LWT / Living   A J
A J Deed - G / QC / W   A J POA - L / D   A J   A J   A J C Other ▼

7

Notarization Date and Time

Date on Document(s)   Reference #

Fees   Paid?
$

A J Compliance Agmt.   A J E & O   A J Proof of ID Aff.   A J Adv. Health. Dir.   A J SDB Verification
A J Correction Agmt.   A J Occ. Aff.   A J Sig./Name Aff.   A J Trust - Irr. / Living   A J Vehicle - O+VIN / TT
A J DOT / Mortgage   A J Own. Aff.   A J Survey Aff.   A J Will - LWT / Living   A J
A J Deed - G / QC / W   A J POA - L / D   A J   A J   A J C Other ▼

8

Notarization Date and Time

Date on Document(s)   Reference #

Fees   Paid?
$

A J Compliance Agmt.   A J E & O   A J Proof of ID Aff.   A J Adv. Health. Dir.   A J SDB Verification
A J Correction Agmt.   A J Occ. Aff.   A J Sig./Name Aff.   A J Trust - Irr. / Living   A J Vehicle - O+VIN / TT
A J DOT / Mortgage   A J Own. Aff.   A J Survey Aff.   A J Will - LWT / Living   A J
A J Deed - G / QC / W   A J POA - L / D   A J   A J   A J C Other ▼

Signer Name and Address	Method of Identification	Signature and Thumbprint	
	☐ Driver's License ☐ Other ID #1 - describe ☐ Personally Known ☐ Passport ☐ Other ID #2 - describe ☐ Credible Witness(es) Ref. #1 Ref. #2	X __SIGN HERE__	Right Thumbprint **1**
	☐ Driver's License ☐ Other ID #1 - describe ☐ Personally Known ☐ Passport ☐ Other ID #2 - describe ☐ Credible Witness(es) Ref. #1 Ref. #2	X __SIGN HERE__	Right Thumbprint **2**
	☐ Driver's License ☐ Other ID #1 - describe ☐ Personally Known ☐ Passport ☐ Other ID #2 - describe ☐ Credible Witness(es) Ref. #1 Ref. #2	X __SIGN HERE__	Right Thumbprint **3**
	☐ Driver's License ☐ Other ID #1 - describe ☐ Personally Known ☐ Passport ☐ Other ID #2 - describe ☐ Credible Witness(es) Ref. #1 Ref. #2	X __SIGN HERE__	Right Thumbprint **4**
	☐ Driver's License ☐ Other ID #1 - describe ☐ Personally Known ☐ Passport ☐ Other ID #2 - describe ☐ Credible Witness(es) Ref. #1 Ref. #2	X __SIGN HERE__	Right Thumbprint **5**
	☐ Driver's License ☐ Other ID #1 - describe ☐ Personally Known ☐ Passport ☐ Other ID #2 - describe ☐ Credible Witness(es) Ref. #1 Ref. #2	X __SIGN HERE__	Right Thumbprint **6**
	☐ Driver's License ☐ Other ID #1 - describe ☐ Personally Known ☐ Passport ☐ Other ID #2 - describe ☐ Credible Witness(es) Ref. #1 Ref. #2	X __SIGN HERE__	Right Thumbprint **7**
	☐ Driver's License ☐ Other ID #1 - describe ☐ Personally Known ☐ Passport ☐ Other ID #2 - describe ☐ Credible Witness(es) Ref. #1 Ref. #2	X __SIGN HERE__	Right Thumbprint **8**

Dates and Fees   Description of Document(s) or Proceeding   Additional Information

1

Notarization Date and Time

Date on Document(s) Reference #

Fees Paid?
$

- A J Compliance Agmt.
- A J Correction Agmt.
- A J DOT / Mortgage
- A J Deed - G / QC / W
- A J E & O
- A J Occ. Aff.
- A J Own. Aff.
- A J POA - L / D
- A J Proof of ID Aff.
- A J Sig./Name Aff.
- A J Survey Aff.
- A J
- A J Adv. Health. Dir.
- A J Trust - Irr. / Living
- A J Will - LWT / Living
- A J
- A J SDB Verification
- A J Vehicle - O+VIN / TT
- A J
- A J C Other ▼

2

Notarization Date and Time

Date on Document(s) Reference #

Fees Paid?
$

- A J Compliance Agmt.
- A J Correction Agmt.
- A J DOT / Mortgage
- A J Deed - G / QC / W
- A J E & O
- A J Occ. Aff.
- A J Own. Aff.
- A J POA - L / D
- A J Proof of ID Aff.
- A J Sig./Name Aff.
- A J Survey Aff.
- A J
- A J Adv. Health. Dir.
- A J Trust - Irr. / Living
- A J Will - LWT / Living
- A J
- A J SDB Verification
- A J Vehicle - O+VIN / TT
- A J
- A J C Other ▼

3

Notarization Date and Time

Date on Document(s) Reference #

Fees Paid?
$

- A J Compliance Agmt.
- A J Correction Agmt.
- A J DOT / Mortgage
- A J Deed - G / QC / W
- A J E & O
- A J Occ. Aff.
- A J Own. Aff.
- A J POA - L / D
- A J Proof of ID Aff.
- A J Sig./Name Aff.
- A J Survey Aff.
- A J
- A J Adv. Health. Dir.
- A J Trust - Irr. / Living
- A J Will - LWT / Living
- A J
- A J SDB Verification
- A J Vehicle - O+VIN / TT
- A J
- A J C Other ▼

4

Notarization Date and Time

Date on Document(s) Reference #

Fees Paid?
$

- A J Compliance Agmt.
- A J Correction Agmt.
- A J DOT / Mortgage
- A J Deed - G / QC / W
- A J E & O
- A J Occ. Aff.
- A J Own. Aff.
- A J POA - L / D
- A J Proof of ID Aff.
- A J Sig./Name Aff.
- A J Survey Aff.
- A J
- A J Adv. Health. Dir.
- A J Trust - Irr. / Living
- A J Will - LWT / Living
- A J
- A J SDB Verification
- A J Vehicle - O+VIN / TT
- A J
- A J C Other ▼

5

Notarization Date and Time

Date on Document(s) Reference #

Fees Paid?
$

- A J Compliance Agmt.
- A J Correction Agmt.
- A J DOT / Mortgage
- A J Deed - G / QC / W
- A J E & O
- A J Occ. Aff.
- A J Own. Aff.
- A J POA - L / D
- A J Proof of ID Aff.
- A J Sig./Name Aff.
- A J Survey Aff.
- A J
- A J Adv. Health. Dir.
- A J Trust - Irr. / Living
- A J Will - LWT / Living
- A J
- A J SDB Verification
- A J Vehicle - O+VIN / TT
- A J
- A J C Other ▼

6

Notarization Date and Time

Date on Document(s) Reference #

Fees Paid?
$

- A J Compliance Agmt.
- A J Correction Agmt.
- A J DOT / Mortgage
- A J Deed - G / QC / W
- A J E & O
- A J Occ. Aff.
- A J Own. Aff.
- A J POA - L / D
- A J Proof of ID Aff.
- A J Sig./Name Aff.
- A J Survey Aff.
- A J
- A J Adv. Health. Dir.
- A J Trust - Irr. / Living
- A J Will - LWT / Living
- A J
- A J SDB Verification
- A J Vehicle - O+VIN / TT
- A J
- A J C Other ▼

7

Notarization Date and Time

Date on Document(s) Reference #

Fees Paid?
$

- A J Compliance Agmt.
- A J Correction Agmt.
- A J DOT / Mortgage
- A J Deed - G / QC / W
- A J E & O
- A J Occ. Aff.
- A J Own. Aff.
- A J POA - L / D
- A J Proof of ID Aff.
- A J Sig./Name Aff.
- A J Survey Aff.
- A J
- A J Adv. Health. Dir.
- A J Trust - Irr. / Living
- A J Will - LWT / Living
- A J
- A J SDB Verification
- A J Vehicle - O+VIN / TT
- A J
- A J C Other ▼

8

Notarization Date and Time

Date on Document(s) Reference #

Fees Paid?
$

- A J Compliance Agmt.
- A J Correction Agmt.
- A J DOT / Mortgage
- A J Deed - G / QC / W
- A J E & O
- A J Occ. Aff.
- A J Own. Aff.
- A J POA - L / D
- A J Proof of ID Aff.
- A J Sig./Name Aff.
- A J Survey Aff.
- A J
- A J Adv. Health. Dir.
- A J Trust - Irr. / Living
- A J Will - LWT / Living
- A J
- A J SDB Verification
- A J Vehicle - O+VIN / TT
- A J
- A J C Other ▼

1

- [ ] Driver's License   [ ] Other ID #1 - describe   [ ] Personally Known
- [ ] Passport   [ ] Other ID #2 - describe   [ ] Credible Witness(es)

Ref. #1

Ref. #2

Right Thumbprint

X ___SIGN HERE___

2

- [ ] Driver's License   [ ] Other ID #1 - describe   [ ] Personally Known
- [ ] Passport   [ ] Other ID #2 - describe   [ ] Credible Witness(es)

Ref. #1

Ref. #2

Right Thumbprint

X ___SIGN HERE___

3

- [ ] Driver's License   [ ] Other ID #1 - describe   [ ] Personally Known
- [ ] Passport   [ ] Other ID #2 - describe   [ ] Credible Witness(es)

Ref. #1

Ref. #2

Right Thumbprint

X ___SIGN HERE___

4

- [ ] Driver's License   [ ] Other ID #1 - describe   [ ] Personally Known
- [ ] Passport   [ ] Other ID #2 - describe   [ ] Credible Witness(es)

Ref. #1

Ref. #2

Right Thumbprint

X ___SIGN HERE___

5

- [ ] Driver's License   [ ] Other ID #1 - describe   [ ] Personally Known
- [ ] Passport   [ ] Other ID #2 - describe   [ ] Credible Witness(es)

Ref. #1

Ref. #2

Right Thumbprint

X ___SIGN HERE___

6

- [ ] Driver's License   [ ] Other ID #1 - describe   [ ] Personally Known
- [ ] Passport   [ ] Other ID #2 - describe   [ ] Credible Witness(es)

Ref. #1

Ref. #2

Right Thumbprint

X ___SIGN HERE___

7

- [ ] Driver's License   [ ] Other ID #1 - describe   [ ] Personally Known
- [ ] Passport   [ ] Other ID #2 - describe   [ ] Credible Witness(es)

Ref. #1

Ref. #2

Right Thumbprint

X ___SIGN HERE___

8

- [ ] Driver's License   [ ] Other ID #1 - describe   [ ] Personally Known
- [ ] Passport   [ ] Other ID #2 - describe   [ ] Credible Witness(es)

Ref. #1

Ref. #2

Right Thumbprint

X ___SIGN HERE___

1

Notarization Date and Time

Date on Document(s) Reference #

Fees $ Paid? ☐

- A J Compliance Agmt.
- A J Correction Agmt.
- A J DOT / Mortgage
- A J Deed - G / QC / W
- A J E & O
- A J Occ. Aff.
- A J Own. Aff.
- A J POA - L / D
- A J Proof of ID Aff.
- A J Sig./Name Aff.
- A J Survey Aff.
- A J
- A J Adv. Health. Dir.
- A J Trust - Irr. / Living
- A J Will - LWT / Living
- A J
- A J SDB Verification
- A J Vehicle - O+VIN / TT
- A J
- A J C ☐ Other ▼

2

Notarization Date and Time

Date on Document(s) Reference #

Fees $ Paid? ☐

- A J Compliance Agmt.
- A J Correction Agmt.
- A J DOT / Mortgage
- A J Deed - G / QC / W
- A J E & O
- A J Occ. Aff.
- A J Own. Aff.
- A J POA - L / D
- A J Proof of ID Aff.
- A J Sig./Name Aff.
- A J Survey Aff.
- A J
- A J Adv. Health. Dir.
- A J Trust - Irr. / Living
- A J Will - LWT / Living
- A J
- A J SDB Verification
- A J Vehicle - O+VIN / TT
- A J
- A J C ☐ Other ▼

3

Notarization Date and Time

Date on Document(s) Reference #

Fees $ Paid? ☐

- A J Compliance Agmt.
- A J Correction Agmt.
- A J DOT / Mortgage
- A J Deed - G / QC / W
- A J E & O
- A J Occ. Aff.
- A J Own. Aff.
- A J POA - L / D
- A J Proof of ID Aff.
- A J Sig./Name Aff.
- A J Survey Aff.
- A J
- A J Adv. Health. Dir.
- A J Trust - Irr. / Living
- A J Will - LWT / Living
- A J
- A J SDB Verification
- A J Vehicle - O+VIN / TT
- A J
- A J C ☐ Other ▼

4

Notarization Date and Time

Date on Document(s) Reference #

Fees $ Paid? ☐

- A J Compliance Agmt.
- A J Correction Agmt.
- A J DOT / Mortgage
- A J Deed - G / QC / W
- A J E & O
- A J Occ. Aff.
- A J Own. Aff.
- A J POA - L / D
- A J Proof of ID Aff.
- A J Sig./Name Aff.
- A J Survey Aff.
- A J
- A J Adv. Health. Dir.
- A J Trust - Irr. / Living
- A J Will - LWT / Living
- A J
- A J SDB Verification
- A J Vehicle - O+VIN / TT
- A J
- A J C ☐ Other ▼

5

Notarization Date and Time

Date on Document(s) Reference #

Fees $ Paid? ☐

- A J Compliance Agmt.
- A J Correction Agmt.
- A J DOT / Mortgage
- A J Deed - G / QC / W
- A J E & O
- A J Occ. Aff.
- A J Own. Aff.
- A J POA - L / D
- A J Proof of ID Aff.
- A J Sig./Name Aff.
- A J Survey Aff.
- A J
- A J Adv. Health. Dir.
- A J Trust - Irr. / Living
- A J Will - LWT / Living
- A J
- A J SDB Verification
- A J Vehicle - O+VIN / TT
- A J
- A J C ☐ Other ▼

6

Notarization Date and Time

Date on Document(s) Reference #

Fees $ Paid? ☐

- A J Compliance Agmt.
- A J Correction Agmt.
- A J DOT / Mortgage
- A J Deed - G / QC / W
- A J E & O
- A J Occ. Aff.
- A J Own. Aff.
- A J POA - L / D
- A J Proof of ID Aff.
- A J Sig./Name Aff.
- A J Survey Aff.
- A J
- A J Adv. Health. Dir.
- A J Trust - Irr. / Living
- A J Will - LWT / Living
- A J
- A J SDB Verification
- A J Vehicle - O+VIN / TT
- A J
- A J C ☐ Other ▼

7

Notarization Date and Time

Date on Document(s) Reference #

Fees $ Paid? ☐

- A J Compliance Agmt.
- A J Correction Agmt.
- A J DOT / Mortgage
- A J Deed - G / QC / W
- A J E & O
- A J Occ. Aff.
- A J Own. Aff.
- A J POA - L / D
- A J Proof of ID Aff.
- A J Sig./Name Aff.
- A J Survey Aff.
- A J
- A J Adv. Health. Dir.
- A J Trust - Irr. / Living
- A J Will - LWT / Living
- A J
- A J SDB Verification
- A J Vehicle - O+VIN / TT
- A J
- A J C ☐ Other ▼

8

Notarization Date and Time

Date on Document(s) Reference #

Fees $ Paid? ☐

- A J Compliance Agmt.
- A J Correction Agmt.
- A J DOT / Mortgage
- A J Deed - G / QC / W
- A J E & O
- A J Occ. Aff.
- A J Own. Aff.
- A J POA - L / D
- A J Proof of ID Aff.
- A J Sig./Name Aff.
- A J Survey Aff.
- A J
- A J Adv. Health. Dir.
- A J Trust - Irr. / Living
- A J Will - LWT / Living
- A J
- A J SDB Verification
- A J Vehicle - O+VIN / TT
- A J
- A J C ☐ Other ▼

1

- [ ] Driver's License
- [ ] Passport
- [ ] Other ID #1 - describe
- [ ] Other ID #2 - describe
- [ ] Personally Known
- [ ] Credible Witness(es)

Ref. #1

Ref. #2

X SIGN HERE

Right Thumbprint

2

- [ ] Driver's License
- [ ] Passport
- [ ] Other ID #1 - describe
- [ ] Other ID #2 - describe
- [ ] Personally Known
- [ ] Credible Witness(es)

Ref. #1

Ref. #2

X SIGN HERE

Right Thumbprint

3

- [ ] Driver's License
- [ ] Passport
- [ ] Other ID #1 - describe
- [ ] Other ID #2 - describe
- [ ] Personally Known
- [ ] Credible Witness(es)

Ref. #1

Ref. #2

X SIGN HERE

Right Thumbprint

4

- [ ] Driver's License
- [ ] Passport
- [ ] Other ID #1 - describe
- [ ] Other ID #2 - describe
- [ ] Personally Known
- [ ] Credible Witness(es)

Ref. #1

Ref. #2

X SIGN HERE

Right Thumbprint

5

- [ ] Driver's License
- [ ] Passport
- [ ] Other ID #1 - describe
- [ ] Other ID #2 - describe
- [ ] Personally Known
- [ ] Credible Witness(es)

Ref. #1

Ref. #2

X SIGN HERE

Right Thumbprint

6

- [ ] Driver's License
- [ ] Passport
- [ ] Other ID #1 - describe
- [ ] Other ID #2 - describe
- [ ] Personally Known
- [ ] Credible Witness(es)

Ref. #1

Ref. #2

X SIGN HERE

Right Thumbprint

7

- [ ] Driver's License
- [ ] Passport
- [ ] Other ID #1 - describe
- [ ] Other ID #2 - describe
- [ ] Personally Known
- [ ] Credible Witness(es)

Ref. #1

Ref. #2

X SIGN HERE

Right Thumbprint

8

- [ ] Driver's License
- [ ] Passport
- [ ] Other ID #1 - describe
- [ ] Other ID #2 - describe
- [ ] Personally Known
- [ ] Credible Witness(es)

Ref. #1

Ref. #2

X SIGN HERE

Right Thumbprint

1

Notarization Date and Time

Date on Document(s)   Reference #

Fees   Paid?
$

A J Compliance Agmt.	A J E & O	A J Proof of ID Aff.	A J Adv. Health. Dir.	A J SDB Verification
A J Correction Agmt.	A J Occ. Aff.	A J Sig./Name Aff.	A J Trust - Irr. / Living	A J Vehicle - O+VIN / TT
A J DOT / Mortgage	A J Own. Aff.	A J Survey Aff.	A J Will - LWT / Living	A J
A J Deed - G / QC / W	A J POA - L / D	A J	A J	A J C Other ▼

2

Notarization Date and Time

Date on Document(s)   Reference #

Fees   Paid?
$

A J Compliance Agmt.	A J E & O	A J Proof of ID Aff.	A J Adv. Health. Dir.	A J SDB Verification
A J Correction Agmt.	A J Occ. Aff.	A J Sig./Name Aff.	A J Trust - Irr. / Living	A J Vehicle - O+VIN / TT
A J DOT / Mortgage	A J Own. Aff.	A J Survey Aff.	A J Will - LWT / Living	A J
A J Deed - G / QC / W	A J POA - L / D	A J	A J	A J C Other ▼

3

Notarization Date and Time

Date on Document(s)   Reference #

Fees   Paid?
$

A J Compliance Agmt.	A J E & O	A J Proof of ID Aff.	A J Adv. Health. Dir.	A J SDB Verification
A J Correction Agmt.	A J Occ. Aff.	A J Sig./Name Aff.	A J Trust - Irr. / Living	A J Vehicle - O+VIN / TT
A J DOT / Mortgage	A J Own. Aff.	A J Survey Aff.	A J Will - LWT / Living	A J
A J Deed - G / QC / W	A J POA - L / D	A J	A J	A J C Other ▼

4

Notarization Date and Time

Date on Document(s)   Reference #

Fees   Paid?
$

A J Compliance Agmt.	A J E & O	A J Proof of ID Aff.	A J Adv. Health. Dir.	A J SDB Verification
A J Correction Agmt.	A J Occ. Aff.	A J Sig./Name Aff.	A J Trust - Irr. / Living	A J Vehicle - O+VIN / TT
A J DOT / Mortgage	A J Own. Aff.	A J Survey Aff.	A J Will - LWT / Living	A J
A J Deed - G / QC / W	A J POA - L / D	A J	A J	A J C Other ▼

5

Notarization Date and Time

Date on Document(s)   Reference #

Fees   Paid?
$

A J Compliance Agmt.	A J E & O	A J Proof of ID Aff.	A J Adv. Health. Dir.	A J SDB Verification
A J Correction Agmt.	A J Occ. Aff.	A J Sig./Name Aff.	A J Trust - Irr. / Living	A J Vehicle - O+VIN / TT
A J DOT / Mortgage	A J Own. Aff.	A J Survey Aff.	A J Will - LWT / Living	A J
A J Deed - G / QC / W	A J POA - L / D	A J	A J	A J C Other ▼

6

Notarization Date and Time

Date on Document(s)   Reference #

Fees   Paid?
$

A J Compliance Agmt.	A J E & O	A J Proof of ID Aff.	A J Adv. Health. Dir.	A J SDB Verification
A J Correction Agmt.	A J Occ. Aff.	A J Sig./Name Aff.	A J Trust - Irr. / Living	A J Vehicle - O+VIN / TT
A J DOT / Mortgage	A J Own. Aff.	A J Survey Aff.	A J Will - LWT / Living	A J
A J Deed - G / QC / W	A J POA - L / D	A J	A J	A J C Other ▼

7

Notarization Date and Time

Date on Document(s)   Reference #

Fees   Paid?
$

A J Compliance Agmt.	A J E & O	A J Proof of ID Aff.	A J Adv. Health. Dir.	A J SDB Verification
A J Correction Agmt.	A J Occ. Aff.	A J Sig./Name Aff.	A J Trust - Irr. / Living	A J Vehicle - O+VIN / TT
A J DOT / Mortgage	A J Own. Aff.	A J Survey Aff.	A J Will - LWT / Living	A J
A J Deed - G / QC / W	A J POA - L / D	A J	A J	A J C Other ▼

8

Notarization Date and Time

Date on Document(s)   Reference #

Fees   Paid?
$

A J Compliance Agmt.	A J E & O	A J Proof of ID Aff.	A J Adv. Health. Dir.	A J SDB Verification
A J Correction Agmt.	A J Occ. Aff.	A J Sig./Name Aff.	A J Trust - Irr. / Living	A J Vehicle - O+VIN / TT
A J DOT / Mortgage	A J Own. Aff.	A J Survey Aff.	A J Will - LWT / Living	A J
A J Deed - G / QC / W	A J POA - L / D	A J	A J	A J C Other ▼

1

- [ ] Driver's License
- [ ] Passport
- [ ] Other ID #1 - describe
- [ ] Other ID #2 - describe
- [ ] Personally Known
- [ ] Credible Witness(es)

Ref. #1

Ref. #2

X SIGN HERE

Right Thumbprint

2

- [ ] Driver's License
- [ ] Passport
- [ ] Other ID #1 - describe
- [ ] Other ID #2 - describe
- [ ] Personally Known
- [ ] Credible Witness(es)

Ref. #1

Ref. #2

X SIGN HERE

Right Thumbprint

3

- [ ] Driver's License
- [ ] Passport
- [ ] Other ID #1 - describe
- [ ] Other ID #2 - describe
- [ ] Personally Known
- [ ] Credible Witness(es)

Ref. #1

Ref. #2

X SIGN HERE

Right Thumbprint

4

- [ ] Driver's License
- [ ] Passport
- [ ] Other ID #1 - describe
- [ ] Other ID #2 - describe
- [ ] Personally Known
- [ ] Credible Witness(es)

Ref. #1

Ref. #2

X SIGN HERE

Right Thumbprint

5

- [ ] Driver's License
- [ ] Passport
- [ ] Other ID #1 - describe
- [ ] Other ID #2 - describe
- [ ] Personally Known
- [ ] Credible Witness(es)

Ref. #1

Ref. #2

X SIGN HERE

Right Thumbprint

6

- [ ] Driver's License
- [ ] Passport
- [ ] Other ID #1 - describe
- [ ] Other ID #2 - describe
- [ ] Personally Known
- [ ] Credible Witness(es)

Ref. #1

Ref. #2

X SIGN HERE

Right Thumbprint

7

- [ ] Driver's License
- [ ] Passport
- [ ] Other ID #1 - describe
- [ ] Other ID #2 - describe
- [ ] Personally Known
- [ ] Credible Witness(es)

Ref. #1

Ref. #2

X SIGN HERE

Right Thumbprint

8

- [ ] Driver's License
- [ ] Passport
- [ ] Other ID #1 - describe
- [ ] Other ID #2 - describe
- [ ] Personally Known
- [ ] Credible Witness(es)

Ref. #1

Ref. #2

X SIGN HERE

Right Thumbprint

95 Dates and Fees   Description of Document(s) or Proceeding   Additional Information

1
Notarization Date and Time

Date on Document(s)   Reference #

Fees   **Paid?**
$

A J Compliance Agmt. A J E & O A J Proof of ID Aff. A J Adv. Health. Dir. A J SDB Verification
A J Correction Agmt. A J Occ. Aff. A J Sig./Name Aff. A J Trust - Irr./Living A J Vehicle - O+VIN/TT
A J DOT / Mortgage A J Own. Aff. A J Survey Aff. A J Will - LWT/Living A J
A J Deed - G/QC/W A J POA - L/D A J A J A J C Other ▼

2
Notarization Date and Time

Date on Document(s)   Reference #

Fees   **Paid?**
$

A J Compliance Agmt. A J E & O A J Proof of ID Aff. A J Adv. Health. Dir. A J SDB Verification
A J Correction Agmt. A J Occ. Aff. A J Sig./Name Aff. A J Trust - Irr./Living A J Vehicle - O+VIN/TT
A J DOT / Mortgage A J Own. Aff. A J Survey Aff. A J Will - LWT/Living A J
A J Deed - G/QC/W A J POA - L/D A J A J A J C Other ▼

3
Notarization Date and Time

Date on Document(s)   Reference #

Fees   **Paid?**
$

A J Compliance Agmt. A J E & O A J Proof of ID Aff. A J Adv. Health. Dir. A J SDB Verification
A J Correction Agmt. A J Occ. Aff. A J Sig./Name Aff. A J Trust - Irr./Living A J Vehicle - O+VIN/TT
A J DOT / Mortgage A J Own. Aff. A J Survey Aff. A J Will - LWT/Living A J
A J Deed - G/QC/W A J POA - L/D A J A J A J C Other ▼

4
Notarization Date and Time

Date on Document(s)   Reference #

Fees   **Paid?**
$

A J Compliance Agmt. A J E & O A J Proof of ID Aff. A J Adv. Health. Dir. A J SDB Verification
A J Correction Agmt. A J Occ. Aff. A J Sig./Name Aff. A J Trust - Irr./Living A J Vehicle - O+VIN/TT
A J DOT / Mortgage A J Own. Aff. A J Survey Aff. A J Will - LWT/Living A J
A J Deed - G/QC/W A J POA - L/D A J A J A J C Other ▼

5
Notarization Date and Time

Date on Document(s)   Reference #

Fees   **Paid?**
$

A J Compliance Agmt. A J E & O A J Proof of ID Aff. A J Adv. Health. Dir. A J SDB Verification
A J Correction Agmt. A J Occ. Aff. A J Sig./Name Aff. A J Trust - Irr./Living A J Vehicle - O+VIN/TT
A J DOT / Mortgage A J Own. Aff. A J Survey Aff. A J Will - LWT/Living A J
A J Deed - G/QC/W A J POA - L/D A J A J A J C Other ▼

6
Notarization Date and Time

Date on Document(s)   Reference #

Fees   **Paid?**
$

A J Compliance Agmt. A J E & O A J Proof of ID Aff. A J Adv. Health. Dir. A J SDB Verification
A J Correction Agmt. A J Occ. Aff. A J Sig./Name Aff. A J Trust - Irr./Living A J Vehicle - O+VIN/TT
A J DOT / Mortgage A J Own. Aff. A J Survey Aff. A J Will - LWT/Living A J
A J Deed - G/QC/W A J POA - L/D A J A J A J C Other ▼

7
Notarization Date and Time

Date on Document(s)   Reference #

Fees   **Paid?**
$

A J Compliance Agmt. A J E & O A J Proof of ID Aff. A J Adv. Health. Dir. A J SDB Verification
A J Correction Agmt. A J Occ. Aff. A J Sig./Name Aff. A J Trust - Irr./Living A J Vehicle - O+VIN/TT
A J DOT / Mortgage A J Own. Aff. A J Survey Aff. A J Will - LWT/Living A J
A J Deed - G/QC/W A J POA - L/D A J A J A J C Other ▼

8
Notarization Date and Time

Date on Document(s)   Reference #

Fees   **Paid?**
$

A J Compliance Agmt. A J E & O A J Proof of ID Aff. A J Adv. Health. Dir. A J SDB Verification
A J Correction Agmt. A J Occ. Aff. A J Sig./Name Aff. A J Trust - Irr./Living A J Vehicle - O+VIN/TT
A J DOT / Mortgage A J Own. Aff. A J Survey Aff. A J Will - LWT/Living A J
A J Deed - G/QC/W A J POA - L/D A J A J A J C Other ▼

1

- [ ] Driver's License [ ] Other ID #1 - describe [ ] Personally Known
- [ ] Passport [ ] Other ID #2 - describe [ ] Credible Witness(es)

Ref. #1

Ref. #2

Right Thumbprint

X SIGN HERE

2

- [ ] Driver's License [ ] Other ID #1 - describe [ ] Personally Known
- [ ] Passport [ ] Other ID #2 - describe [ ] Credible Witness(es)

Ref. #1

Ref. #2

Right Thumbprint

X SIGN HERE

3

- [ ] Driver's License [ ] Other ID #1 - describe [ ] Personally Known
- [ ] Passport [ ] Other ID #2 - describe [ ] Credible Witness(es)

Ref. #1

Ref. #2

Right Thumbprint

X SIGN HERE

4

- [ ] Driver's License [ ] Other ID #1 - describe [ ] Personally Known
- [ ] Passport [ ] Other ID #2 - describe [ ] Credible Witness(es)

Ref. #1

Ref. #2

Right Thumbprint

X SIGN HERE

5

- [ ] Driver's License [ ] Other ID #1 - describe [ ] Personally Known
- [ ] Passport [ ] Other ID #2 - describe [ ] Credible Witness(es)

Ref. #1

Ref. #2

Right Thumbprint

X SIGN HERE

6

- [ ] Driver's License [ ] Other ID #1 - describe [ ] Personally Known
- [ ] Passport [ ] Other ID #2 - describe [ ] Credible Witness(es)

Ref. #1

Ref. #2

Right Thumbprint

X SIGN HERE

7

- [ ] Driver's License [ ] Other ID #1 - describe [ ] Personally Known
- [ ] Passport [ ] Other ID #2 - describe [ ] Credible Witness(es)

Ref. #1

Ref. #2

Right Thumbprint

X SIGN HERE

8

- [ ] Driver's License [ ] Other ID #1 - describe [ ] Personally Known
- [ ] Passport [ ] Other ID #2 - describe [ ] Credible Witness(es)

Ref. #1

Ref. #2

Right Thumbprint

X SIGN HERE

1

Notarization Date and Time

Date on Document(s) Reference #

Fees Paid?
$

- A J Compliance Agmt. A J E & O A J Proof of ID Aff. A J Adv. Health. Dir. A J SDB Verification
- A J Correction Agmt. A J Occ. Aff. A J Sig./Name Aff. A J Trust - Irr. / Living A J Vehicle - O+VIN / TT
- A J DOT / Mortgage A J Own. Aff. A J Survey Aff. A J Will - LWT / Living A J
- A J Deed - G / QC / W A J POA - L / D A J A J A J C Other ▼

2

Notarization Date and Time

Date on Document(s) Reference #

Fees Paid?
$

- A J Compliance Agmt. A J E & O A J Proof of ID Aff. A J Adv. Health. Dir. A J SDB Verification
- A J Correction Agmt. A J Occ. Aff. A J Sig./Name Aff. A J Trust - Irr. / Living A J Vehicle - O+VIN / TT
- A J DOT / Mortgage A J Own. Aff. A J Survey Aff. A J Will - LWT / Living A J
- A J Deed - G / QC / W A J POA - L / D A J A J A J C Other ▼

3

Notarization Date and Time

Date on Document(s) Reference #

Fees Paid?
$

- A J Compliance Agmt. A J E & O A J Proof of ID Aff. A J Adv. Health. Dir. A J SDB Verification
- A J Correction Agmt. A J Occ. Aff. A J Sig./Name Aff. A J Trust - Irr. / Living A J Vehicle - O+VIN / TT
- A J DOT / Mortgage A J Own. Aff. A J Survey Aff. A J Will - LWT / Living A J
- A J Deed - G / QC / W A J POA - L / D A J A J A J C Other ▼

4

Notarization Date and Time

Date on Document(s) Reference #

Fees Paid?
$

- A J Compliance Agmt. A J E & O A J Proof of ID Aff. A J Adv. Health. Dir. A J SDB Verification
- A J Correction Agmt. A J Occ. Aff. A J Sig./Name Aff. A J Trust - Irr. / Living A J Vehicle - O+VIN / TT
- A J DOT / Mortgage A J Own. Aff. A J Survey Aff. A J Will - LWT / Living A J
- A J Deed - G / QC / W A J POA - L / D A J A J A J C Other ▼

5

Notarization Date and Time

Date on Document(s) Reference #

Fees Paid?
$

- A J Compliance Agmt. A J E & O A J Proof of ID Aff. A J Adv. Health. Dir. A J SDB Verification
- A J Correction Agmt. A J Occ. Aff. A J Sig./Name Aff. A J Trust - Irr. / Living A J Vehicle - O+VIN / TT
- A J DOT / Mortgage A J Own. Aff. A J Survey Aff. A J Will - LWT / Living A J
- A J Deed - G / QC / W A J POA - L / D A J A J A J C Other ▼

6

Notarization Date and Time

Date on Document(s) Reference #

Fees Paid?
$

- A J Compliance Agmt. A J E & O A J Proof of ID Aff. A J Adv. Health. Dir. A J SDB Verification
- A J Correction Agmt. A J Occ. Aff. A J Sig./Name Aff. A J Trust - Irr. / Living A J Vehicle - O+VIN / TT
- A J DOT / Mortgage A J Own. Aff. A J Survey Aff. A J Will - LWT / Living A J
- A J Deed - G / QC / W A J POA - L / D A J A J A J C Other ▼

7

Notarization Date and Time

Date on Document(s) Reference #

Fees Paid?
$

- A J Compliance Agmt. A J E & O A J Proof of ID Aff. A J Adv. Health. Dir. A J SDB Verification
- A J Correction Agmt. A J Occ. Aff. A J Sig./Name Aff. A J Trust - Irr. / Living A J Vehicle - O+VIN / TT
- A J DOT / Mortgage A J Own. Aff. A J Survey Aff. A J Will - LWT / Living A J
- A J Deed - G / QC / W A J POA - L / D A J A J A J C Other ▼

8

Notarization Date and Time

Date on Document(s) Reference #

Fees Paid?
$

- A J Compliance Agmt. A J E & O A J Proof of ID Aff. A J Adv. Health. Dir. A J SDB Verification
- A J Correction Agmt. A J Occ. Aff. A J Sig./Name Aff. A J Trust - Irr. / Living A J Vehicle - O+VIN / TT
- A J DOT / Mortgage A J Own. Aff. A J Survey Aff. A J Will - LWT / Living A J
- A J Deed - G / QC / W A J POA - L / D A J A J A J C Other ▼

1

Signer Name and Address

Method of Identification:
- ☐ Driver's License
- ☐ Passport
- ☐ Other ID #1 - describe
- ☐ Other ID #2 - describe
- ☐ Personally Known
- ☐ Credible Witness(es)

Ref. #1

Ref. #2

X _SIGN HERE_

Right Thumbprint

2

Method of Identification:
- ☐ Driver's License
- ☐ Passport
- ☐ Other ID #1 - describe
- ☐ Other ID #2 - describe
- ☐ Personally Known
- ☐ Credible Witness(es)

Ref. #1

Ref. #2

X _SIGN HERE_

Right Thumbprint

3

Method of Identification:
- ☐ Driver's License
- ☐ Passport
- ☐ Other ID #1 - describe
- ☐ Other ID #2 - describe
- ☐ Personally Known
- ☐ Credible Witness(es)

Ref. #1

Ref. #2

X _SIGN HERE_

Right Thumbprint

4

Method of Identification:
- ☐ Driver's License
- ☐ Passport
- ☐ Other ID #1 - describe
- ☐ Other ID #2 - describe
- ☐ Personally Known
- ☐ Credible Witness(es)

Ref. #1

Ref. #2

X _SIGN HERE_

Right Thumbprint

5

Method of Identification:
- ☐ Driver's License
- ☐ Passport
- ☐ Other ID #1 - describe
- ☐ Other ID #2 - describe
- ☐ Personally Known
- ☐ Credible Witness(es)

Ref. #1

Ref. #2

X _SIGN HERE_

Right Thumbprint

6

Method of Identification:
- ☐ Driver's License
- ☐ Passport
- ☐ Other ID #1 - describe
- ☐ Other ID #2 - describe
- ☐ Personally Known
- ☐ Credible Witness(es)

Ref. #1

Ref. #2

X _SIGN HERE_

Right Thumbprint

7

Method of Identification:
- ☐ Driver's License
- ☐ Passport
- ☐ Other ID #1 - describe
- ☐ Other ID #2 - describe
- ☐ Personally Known
- ☐ Credible Witness(es)

Ref. #1

Ref. #2

X _SIGN HERE_

Right Thumbprint

8

Method of Identification:
- ☐ Driver's License
- ☐ Passport
- ☐ Other ID #1 - describe
- ☐ Other ID #2 - describe
- ☐ Personally Known
- ☐ Credible Witness(es)

Ref. #1

Ref. #2

X _SIGN HERE_

Right Thumbprint

1

Notarization Date and Time

Date on Document(s)   Reference #

Fees $ Paid? ☐

A J Compliance Agmt.   A J E & O   A J Proof of ID Aff.   A J Adv. Health. Dir.   A J SDB Verification
A J Correction Agmt.   A J Occ. Aff.   A J Sig./Name Aff.   A J Trust - Irr. / Living   A J Vehicle - O+VIN / TT
A J DOT / Mortgage   A J Own. Aff.   A J Survey Aff.   A J Will - LWT / Living   A J
A J Deed - G / QC / W   A J POA - L / D   A J   A J   A J C ☐ Other ▼

2

Notarization Date and Time

Date on Document(s)   Reference #

Fees $ Paid? ☐

A J Compliance Agmt.   A J E & O   A J Proof of ID Aff.   A J Adv. Health. Dir.   A J SDB Verification
A J Correction Agmt.   A J Occ. Aff.   A J Sig./Name Aff.   A J Trust - Irr. / Living   A J Vehicle - O+VIN / TT
A J DOT / Mortgage   A J Own. Aff.   A J Survey Aff.   A J Will - LWT / Living   A J
A J Deed - G / QC / W   A J POA - L / D   A J   A J   A J C ☐ Other ▼

3

Notarization Date and Time

Date on Document(s)   Reference #

Fees $ Paid? ☐

A J Compliance Agmt.   A J E & O   A J Proof of ID Aff.   A J Adv. Health. Dir.   A J SDB Verification
A J Correction Agmt.   A J Occ. Aff.   A J Sig./Name Aff.   A J Trust - Irr. / Living   A J Vehicle - O+VIN / TT
A J DOT / Mortgage   A J Own. Aff.   A J Survey Aff.   A J Will - LWT / Living   A J
A J Deed - G / QC / W   A J POA - L / D   A J   A J   A J C ☐ Other ▼

4

Notarization Date and Time

Date on Document(s)   Reference #

Fees $ Paid? ☐

A J Compliance Agmt.   A J E & O   A J Proof of ID Aff.   A J Adv. Health. Dir.   A J SDB Verification
A J Correction Agmt.   A J Occ. Aff.   A J Sig./Name Aff.   A J Trust - Irr. / Living   A J Vehicle - O+VIN / TT
A J DOT / Mortgage   A J Own. Aff.   A J Survey Aff.   A J Will - LWT / Living   A J
A J Deed - G / QC / W   A J POA - L / D   A J   A J   A J C ☐ Other ▼

5

Notarization Date and Time

Date on Document(s)   Reference #

Fees $ Paid? ☐

A J Compliance Agmt.   A J E & O   A J Proof of ID Aff.   A J Adv. Health. Dir.   A J SDB Verification
A J Correction Agmt.   A J Occ. Aff.   A J Sig./Name Aff.   A J Trust - Irr. / Living   A J Vehicle - O+VIN / TT
A J DOT / Mortgage   A J Own. Aff.   A J Survey Aff.   A J Will - LWT / Living   A J
A J Deed - G / QC / W   A J POA - L / D   A J   A J   A J C ☐ Other ▼

6

Notarization Date and Time

Date on Document(s)   Reference #

Fees $ Paid? ☐

A J Compliance Agmt.   A J E & O   A J Proof of ID Aff.   A J Adv. Health. Dir.   A J SDB Verification
A J Correction Agmt.   A J Occ. Aff.   A J Sig./Name Aff.   A J Trust - Irr. / Living   A J Vehicle - O+VIN / TT
A J DOT / Mortgage   A J Own. Aff.   A J Survey Aff.   A J Will - LWT / Living   A J
A J Deed - G / QC / W   A J POA - L / D   A J   A J   A J C ☐ Other ▼

7

Notarization Date and Time

Date on Document(s)   Reference #

Fees $ Paid? ☐

A J Compliance Agmt.   A J E & O   A J Proof of ID Aff.   A J Adv. Health. Dir.   A J SDB Verification
A J Correction Agmt.   A J Occ. Aff.   A J Sig./Name Aff.   A J Trust - Irr. / Living   A J Vehicle - O+VIN / TT
A J DOT / Mortgage   A J Own. Aff.   A J Survey Aff.   A J Will - LWT / Living   A J
A J Deed - G / QC / W   A J POA - L / D   A J   A J   A J C ☐ Other ▼

8

Notarization Date and Time

Date on Document(s)   Reference #

Fees $ Paid? ☐

A J Compliance Agmt.   A J E & O   A J Proof of ID Aff.   A J Adv. Health. Dir.   A J SDB Verification
A J Correction Agmt.   A J Occ. Aff.   A J Sig./Name Aff.   A J Trust - Irr. / Living   A J Vehicle - O+VIN / TT
A J DOT / Mortgage   A J Own. Aff.   A J Survey Aff.   A J Will - LWT / Living   A J
A J Deed - G / QC / W   A J POA - L / D   A J   A J   A J C ☐ Other ▼

Signer Name and Address	Method of Identification	Signature and Thumbprint	**100**

Signer Name and Address — **Method of Identification** — **Signature and Thumbprint** — **100**

1

☐ Driver's License ☐ Other ID #1 - describe ☐ Personally Known
☐ Passport ☐ Other ID #2 - describe ☐ Credible Witness(es)

Ref. #1

Ref. #2

X SIGN HERE

Right Thumbprint

2

☐ Driver's License ☐ Other ID #1 - describe ☐ Personally Known
☐ Passport ☐ Other ID #2 - describe ☐ Credible Witness(es)

Ref. #1

Ref. #2

X SIGN HERE

Right Thumbprint

3

☐ Driver's License ☐ Other ID #1 - describe ☐ Personally Known
☐ Passport ☐ Other ID #2 - describe ☐ Credible Witness(es)

Ref. #1

Ref. #2

X SIGN HERE

Right Thumbprint

4

☐ Driver's License ☐ Other ID #1 - describe ☐ Personally Known
☐ Passport ☐ Other ID #2 - describe ☐ Credible Witness(es)

Ref. #1

Ref. #2

X SIGN HERE

Right Thumbprint

5

☐ Driver's License ☐ Other ID #1 - describe ☐ Personally Known
☐ Passport ☐ Other ID #2 - describe ☐ Credible Witness(es)

Ref. #1

Ref. #2

X SIGN HERE

Right Thumbprint

6

☐ Driver's License ☐ Other ID #1 - describe ☐ Personally Known
☐ Passport ☐ Other ID #2 - describe ☐ Credible Witness(es)

Ref. #1

Ref. #2

X SIGN HERE

Right Thumbprint

7

☐ Driver's License ☐ Other ID #1 - describe ☐ Personally Known
☐ Passport ☐ Other ID #2 - describe ☐ Credible Witness(es)

Ref. #1

Ref. #2

X SIGN HERE

Right Thumbprint

8

☐ Driver's License ☐ Other ID #1 - describe ☐ Personally Known
☐ Passport ☐ Other ID #2 - describe ☐ Credible Witness(es)

Ref. #1

Ref. #2

X SIGN HERE

Right Thumbprint

1

Notarization Date and Time

Date on Document(s)   Reference #

Fees   Paid?
$

A J	Compliance Agmt.	A J	E & O	A J	Proof of ID Aff.	A J	Adv. Health. Dir.	A J	SDB Verification
A J	Correction Agmt.	A J	Occ. Aff.	A J	Sig./Name Aff.	A J	Trust - Irr. / Living	A J	Vehicle - O+VIN / TT
A J	DOT / Mortgage	A J	Own. Aff.	A J	Survey Aff.	A J	Will - LWT / Living	A J	
A J	Deed - G / QC / W	A J	POA - L / D	A J		A J		A J C	Other ▼

2

Notarization Date and Time

Date on Document(s)   Reference #

Fees   Paid?
$

A J	Compliance Agmt.	A J	E & O	A J	Proof of ID Aff.	A J	Adv. Health. Dir.	A J	SDB Verification
A J	Correction Agmt.	A J	Occ. Aff.	A J	Sig./Name Aff.	A J	Trust - Irr. / Living	A J	Vehicle - O+VIN / TT
A J	DOT / Mortgage	A J	Own. Aff.	A J	Survey Aff.	A J	Will - LWT / Living	A J	
A J	Deed - G / QC / W	A J	POA - L / D	A J		A J		A J C	Other ▼

3

Notarization Date and Time

Date on Document(s)   Reference #

Fees   Paid?
$

A J	Compliance Agmt.	A J	E & O	A J	Proof of ID Aff.	A J	Adv. Health. Dir.	A J	SDB Verification
A J	Correction Agmt.	A J	Occ. Aff.	A J	Sig./Name Aff.	A J	Trust - Irr. / Living	A J	Vehicle - O+VIN / TT
A J	DOT / Mortgage	A J	Own. Aff.	A J	Survey Aff.	A J	Will - LWT / Living	A J	
A J	Deed - G / QC / W	A J	POA - L / D	A J		A J		A J C	Other ▼

4

Notarization Date and Time

Date on Document(s)   Reference #

Fees   Paid?
$

A J	Compliance Agmt.	A J	E & O	A J	Proof of ID Aff.	A J	Adv. Health. Dir.	A J	SDB Verification
A J	Correction Agmt.	A J	Occ. Aff.	A J	Sig./Name Aff.	A J	Trust - Irr. / Living	A J	Vehicle - O+VIN / TT
A J	DOT / Mortgage	A J	Own. Aff.	A J	Survey Aff.	A J	Will - LWT / Living	A J	
A J	Deed - G / QC / W	A J	POA - L / D	A J		A J		A J C	Other ▼

5

Notarization Date and Time

Date on Document(s)   Reference #

Fees   Paid?
$

A J	Compliance Agmt.	A J	E & O	A J	Proof of ID Aff.	A J	Adv. Health. Dir.	A J	SDB Verification
A J	Correction Agmt.	A J	Occ. Aff.	A J	Sig./Name Aff.	A J	Trust - Irr. / Living	A J	Vehicle - O+VIN / TT
A J	DOT / Mortgage	A J	Own. Aff.	A J	Survey Aff.	A J	Will - LWT / Living	A J	
A J	Deed - G / QC / W	A J	POA - L / D	A J		A J		A J C	Other ▼

6

Notarization Date and Time

Date on Document(s)   Reference #

Fees   Paid?
$

A J	Compliance Agmt.	A J	E & O	A J	Proof of ID Aff.	A J	Adv. Health. Dir.	A J	SDB Verification
A J	Correction Agmt.	A J	Occ. Aff.	A J	Sig./Name Aff.	A J	Trust - Irr. / Living	A J	Vehicle - O+VIN / TT
A J	DOT / Mortgage	A J	Own. Aff.	A J	Survey Aff.	A J	Will - LWT / Living	A J	
A J	Deed - G / QC / W	A J	POA - L / D	A J		A J		A J C	Other ▼

7

Notarization Date and Time

Date on Document(s)   Reference #

Fees   Paid?
$

A J	Compliance Agmt.	A J	E & O	A J	Proof of ID Aff.	A J	Adv. Health. Dir.	A J	SDB Verification
A J	Correction Agmt.	A J	Occ. Aff.	A J	Sig./Name Aff.	A J	Trust - Irr. / Living	A J	Vehicle - O+VIN / TT
A J	DOT / Mortgage	A J	Own. Aff.	A J	Survey Aff.	A J	Will - LWT / Living	A J	
A J	Deed - G / QC / W	A J	POA - L / D	A J		A J		A J C	Other ▼

8

Notarization Date and Time

Date on Document(s)   Reference #

Fees   Paid?
$

A J	Compliance Agmt.	A J	E & O	A J	Proof of ID Aff.	A J	Adv. Health. Dir.	A J	SDB Verification
A J	Correction Agmt.	A J	Occ. Aff.	A J	Sig./Name Aff.	A J	Trust - Irr. / Living	A J	Vehicle - O+VIN / TT
A J	DOT / Mortgage	A J	Own. Aff.	A J	Survey Aff.	A J	Will - LWT / Living	A J	
A J	Deed - G / QC / W	A J	POA - L / D	A J		A J		A J C	Other ▼

1

☐ Driver's License ☐ Other ID #1 - describe ☐ Personally Known
☐ Passport ☐ Other ID #2 - describe ☐ Credible Witness(es)

Ref. #1

Ref. #2

Right Thumbprint

X *SIGN HERE*

2

☐ Driver's License ☐ Other ID #1 - describe ☐ Personally Known
☐ Passport ☐ Other ID #2 - describe ☐ Credible Witness(es)

Ref. #1

Ref. #2

Right Thumbprint

X *SIGN HERE*

3

☐ Driver's License ☐ Other ID #1 - describe ☐ Personally Known
☐ Passport ☐ Other ID #2 - describe ☐ Credible Witness(es)

Ref. #1

Ref. #2

Right Thumbprint

X *SIGN HERE*

4

☐ Driver's License ☐ Other ID #1 - describe ☐ Personally Known
☐ Passport ☐ Other ID #2 - describe ☐ Credible Witness(es)

Ref. #1

Ref. #2

Right Thumbprint

X *SIGN HERE*

5

☐ Driver's License ☐ Other ID #1 - describe ☐ Personally Known
☐ Passport ☐ Other ID #2 - describe ☐ Credible Witness(es)

Ref. #1

Ref. #2

Right Thumbprint

X *SIGN HERE*

6

☐ Driver's License ☐ Other ID #1 - describe ☐ Personally Known
☐ Passport ☐ Other ID #2 - describe ☐ Credible Witness(es)

Ref. #1

Ref. #2

Right Thumbprint

X *SIGN HERE*

7

☐ Driver's License ☐ Other ID #1 - describe ☐ Personally Known
☐ Passport ☐ Other ID #2 - describe ☐ Credible Witness(es)

Ref. #1

Ref. #2

Right Thumbprint

X *SIGN HERE*

8

☐ Driver's License ☐ Other ID #1 - describe ☐ Personally Known
☐ Passport ☐ Other ID #2 - describe ☐ Credible Witness(es)

Ref. #1

Ref. #2

Right Thumbprint

X *SIGN HERE*

1

Notarization Date and Time

Date on Document(s) **Reference #**

Fees $ **Paid?** ☐

A J Compliance Agmt.	A J E & O	A J Proof of ID Aff.	A J Adv. Health. Dir.	A J SDB Verification
A J Correction Agmt.	A J Occ. Aff.	A J Sig./Name Aff.	A J Trust - Irr. / Living	A J Vehicle - O+VIN / TT
A J DOT / Mortgage	A J Own. Aff.	A J Survey Aff.	A J Will - LWT / Living	A J
A J Deed - G / QC / W	A J POA - L / D	A J	A J	A J C ☐ Other ▼

2

Notarization Date and Time

Date on Document(s) **Reference #**

Fees $ **Paid?** ☐

A J Compliance Agmt.	A J E & O	A J Proof of ID Aff.	A J Adv. Health. Dir.	A J SDB Verification
A J Correction Agmt.	A J Occ. Aff.	A J Sig./Name Aff.	A J Trust - Irr. / Living	A J Vehicle - O+VIN / TT
A J DOT / Mortgage	A J Own. Aff.	A J Survey Aff.	A J Will - LWT / Living	A J
A J Deed - G / QC / W	A J POA - L / D	A J	A J	A J C ☐ Other ▼

3

Notarization Date and Time

Date on Document(s) **Reference #**

Fees $ **Paid?** ☐

A J Compliance Agmt.	A J E & O	A J Proof of ID Aff.	A J Adv. Health. Dir.	A J SDB Verification
A J Correction Agmt.	A J Occ. Aff.	A J Sig./Name Aff.	A J Trust - Irr. / Living	A J Vehicle - O+VIN / TT
A J DOT / Mortgage	A J Own. Aff.	A J Survey Aff.	A J Will - LWT / Living	A J
A J Deed - G / QC / W	A J POA - L / D	A J	A J	A J C ☐ Other ▼

4

Notarization Date and Time

Date on Document(s) **Reference #**

Fees $ **Paid?** ☐

A J Compliance Agmt.	A J E & O	A J Proof of ID Aff.	A J Adv. Health. Dir.	A J SDB Verification
A J Correction Agmt.	A J Occ. Aff.	A J Sig./Name Aff.	A J Trust - Irr. / Living	A J Vehicle - O+VIN / TT
A J DOT / Mortgage	A J Own. Aff.	A J Survey Aff.	A J Will - LWT / Living	A J
A J Deed - G / QC / W	A J POA - L / D	A J	A J	A J C ☐ Other ▼

5

Notarization Date and Time

Date on Document(s) **Reference #**

Fees $ **Paid?** ☐

A J Compliance Agmt.	A J E & O	A J Proof of ID Aff.	A J Adv. Health. Dir.	A J SDB Verification
A J Correction Agmt.	A J Occ. Aff.	A J Sig./Name Aff.	A J Trust - Irr. / Living	A J Vehicle - O+VIN / TT
A J DOT / Mortgage	A J Own. Aff.	A J Survey Aff.	A J Will - LWT / Living	A J
A J Deed - G / QC / W	A J POA - L / D	A J	A J	A J C ☐ Other ▼

6

Notarization Date and Time

Date on Document(s) **Reference #**

Fees $ **Paid?** ☐

A J Compliance Agmt.	A J E & O	A J Proof of ID Aff.	A J Adv. Health. Dir.	A J SDB Verification
A J Correction Agmt.	A J Occ. Aff.	A J Sig./Name Aff.	A J Trust - Irr. / Living	A J Vehicle - O+VIN / TT
A J DOT / Mortgage	A J Own. Aff.	A J Survey Aff.	A J Will - LWT / Living	A J
A J Deed - G / QC / W	A J POA - L / D	A J	A J	A J C ☐ Other ▼

7

Notarization Date and Time

Date on Document(s) **Reference #**

Fees $ **Paid?** ☐

A J Compliance Agmt.	A J E & O	A J Proof of ID Aff.	A J Adv. Health. Dir.	A J SDB Verification
A J Correction Agmt.	A J Occ. Aff.	A J Sig./Name Aff.	A J Trust - Irr. / Living	A J Vehicle - O+VIN / TT
A J DOT / Mortgage	A J Own. Aff.	A J Survey Aff.	A J Will - LWT / Living	A J
A J Deed - G / QC / W	A J POA - L / D	A J	A J	A J C ☐ Other ▼

8

Notarization Date and Time

Date on Document(s) **Reference #**

Fees $ **Paid?** ☐

A J Compliance Agmt.	A J E & O	A J Proof of ID Aff.	A J Adv. Health. Dir.	A J SDB Verification
A J Correction Agmt.	A J Occ. Aff.	A J Sig./Name Aff.	A J Trust - Irr. / Living	A J Vehicle - O+VIN / TT
A J DOT / Mortgage	A J Own. Aff.	A J Survey Aff.	A J Will - LWT / Living	A J
A J Deed - G / QC / W	A J POA - L / D	A J	A J	A J C ☐ Other ▼

1

- ☐ Driver's License
- ☐ Passport
- ☐ Other ID #1 - describe
- ☐ Other ID #2 - describe
- ☐ Personally Known
- ☐ Credible Witness(es)

Ref. #1

Ref. #2

X SIGN HERE

Right Thumbprint

2

- ☐ Driver's License
- ☐ Passport
- ☐ Other ID #1 - describe
- ☐ Other ID #2 - describe
- ☐ Personally Known
- ☐ Credible Witness(es)

Ref. #1

Ref. #2

X SIGN HERE

Right Thumbprint

3

- ☐ Driver's License
- ☐ Passport
- ☐ Other ID #1 - describe
- ☐ Other ID #2 - describe
- ☐ Personally Known
- ☐ Credible Witness(es)

Ref. #1

Ref. #2

X SIGN HERE

Right Thumbprint

4

- ☐ Driver's License
- ☐ Passport
- ☐ Other ID #1 - describe
- ☐ Other ID #2 - describe
- ☐ Personally Known
- ☐ Credible Witness(es)

Ref. #1

Ref. #2

X SIGN HERE

Right Thumbprint

5

- ☐ Driver's License
- ☐ Passport
- ☐ Other ID #1 - describe
- ☐ Other ID #2 - describe
- ☐ Personally Known
- ☐ Credible Witness(es)

Ref. #1

Ref. #2

X SIGN HERE

Right Thumbprint

6

- ☐ Driver's License
- ☐ Passport
- ☐ Other ID #1 - describe
- ☐ Other ID #2 - describe
- ☐ Personally Known
- ☐ Credible Witness(es)

Ref. #1

Ref. #2

X SIGN HERE

Right Thumbprint

7

- ☐ Driver's License
- ☐ Passport
- ☐ Other ID #1 - describe
- ☐ Other ID #2 - describe
- ☐ Personally Known
- ☐ Credible Witness(es)

Ref. #1

Ref. #2

X SIGN HERE

Right Thumbprint

8

- ☐ Driver's License
- ☐ Passport
- ☐ Other ID #1 - describe
- ☐ Other ID #2 - describe
- ☐ Personally Known
- ☐ Credible Witness(es)

Ref. #1

Ref. #2

X SIGN HERE

Right Thumbprint

Entry 1

Notarization Date and Time

Date on Document(s)   Reference #

Fees $ Paid?

A J Compliance Agmt.   A J E & O   A J Proof of ID Aff.   A J Adv. Health. Dir.   A J SDB Verification
A J Correction Agmt.   A J Occ. Aff.   A J Sig./Name Aff.   A J Trust - Irr. / Living   A J Vehicle - O+VIN / TT
A J DOT / Mortgage   A J Own. Aff.   A J Survey Aff.   A J Will - LWT / Living   A J
A J Deed - G / QC / W   A J POA - L / D   A J   A J   A J C   Other ▼

Entry 2

Notarization Date and Time

Date on Document(s)   Reference #

Fees $ Paid?

A J Compliance Agmt.   A J E & O   A J Proof of ID Aff.   A J Adv. Health. Dir.   A J SDB Verification
A J Correction Agmt.   A J Occ. Aff.   A J Sig./Name Aff.   A J Trust - Irr. / Living   A J Vehicle - O+VIN / TT
A J DOT / Mortgage   A J Own. Aff.   A J Survey Aff.   A J Will - LWT / Living   A J
A J Deed - G / QC / W   A J POA - L / D   A J   A J   A J C   Other ▼

Entry 3

Notarization Date and Time

Date on Document(s)   Reference #

Fees $ Paid?

A J Compliance Agmt.   A J E & O   A J Proof of ID Aff.   A J Adv. Health. Dir.   A J SDB Verification
A J Correction Agmt.   A J Occ. Aff.   A J Sig./Name Aff.   A J Trust - Irr. / Living   A J Vehicle - O+VIN / TT
A J DOT / Mortgage   A J Own. Aff.   A J Survey Aff.   A J Will - LWT / Living   A J
A J Deed - G / QC / W   A J POA - L / D   A J   A J   A J C   Other ▼

Entry 4

Notarization Date and Time

Date on Document(s)   Reference #

Fees $ Paid?

A J Compliance Agmt.   A J E & O   A J Proof of ID Aff.   A J Adv. Health. Dir.   A J SDB Verification
A J Correction Agmt.   A J Occ. Aff.   A J Sig./Name Aff.   A J Trust - Irr. / Living   A J Vehicle - O+VIN / TT
A J DOT / Mortgage   A J Own. Aff.   A J Survey Aff.   A J Will - LWT / Living   A J
A J Deed - G / QC / W   A J POA - L / D   A J   A J   A J C   Other ▼

Entry 5

Notarization Date and Time

Date on Document(s)   Reference #

Fees $ Paid?

A J Compliance Agmt.   A J E & O   A J Proof of ID Aff.   A J Adv. Health. Dir.   A J SDB Verification
A J Correction Agmt.   A J Occ. Aff.   A J Sig./Name Aff.   A J Trust - Irr. / Living   A J Vehicle - O+VIN / TT
A J DOT / Mortgage   A J Own. Aff.   A J Survey Aff.   A J Will - LWT / Living   A J
A J Deed - G / QC / W   A J POA - L / D   A J   A J   A J C   Other ▼

Entry 6

Notarization Date and Time

Date on Document(s)   Reference #

Fees $ Paid?

A J Compliance Agmt.   A J E & O   A J Proof of ID Aff.   A J Adv. Health. Dir.   A J SDB Verification
A J Correction Agmt.   A J Occ. Aff.   A J Sig./Name Aff.   A J Trust - Irr. / Living   A J Vehicle - O+VIN / TT
A J DOT / Mortgage   A J Own. Aff.   A J Survey Aff.   A J Will - LWT / Living   A J
A J Deed - G / QC / W   A J POA - L / D   A J   A J   A J C   Other ▼

Entry 7

Notarization Date and Time

Date on Document(s)   Reference #

Fees $ Paid?

A J Compliance Agmt.   A J E & O   A J Proof of ID Aff.   A J Adv. Health. Dir.   A J SDB Verification
A J Correction Agmt.   A J Occ. Aff.   A J Sig./Name Aff.   A J Trust - Irr. / Living   A J Vehicle - O+VIN / TT
A J DOT / Mortgage   A J Own. Aff.   A J Survey Aff.   A J Will - LWT / Living   A J
A J Deed - G / QC / W   A J POA - L / D   A J   A J   A J C   Other ▼

Entry 8

Notarization Date and Time

Date on Document(s)   Reference #

Fees $ Paid?

A J Compliance Agmt.   A J E & O   A J Proof of ID Aff.   A J Adv. Health. Dir.   A J SDB Verification
A J Correction Agmt.   A J Occ. Aff.   A J Sig./Name Aff.   A J Trust - Irr. / Living   A J Vehicle - O+VIN / TT
A J DOT / Mortgage   A J Own. Aff.   A J Survey Aff.   A J Will - LWT / Living   A J
A J Deed - G / QC / W   A J POA - L / D   A J   A J   A J C   Other ▼

1

☐ Driver's License ☐ Other ID #1 - describe ☐ Personally Known
☐ Passport ☐ Other ID #2 - describe ☐ Credible Witness(es)

Ref. #1

Ref. #2

Right Thumbprint

X _SIGN HERE_

2

☐ Driver's License ☐ Other ID #1 - describe ☐ Personally Known
☐ Passport ☐ Other ID #2 - describe ☐ Credible Witness(es)

Ref. #1

Ref. #2

Right Thumbprint

X _SIGN HERE_

3

☐ Driver's License ☐ Other ID #1 - describe ☐ Personally Known
☐ Passport ☐ Other ID #2 - describe ☐ Credible Witness(es)

Ref. #1

Ref. #2

Right Thumbprint

X _SIGN HERE_

4

☐ Driver's License ☐ Other ID #1 - describe ☐ Personally Known
☐ Passport ☐ Other ID #2 - describe ☐ Credible Witness(es)

Ref. #1

Ref. #2

Right Thumbprint

X _SIGN HERE_

5

☐ Driver's License ☐ Other ID #1 - describe ☐ Personally Known
☐ Passport ☐ Other ID #2 - describe ☐ Credible Witness(es)

Ref. #1

Ref. #2

Right Thumbprint

X _SIGN HERE_

6

☐ Driver's License ☐ Other ID #1 - describe ☐ Personally Known
☐ Passport ☐ Other ID #2 - describe ☐ Credible Witness(es)

Ref. #1

Ref. #2

Right Thumbprint

X _SIGN HERE_

7

☐ Driver's License ☐ Other ID #1 - describe ☐ Personally Known
☐ Passport ☐ Other ID #2 - describe ☐ Credible Witness(es)

Ref. #1

Ref. #2

Right Thumbprint

X _SIGN HERE_

8

☐ Driver's License ☐ Other ID #1 - describe ☐ Personally Known
☐ Passport ☐ Other ID #2 - describe ☐ Credible Witness(es)

Ref. #1

Ref. #2

Right Thumbprint

X _SIGN HERE_

1

Notarization Date and Time

Date on Document(s)   Reference #

Fees $ Paid? ☐

A J Compliance Agmt.	A J E & O	A J Proof of ID Aff.	A J Adv. Health. Dir.	A J SDB Verification	
A J Correction Agmt.	A J Occ. Aff.	A J Sig./Name Aff.	A J Trust - Irr. / Living	A J Vehicle - O+VIN / TT	
A J DOT / Mortgage	A J Own. Aff.	A J Survey Aff.	A J Will - LWT / Living	A J	
A J Deed - G / QC / W	A J POA - L / D	A J	A J	A J C ☐ Other ▼	

2

Notarization Date and Time

Date on Document(s)   Reference #

Fees $ Paid? ☐

A J Compliance Agmt.	A J E & O	A J Proof of ID Aff.	A J Adv. Health. Dir.	A J SDB Verification	
A J Correction Agmt.	A J Occ. Aff.	A J Sig./Name Aff.	A J Trust - Irr. / Living	A J Vehicle - O+VIN / TT	
A J DOT / Mortgage	A J Own. Aff.	A J Survey Aff.	A J Will - LWT / Living	A J	
A J Deed - G / QC / W	A J POA - L / D	A J	A J	A J C ☐ Other ▼	

3

Notarization Date and Time

Date on Document(s)   Reference #

Fees $ Paid? ☐

A J Compliance Agmt.	A J E & O	A J Proof of ID Aff.	A J Adv. Health. Dir.	A J SDB Verification	
A J Correction Agmt.	A J Occ. Aff.	A J Sig./Name Aff.	A J Trust - Irr. / Living	A J Vehicle - O+VIN / TT	
A J DOT / Mortgage	A J Own. Aff.	A J Survey Aff.	A J Will - LWT / Living	A J	
A J Deed - G / QC / W	A J POA - L / D	A J	A J	A J C ☐ Other ▼	

4

Notarization Date and Time

Date on Document(s)   Reference #

Fees $ Paid? ☐

A J Compliance Agmt.	A J E & O	A J Proof of ID Aff.	A J Adv. Health. Dir.	A J SDB Verification	
A J Correction Agmt.	A J Occ. Aff.	A J Sig./Name Aff.	A J Trust - Irr. / Living	A J Vehicle - O+VIN / TT	
A J DOT / Mortgage	A J Own. Aff.	A J Survey Aff.	A J Will - LWT / Living	A J	
A J Deed - G / QC / W	A J POA - L / D	A J	A J	A J C ☐ Other ▼	

5

Notarization Date and Time

Date on Document(s)   Reference #

Fees $ Paid? ☐

A J Compliance Agmt.	A J E & O	A J Proof of ID Aff.	A J Adv. Health. Dir.	A J SDB Verification	
A J Correction Agmt.	A J Occ. Aff.	A J Sig./Name Aff.	A J Trust - Irr. / Living	A J Vehicle - O+VIN / TT	
A J DOT / Mortgage	A J Own. Aff.	A J Survey Aff.	A J Will - LWT / Living	A J	
A J Deed - G / QC / W	A J POA - L / D	A J	A J	A J C ☐ Other ▼	

6

Notarization Date and Time

Date on Document(s)   Reference #

Fees $ Paid? ☐

A J Compliance Agmt.	A J E & O	A J Proof of ID Aff.	A J Adv. Health. Dir.	A J SDB Verification	
A J Correction Agmt.	A J Occ. Aff.	A J Sig./Name Aff.	A J Trust - Irr. / Living	A J Vehicle - O+VIN / TT	
A J DOT / Mortgage	A J Own. Aff.	A J Survey Aff.	A J Will - LWT / Living	A J	
A J Deed - G / QC / W	A J POA - L / D	A J	A J	A J C ☐ Other ▼	

7

Notarization Date and Time

Date on Document(s)   Reference #

Fees $ Paid? ☐

A J Compliance Agmt.	A J E & O	A J Proof of ID Aff.	A J Adv. Health. Dir.	A J SDB Verification	
A J Correction Agmt.	A J Occ. Aff.	A J Sig./Name Aff.	A J Trust - Irr. / Living	A J Vehicle - O+VIN / TT	
A J DOT / Mortgage	A J Own. Aff.	A J Survey Aff.	A J Will - LWT / Living	A J	
A J Deed - G / QC / W	A J POA - L / D	A J	A J	A J C ☐ Other ▼	

8

Notarization Date and Time

Date on Document(s)   Reference #

Fees $ Paid? ☐

A J Compliance Agmt.	A J E & O	A J Proof of ID Aff.	A J Adv. Health. Dir.	A J SDB Verification	
A J Correction Agmt.	A J Occ. Aff.	A J Sig./Name Aff.	A J Trust - Irr. / Living	A J Vehicle - O+VIN / TT	
A J DOT / Mortgage	A J Own. Aff.	A J Survey Aff.	A J Will - LWT / Living	A J	
A J Deed - G / QC / W	A J POA - L / D	A J	A J	A J C ☐ Other ▼	

	Driver's License ☐ Other ID #1 - describe ☐ Personally Known ☐ Passport ☐ Other ID #2 - describe ☐ Credible Witness(es) ☐ Ref. #1 Ref. #2	X **SIGN HERE**	Right Thumbprint	**1**
	Driver's License ☐ Other ID #1 - describe ☐ Personally Known ☐ Passport ☐ Other ID #2 - describe ☐ Credible Witness(es) ☐ Ref. #1 Ref. #2	X **SIGN HERE**	Right Thumbprint	**2**
	Driver's License ☐ Other ID #1 - describe ☐ Personally Known ☐ Passport ☐ Other ID #2 - describe ☐ Credible Witness(es) ☐ Ref. #1 Ref. #2	X **SIGN HERE**	Right Thumbprint	**3**
	Driver's License ☐ Other ID #1 - describe ☐ Personally Known ☐ Passport ☐ Other ID #2 - describe ☐ Credible Witness(es) ☐ Ref. #1 Ref. #2	X **SIGN HERE**	Right Thumbprint	**4**
	Driver's License ☐ Other ID #1 - describe ☐ Personally Known ☐ Passport ☐ Other ID #2 - describe ☐ Credible Witness(es) ☐ Ref. #1 Ref. #2	X **SIGN HERE**	Right Thumbprint	**5**
	Driver's License ☐ Other ID #1 - describe ☐ Personally Known ☐ Passport ☐ Other ID #2 - describe ☐ Credible Witness(es) ☐ Ref. #1 Ref. #2	X **SIGN HERE**	Right Thumbprint	**6**
	Driver's License ☐ Other ID #1 - describe ☐ Personally Known ☐ Passport ☐ Other ID #2 - describe ☐ Credible Witness(es) ☐ Ref. #1 Ref. #2	X **SIGN HERE**	Right Thumbprint	**7**
	Driver's License ☐ Other ID #1 - describe ☐ Personally Known ☐ Passport ☐ Other ID #2 - describe ☐ Credible Witness(es) ☐ Ref. #1 Ref. #2	X **SIGN HERE**	Right Thumbprint	**8**

1

Notarization Date and Time

Date on Document(s) Reference #

Fees Paid?
$

A J	Compliance Agmt.	A J	E & O	A J	Proof of ID Aff.	A J	Adv. Health. Dir.	A J	SDB Verification
A J	Correction Agmt.	A J	Occ. Aff.	A J	Sig./Name Aff.	A J	Trust - Irr. / Living	A J	Vehicle - O+VIN / TT
A J	DOT / Mortgage	A J	Own. Aff.	A J	Survey Aff.	A J	Will - LWT / Living	A J	
A J	Deed - G / QC / W	A J	POA - L / D	A J		A J		A J C	Other

2

Notarization Date and Time

Date on Document(s) Reference #

Fees Paid?
$

A J	Compliance Agmt.	A J	E & O	A J	Proof of ID Aff.	A J	Adv. Health. Dir.	A J	SDB Verification
A J	Correction Agmt.	A J	Occ. Aff.	A J	Sig./Name Aff.	A J	Trust - Irr. / Living	A J	Vehicle - O+VIN / TT
A J	DOT / Mortgage	A J	Own. Aff.	A J	Survey Aff.	A J	Will - LWT / Living	A J	
A J	Deed - G / QC / W	A J	POA - L / D	A J		A J		A J C	Other

3

Notarization Date and Time

Date on Document(s) Reference #

Fees Paid?
$

A J	Compliance Agmt.	A J	E & O	A J	Proof of ID Aff.	A J	Adv. Health. Dir.	A J	SDB Verification
A J	Correction Agmt.	A J	Occ. Aff.	A J	Sig./Name Aff.	A J	Trust - Irr. / Living	A J	Vehicle - O+VIN / TT
A J	DOT / Mortgage	A J	Own. Aff.	A J	Survey Aff.	A J	Will - LWT / Living	A J	
A J	Deed - G / QC / W	A J	POA - L / D	A J		A J		A J C	Other

4

Notarization Date and Time

Date on Document(s) Reference #

Fees Paid?
$

A J	Compliance Agmt.	A J	E & O	A J	Proof of ID Aff.	A J	Adv. Health. Dir.	A J	SDB Verification
A J	Correction Agmt.	A J	Occ. Aff.	A J	Sig./Name Aff.	A J	Trust - Irr. / Living	A J	Vehicle - O+VIN / TT
A J	DOT / Mortgage	A J	Own. Aff.	A J	Survey Aff.	A J	Will - LWT / Living	A J	
A J	Deed - G / QC / W	A J	POA - L / D	A J		A J		A J C	Other

5

Notarization Date and Time

Date on Document(s) Reference #

Fees Paid?
$

A J	Compliance Agmt.	A J	E & O	A J	Proof of ID Aff.	A J	Adv. Health. Dir.	A J	SDB Verification
A J	Correction Agmt.	A J	Occ. Aff.	A J	Sig./Name Aff.	A J	Trust - Irr. / Living	A J	Vehicle - O+VIN / TT
A J	DOT / Mortgage	A J	Own. Aff.	A J	Survey Aff.	A J	Will - LWT / Living	A J	
A J	Deed - G / QC / W	A J	POA - L / D	A J		A J		A J C	Other

6

Notarization Date and Time

Date on Document(s) Reference #

Fees Paid?
$

A J	Compliance Agmt.	A J	E & O	A J	Proof of ID Aff.	A J	Adv. Health. Dir.	A J	SDB Verification
A J	Correction Agmt.	A J	Occ. Aff.	A J	Sig./Name Aff.	A J	Trust - Irr. / Living	A J	Vehicle - O+VIN / TT
A J	DOT / Mortgage	A J	Own. Aff.	A J	Survey Aff.	A J	Will - LWT / Living	A J	
A J	Deed - G / QC / W	A J	POA - L / D	A J		A J		A J C	Other

7

Notarization Date and Time

Date on Document(s) Reference #

Fees Paid?
$

A J	Compliance Agmt.	A J	E & O	A J	Proof of ID Aff.	A J	Adv. Health. Dir.	A J	SDB Verification
A J	Correction Agmt.	A J	Occ. Aff.	A J	Sig./Name Aff.	A J	Trust - Irr. / Living	A J	Vehicle - O+VIN / TT
A J	DOT / Mortgage	A J	Own. Aff.	A J	Survey Aff.	A J	Will - LWT / Living	A J	
A J	Deed - G / QC / W	A J	POA - L / D	A J		A J		A J C	Other

8

Notarization Date and Time

Date on Document(s) Reference #

Fees Paid?
$

A J	Compliance Agmt.	A J	E & O	A J	Proof of ID Aff.	A J	Adv. Health. Dir.	A J	SDB Verification
A J	Correction Agmt.	A J	Occ. Aff.	A J	Sig./Name Aff.	A J	Trust - Irr. / Living	A J	Vehicle - O+VIN / TT
A J	DOT / Mortgage	A J	Own. Aff.	A J	Survey Aff.	A J	Will - LWT / Living	A J	
A J	Deed - G / QC / W	A J	POA - L / D	A J		A J		A J C	Other

1

☐ Driver's License ☐ Other ID #1 - describe ☐ Personally Known
☐ Passport ☐ Other ID #2 - describe ☐ Credible Witness(es)

Ref. #1

Ref. #2

Right Thumbprint

X SIGN HERE

2

☐ Driver's License ☐ Other ID #1 - describe ☐ Personally Known
☐ Passport ☐ Other ID #2 - describe ☐ Credible Witness(es)

Ref. #1

Ref. #2

Right Thumbprint

X SIGN HERE

3

☐ Driver's License ☐ Other ID #1 - describe ☐ Personally Known
☐ Passport ☐ Other ID #2 - describe ☐ Credible Witness(es)

Ref. #1

Ref. #2

Right Thumbprint

X SIGN HERE

4

☐ Driver's License ☐ Other ID #1 - describe ☐ Personally Known
☐ Passport ☐ Other ID #2 - describe ☐ Credible Witness(es)

Ref. #1

Ref. #2

Right Thumbprint

X SIGN HERE

5

☐ Driver's License ☐ Other ID #1 - describe ☐ Personally Known
☐ Passport ☐ Other ID #2 - describe ☐ Credible Witness(es)

Ref. #1

Ref. #2

Right Thumbprint

X SIGN HERE

6

☐ Driver's License ☐ Other ID #1 - describe ☐ Personally Known
☐ Passport ☐ Other ID #2 - describe ☐ Credible Witness(es)

Ref. #1

Ref. #2

Right Thumbprint

X SIGN HERE

7

☐ Driver's License ☐ Other ID #1 - describe ☐ Personally Known
☐ Passport ☐ Other ID #2 - describe ☐ Credible Witness(es)

Ref. #1

Ref. #2

Right Thumbprint

X SIGN HERE

8

☐ Driver's License ☐ Other ID #1 - describe ☐ Personally Known
☐ Passport ☐ Other ID #2 - describe ☐ Credible Witness(es)

Ref. #1

Ref. #2

Right Thumbprint

X SIGN HERE

1

Notarization Date and Time

Date on Document(s) Reference #

Fees $ Paid? □

A J Compliance Agmt.	A J E & O	A J Proof of ID Aff.	A J Adv. Health. Dir.	A J SDB Verification
A J Correction Agmt.	A J Occ. Aff.	A J Sig./Name Aff.	A J Trust - Irr. / Living	A J Vehicle - O+VIN / TT
A J DOT / Mortgage	A J Own. Aff.	A J Survey Aff.	A J Will - LWT / Living	A J
A J Deed - G / QC / W	A J POA - L / D	A J	A J	A J C □ Other ▼

2

Notarization Date and Time

Date on Document(s) Reference #

Fees $ Paid? □

A J Compliance Agmt.	A J E & O	A J Proof of ID Aff.	A J Adv. Health. Dir.	A J SDB Verification
A J Correction Agmt.	A J Occ. Aff.	A J Sig./Name Aff.	A J Trust - Irr. / Living	A J Vehicle - O+VIN / TT
A J DOT / Mortgage	A J Own. Aff.	A J Survey Aff.	A J Will - LWT / Living	A J
A J Deed - G / QC / W	A J POA - L / D	A J	A J	A J C □ Other ▼

3

Notarization Date and Time

Date on Document(s) Reference #

Fees $ Paid? □

A J Compliance Agmt.	A J E & O	A J Proof of ID Aff.	A J Adv. Health. Dir.	A J SDB Verification
A J Correction Agmt.	A J Occ. Aff.	A J Sig./Name Aff.	A J Trust - Irr. / Living	A J Vehicle - O+VIN / TT
A J DOT / Mortgage	A J Own. Aff.	A J Survey Aff.	A J Will - LWT / Living	A J
A J Deed - G / QC / W	A J POA - L / D	A J	A J	A J C □ Other ▼

4

Notarization Date and Time

Date on Document(s) Reference #

Fees $ Paid? □

A J Compliance Agmt.	A J E & O	A J Proof of ID Aff.	A J Adv. Health. Dir.	A J SDB Verification
A J Correction Agmt.	A J Occ. Aff.	A J Sig./Name Aff.	A J Trust - Irr. / Living	A J Vehicle - O+VIN / TT
A J DOT / Mortgage	A J Own. Aff.	A J Survey Aff.	A J Will - LWT / Living	A J
A J Deed - G / QC / W	A J POA - L / D	A J	A J	A J C □ Other ▼

5

Notarization Date and Time

Date on Document(s) Reference #

Fees $ Paid? □

A J Compliance Agmt.	A J E & O	A J Proof of ID Aff.	A J Adv. Health. Dir.	A J SDB Verification
A J Correction Agmt.	A J Occ. Aff.	A J Sig./Name Aff.	A J Trust - Irr. / Living	A J Vehicle - O+VIN / TT
A J DOT / Mortgage	A J Own. Aff.	A J Survey Aff.	A J Will - LWT / Living	A J
A J Deed - G / QC / W	A J POA - L / D	A J	A J	A J C □ Other ▼

6

Notarization Date and Time

Date on Document(s) Reference #

Fees $ Paid? □

A J Compliance Agmt.	A J E & O	A J Proof of ID Aff.	A J Adv. Health. Dir.	A J SDB Verification
A J Correction Agmt.	A J Occ. Aff.	A J Sig./Name Aff.	A J Trust - Irr. / Living	A J Vehicle - O+VIN / TT
A J DOT / Mortgage	A J Own. Aff.	A J Survey Aff.	A J Will - LWT / Living	A J
A J Deed - G / QC / W	A J POA - L / D	A J	A J	A J C □ Other ▼

7

Notarization Date and Time

Date on Document(s) Reference #

Fees $ Paid? □

A J Compliance Agmt.	A J E & O	A J Proof of ID Aff.	A J Adv. Health. Dir.	A J SDB Verification
A J Correction Agmt.	A J Occ. Aff.	A J Sig./Name Aff.	A J Trust - Irr. / Living	A J Vehicle - O+VIN / TT
A J DOT / Mortgage	A J Own. Aff.	A J Survey Aff.	A J Will - LWT / Living	A J
A J Deed - G / QC / W	A J POA - L / D	A J	A J	A J C □ Other ▼

8

Notarization Date and Time

Date on Document(s) Reference #

Fees $ Paid? □

A J Compliance Agmt.	A J E & O	A J Proof of ID Aff.	A J Adv. Health. Dir.	A J SDB Verification
A J Correction Agmt.	A J Occ. Aff.	A J Sig./Name Aff.	A J Trust - Irr. / Living	A J Vehicle - O+VIN / TT
A J DOT / Mortgage	A J Own. Aff.	A J Survey Aff.	A J Will - LWT / Living	A J
A J Deed - G / QC / W	A J POA - L / D	A J	A J	A J C □ Other ▼

1

Driver's License ☐   Other ID #1 - describe ☐   Personally Known ☐
Passport ☐   Other ID #2 - describe ☐   Credible Witness(es) ☐

Ref. #1

Ref. #2

X SIGN HERE _____

Right Thumbprint

2

Driver's License ☐   Other ID #1 - describe ☐   Personally Known ☐
Passport ☐   Other ID #2 - describe ☐   Credible Witness(es) ☐

Ref. #1

Ref. #2

X SIGN HERE _____

Right Thumbprint

3

Driver's License ☐   Other ID #1 - describe ☐   Personally Known ☐
Passport ☐   Other ID #2 - describe ☐   Credible Witness(es) ☐

Ref. #1

Ref. #2

X SIGN HERE _____

Right Thumbprint

4

Driver's License ☐   Other ID #1 - describe ☐   Personally Known ☐
Passport ☐   Other ID #2 - describe ☐   Credible Witness(es) ☐

Ref. #1

Ref. #2

X SIGN HERE _____

Right Thumbprint

5

Driver's License ☐   Other ID #1 - describe ☐   Personally Known ☐
Passport ☐   Other ID #2 - describe ☐   Credible Witness(es) ☐

Ref. #1

Ref. #2

X SIGN HERE _____

Right Thumbprint

6

Driver's License ☐   Other ID #1 - describe ☐   Personally Known ☐
Passport ☐   Other ID #2 - describe ☐   Credible Witness(es) ☐

Ref. #1

Ref. #2

X SIGN HERE _____

Right Thumbprint

7

Driver's License ☐   Other ID #1 - describe ☐   Personally Known ☐
Passport ☐   Other ID #2 - describe ☐   Credible Witness(es) ☐

Ref. #1

Ref. #2

X SIGN HERE _____

Right Thumbprint

8

Driver's License ☐   Other ID #1 - describe ☐   Personally Known ☐
Passport ☐   Other ID #2 - describe ☐   Credible Witness(es) ☐

Ref. #1

Ref. #2

X SIGN HERE _____

Right Thumbprint

1

Notarization Date and Time

Date on Document(s)   Reference #

Fees $ Paid? ☐

A J	Compliance Agmt.	A J	E & O	A J	Proof of ID Aff.	A J	Adv. Health. Dir.	A J	SDB Verification
A J	Correction Agmt.	A J	Occ. Aff.	A J	Sig./Name Aff.	A J	Trust - Irr. / Living	A J	Vehicle - O+VIN / TT
A J	DOT / Mortgage	A J	Own. Aff.	A J	Survey Aff.	A J	Will - LWT / Living	A J	
A J	Deed - G / QC / W	A J	POA - L / D	A J		A J		A J C ☐	Other ▼

2

Notarization Date and Time

Date on Document(s)   Reference #

Fees $ Paid? ☐

A J	Compliance Agmt.	A J	E & O	A J	Proof of ID Aff.	A J	Adv. Health. Dir.	A J	SDB Verification
A J	Correction Agmt.	A J	Occ. Aff.	A J	Sig./Name Aff.	A J	Trust - Irr. / Living	A J	Vehicle - O+VIN / TT
A J	DOT / Mortgage	A J	Own. Aff.	A J	Survey Aff.	A J	Will - LWT / Living	A J	
A J	Deed - G / QC / W	A J	POA - L / D	A J		A J		A J C ☐	Other ▼

3

Notarization Date and Time

Date on Document(s)   Reference #

Fees $ Paid? ☐

A J	Compliance Agmt.	A J	E & O	A J	Proof of ID Aff.	A J	Adv. Health. Dir.	A J	SDB Verification
A J	Correction Agmt.	A J	Occ. Aff.	A J	Sig./Name Aff.	A J	Trust - Irr. / Living	A J	Vehicle - O+VIN / TT
A J	DOT / Mortgage	A J	Own. Aff.	A J	Survey Aff.	A J	Will - LWT / Living	A J	
A J	Deed - G / QC / W	A J	POA - L / D	A J		A J		A J C ☐	Other ▼

4

Notarization Date and Time

Date on Document(s)   Reference #

Fees $ Paid? ☐

A J	Compliance Agmt.	A J	E & O	A J	Proof of ID Aff.	A J	Adv. Health. Dir.	A J	SDB Verification
A J	Correction Agmt.	A J	Occ. Aff.	A J	Sig./Name Aff.	A J	Trust - Irr. / Living	A J	Vehicle - O+VIN / TT
A J	DOT / Mortgage	A J	Own. Aff.	A J	Survey Aff.	A J	Will - LWT / Living	A J	
A J	Deed - G / QC / W	A J	POA - L / D	A J		A J		A J C ☐	Other ▼

5

Notarization Date and Time

Date on Document(s)   Reference #

Fees $ Paid? ☐

A J	Compliance Agmt.	A J	E & O	A J	Proof of ID Aff.	A J	Adv. Health. Dir.	A J	SDB Verification
A J	Correction Agmt.	A J	Occ. Aff.	A J	Sig./Name Aff.	A J	Trust - Irr. / Living	A J	Vehicle - O+VIN / TT
A J	DOT / Mortgage	A J	Own. Aff.	A J	Survey Aff.	A J	Will - LWT / Living	A J	
A J	Deed - G / QC / W	A J	POA - L / D	A J		A J		A J C ☐	Other ▼

6

Notarization Date and Time

Date on Document(s)   Reference #

Fees $ Paid? ☐

A J	Compliance Agmt.	A J	E & O	A J	Proof of ID Aff.	A J	Adv. Health. Dir.	A J	SDB Verification
A J	Correction Agmt.	A J	Occ. Aff.	A J	Sig./Name Aff.	A J	Trust - Irr. / Living	A J	Vehicle - O+VIN / TT
A J	DOT / Mortgage	A J	Own. Aff.	A J	Survey Aff.	A J	Will - LWT / Living	A J	
A J	Deed - G / QC / W	A J	POA - L / D	A J		A J		A J C ☐	Other ▼

7

Notarization Date and Time

Date on Document(s)   Reference #

Fees $ Paid? ☐

A J	Compliance Agmt.	A J	E & O	A J	Proof of ID Aff.	A J	Adv. Health. Dir.	A J	SDB Verification
A J	Correction Agmt.	A J	Occ. Aff.	A J	Sig./Name Aff.	A J	Trust - Irr. / Living	A J	Vehicle - O+VIN / TT
A J	DOT / Mortgage	A J	Own. Aff.	A J	Survey Aff.	A J	Will - LWT / Living	A J	
A J	Deed - G / QC / W	A J	POA - L / D	A J		A J		A J C ☐	Other ▼

8

Notarization Date and Time

Date on Document(s)   Reference #

Fees $ Paid? ☐

A J	Compliance Agmt.	A J	E & O	A J	Proof of ID Aff.	A J	Adv. Health. Dir.	A J	SDB Verification
A J	Correction Agmt.	A J	Occ. Aff.	A J	Sig./Name Aff.	A J	Trust - Irr. / Living	A J	Vehicle - O+VIN / TT
A J	DOT / Mortgage	A J	Own. Aff.	A J	Survey Aff.	A J	Will - LWT / Living	A J	
A J	Deed - G / QC / W	A J	POA - L / D	A J		A J		A J C ☐	Other ▼

1

- [ ] Driver's License
- [ ] Passport
- [ ] Other ID #1 - describe
- [ ] Other ID #2 - describe
- [ ] Personally Known
- [ ] Credible Witness(es)

Ref. #1

Ref. #2

X _____ SIGN HERE

Right Thumbprint

2

- [ ] Driver's License
- [ ] Passport
- [ ] Other ID #1 - describe
- [ ] Other ID #2 - describe
- [ ] Personally Known
- [ ] Credible Witness(es)

Ref. #1

Ref. #2

X _____ SIGN HERE

Right Thumbprint

3

- [ ] Driver's License
- [ ] Passport
- [ ] Other ID #1 - describe
- [ ] Other ID #2 - describe
- [ ] Personally Known
- [ ] Credible Witness(es)

Ref. #1

Ref. #2

X _____ SIGN HERE

Right Thumbprint

4

- [ ] Driver's License
- [ ] Passport
- [ ] Other ID #1 - describe
- [ ] Other ID #2 - describe
- [ ] Personally Known
- [ ] Credible Witness(es)

Ref. #1

Ref. #2

X _____ SIGN HERE

Right Thumbprint

5

- [ ] Driver's License
- [ ] Passport
- [ ] Other ID #1 - describe
- [ ] Other ID #2 - describe
- [ ] Personally Known
- [ ] Credible Witness(es)

Ref. #1

Ref. #2

X _____ SIGN HERE

Right Thumbprint

6

- [ ] Driver's License
- [ ] Passport
- [ ] Other ID #1 - describe
- [ ] Other ID #2 - describe
- [ ] Personally Known
- [ ] Credible Witness(es)

Ref. #1

Ref. #2

X _____ SIGN HERE

Right Thumbprint

7

- [ ] Driver's License
- [ ] Passport
- [ ] Other ID #1 - describe
- [ ] Other ID #2 - describe
- [ ] Personally Known
- [ ] Credible Witness(es)

Ref. #1

Ref. #2

X _____ SIGN HERE

Right Thumbprint

8

- [ ] Driver's License
- [ ] Passport
- [ ] Other ID #1 - describe
- [ ] Other ID #2 - describe
- [ ] Personally Known
- [ ] Credible Witness(es)

Ref. #1

Ref. #2

X _____ SIGN HERE

Right Thumbprint

1

Notarization Date and Time

Date on Document(s) | Reference #

Fees: $ Paid? ☐

- [A] [J] Compliance Agmt.
- [A] [J] Correction Agmt.
- [A] [J] DOT / Mortgage
- [A] [J] Deed - G / QC / W
- [A] [J] E & O
- [A] [J] Occ. Aff.
- [A] [J] Own. Aff.
- [A] [J] POA - L / D
- [A] [J] Proof of ID Aff.
- [A] [J] Sig. / Name Aff.
- [A] [J] Survey Aff.
- [A] [J]
- [A] [J] Adv. Health. Dir.
- [A] [J] Trust - Irr. / Living
- [A] [J] Will - LWT / Living
- [A] [J]
- [A] [J] SDB Verification
- [A] [J] Vehicle - O+VIN / TT
- [A] [J] [C] ☐ Other ▼

2

Notarization Date and Time

Date on Document(s) | Reference #

Fees: $ Paid? ☐

- [A] [J] Compliance Agmt.
- [A] [J] Correction Agmt.
- [A] [J] DOT / Mortgage
- [A] [J] Deed - G / QC / W
- [A] [J] E & O
- [A] [J] Occ. Aff.
- [A] [J] Own. Aff.
- [A] [J] POA - L / D
- [A] [J] Proof of ID Aff.
- [A] [J] Sig. / Name Aff.
- [A] [J] Survey Aff.
- [A] [J]
- [A] [J] Adv. Health. Dir.
- [A] [J] Trust - Irr. / Living
- [A] [J] Will - LWT / Living
- [A] [J]
- [A] [J] SDB Verification
- [A] [J] Vehicle - O+VIN / TT
- [A] [J] [C] ☐ Other ▼

3

Notarization Date and Time

Date on Document(s) | Reference #

Fees: $ Paid? ☐

- [A] [J] Compliance Agmt.
- [A] [J] Correction Agmt.
- [A] [J] DOT / Mortgage
- [A] [J] Deed - G / QC / W
- [A] [J] E & O
- [A] [J] Occ. Aff.
- [A] [J] Own. Aff.
- [A] [J] POA - L / D
- [A] [J] Proof of ID Aff.
- [A] [J] Sig. / Name Aff.
- [A] [J] Survey Aff.
- [A] [J]
- [A] [J] Adv. Health. Dir.
- [A] [J] Trust - Irr. / Living
- [A] [J] Will - LWT / Living
- [A] [J]
- [A] [J] SDB Verification
- [A] [J] Vehicle - O+VIN / TT
- [A] [J] [C] ☐ Other ▼

4

Notarization Date and Time

Date on Document(s) | Reference #

Fees: $ Paid? ☐

- [A] [J] Compliance Agmt.
- [A] [J] Correction Agmt.
- [A] [J] DOT / Mortgage
- [A] [J] Deed - G / QC / W
- [A] [J] E & O
- [A] [J] Occ. Aff.
- [A] [J] Own. Aff.
- [A] [J] POA - L / D
- [A] [J] Proof of ID Aff.
- [A] [J] Sig. / Name Aff.
- [A] [J] Survey Aff.
- [A] [J]
- [A] [J] Adv. Health. Dir.
- [A] [J] Trust - Irr. / Living
- [A] [J] Will - LWT / Living
- [A] [J]
- [A] [J] SDB Verification
- [A] [J] Vehicle - O+VIN / TT
- [A] [J] [C] ☐ Other ▼

5

Notarization Date and Time

Date on Document(s) | Reference #

Fees: $ Paid? ☐

- [A] [J] Compliance Agmt.
- [A] [J] Correction Agmt.
- [A] [J] DOT / Mortgage
- [A] [J] Deed - G / QC / W
- [A] [J] E & O
- [A] [J] Occ. Aff.
- [A] [J] Own. Aff.
- [A] [J] POA - L / D
- [A] [J] Proof of ID Aff.
- [A] [J] Sig. / Name Aff.
- [A] [J] Survey Aff.
- [A] [J]
- [A] [J] Adv. Health. Dir.
- [A] [J] Trust - Irr. / Living
- [A] [J] Will - LWT / Living
- [A] [J]
- [A] [J] SDB Verification
- [A] [J] Vehicle - O+VIN / TT
- [A] [J] [C] ☐ Other ▼

6

Notarization Date and Time

Date on Document(s) | Reference #

Fees: $ Paid? ☐

- [A] [J] Compliance Agmt.
- [A] [J] Correction Agmt.
- [A] [J] DOT / Mortgage
- [A] [J] Deed - G / QC / W
- [A] [J] E & O
- [A] [J] Occ. Aff.
- [A] [J] Own. Aff.
- [A] [J] POA - L / D
- [A] [J] Proof of ID Aff.
- [A] [J] Sig. / Name Aff.
- [A] [J] Survey Aff.
- [A] [J]
- [A] [J] Adv. Health. Dir.
- [A] [J] Trust - Irr. / Living
- [A] [J] Will - LWT / Living
- [A] [J]
- [A] [J] SDB Verification
- [A] [J] Vehicle - O+VIN / TT
- [A] [J] [C] ☐ Other ▼

7

Notarization Date and Time

Date on Document(s) | Reference #

Fees: $ Paid? ☐

- [A] [J] Compliance Agmt.
- [A] [J] Correction Agmt.
- [A] [J] DOT / Mortgage
- [A] [J] Deed - G / QC / W
- [A] [J] E & O
- [A] [J] Occ. Aff.
- [A] [J] Own. Aff.
- [A] [J] POA - L / D
- [A] [J] Proof of ID Aff.
- [A] [J] Sig. / Name Aff.
- [A] [J] Survey Aff.
- [A] [J]
- [A] [J] Adv. Health. Dir.
- [A] [J] Trust - Irr. / Living
- [A] [J] Will - LWT / Living
- [A] [J]
- [A] [J] SDB Verification
- [A] [J] Vehicle - O+VIN / TT
- [A] [J] [C] ☐ Other ▼

8

Notarization Date and Time

Date on Document(s) | Reference #

Fees: $ Paid? ☐

- [A] [J] Compliance Agmt.
- [A] [J] Correction Agmt.
- [A] [J] DOT / Mortgage
- [A] [J] Deed - G / QC / W
- [A] [J] E & O
- [A] [J] Occ. Aff.
- [A] [J] Own. Aff.
- [A] [J] POA - L / D
- [A] [J] Proof of ID Aff.
- [A] [J] Sig. / Name Aff.
- [A] [J] Survey Aff.
- [A] [J]
- [A] [J] Adv. Health. Dir.
- [A] [J] Trust - Irr. / Living
- [A] [J] Will - LWT / Living
- [A] [J]
- [A] [J] SDB Verification
- [A] [J] Vehicle - O+VIN / TT
- [A] [J] [C] ☐ Other ▼

Signer Name and Address	Method of Identification	Signature and Thumbprint	
	☐ Driver's License ☐ Other ID #1 - describe ☐ Personally Known ☐ Passport ☐ Other ID #2 - describe ☐ Credible Witness(es) Ref. #1 Ref. #2	Right Thumbprint X ___SIGN HERE___	1
	☐ Driver's License ☐ Other ID #1 - describe ☐ Personally Known ☐ Passport ☐ Other ID #2 - describe ☐ Credible Witness(es) Ref. #1 Ref. #2	Right Thumbprint X ___SIGN HERE___	2
	☐ Driver's License ☐ Other ID #1 - describe ☐ Personally Known ☐ Passport ☐ Other ID #2 - describe ☐ Credible Witness(es) Ref. #1 Ref. #2	Right Thumbprint X ___SIGN HERE___	3
	☐ Driver's License ☐ Other ID #1 - describe ☐ Personally Known ☐ Passport ☐ Other ID #2 - describe ☐ Credible Witness(es) Ref. #1 Ref. #2	Right Thumbprint X ___SIGN HERE___	4
	☐ Driver's License ☐ Other ID #1 - describe ☐ Personally Known ☐ Passport ☐ Other ID #2 - describe ☐ Credible Witness(es) Ref. #1 Ref. #2	Right Thumbprint X ___SIGN HERE___	5
	☐ Driver's License ☐ Other ID #1 - describe ☐ Personally Known ☐ Passport ☐ Other ID #2 - describe ☐ Credible Witness(es) Ref. #1 Ref. #2	Right Thumbprint X ___SIGN HERE___	6
	☐ Driver's License ☐ Other ID #1 - describe ☐ Personally Known ☐ Passport ☐ Other ID #2 - describe ☐ Credible Witness(es) Ref. #1 Ref. #2	Right Thumbprint X ___SIGN HERE___	7
	☐ Driver's License ☐ Other ID #1 - describe ☐ Personally Known ☐ Passport ☐ Other ID #2 - describe ☐ Credible Witness(es) Ref. #1 Ref. #2	Right Thumbprint X ___SIGN HERE___	8

1

Notarization Date and Time

Date on Document(s)   Reference #

Fees   Paid?
$

A J Compliance Agmt.   A J E & O   A J Proof of ID Aff.   A J Adv. Health. Dir.   A J SDB Verification
A J Correction Agmt.   A J Occ. Aff.   A J Sig./Name Aff.   A J Trust - Irr. / Living   A J Vehicle - O+VIN / TT
A J DOT / Mortgage   A J Own. Aff.   A J Survey Aff.   A J Will - LWT / Living   A J
A J Deed - G / QC / W   A J POA - L / D   A J   A J   A J C Other

---

2

Notarization Date and Time

Date on Document(s)   Reference #

Fees   Paid?
$

A J Compliance Agmt.   A J E & O   A J Proof of ID Aff.   A J Adv. Health. Dir.   A J SDB Verification
A J Correction Agmt.   A J Occ. Aff.   A J Sig./Name Aff.   A J Trust - Irr. / Living   A J Vehicle - O+VIN / TT
A J DOT / Mortgage   A J Own. Aff.   A J Survey Aff.   A J Will - LWT / Living   A J
A J Deed - G / QC / W   A J POA - L / D   A J   A J   A J C Other

---

3

Notarization Date and Time

Date on Document(s)   Reference #

Fees   Paid?
$

A J Compliance Agmt.   A J E & O   A J Proof of ID Aff.   A J Adv. Health. Dir.   A J SDB Verification
A J Correction Agmt.   A J Occ. Aff.   A J Sig./Name Aff.   A J Trust - Irr. / Living   A J Vehicle - O+VIN / TT
A J DOT / Mortgage   A J Own. Aff.   A J Survey Aff.   A J Will - LWT / Living   A J
A J Deed - G / QC / W   A J POA - L / D   A J   A J   A J C Other

---

4

Notarization Date and Time

Date on Document(s)   Reference #

Fees   Paid?
$

A J Compliance Agmt.   A J E & O   A J Proof of ID Aff.   A J Adv. Health. Dir.   A J SDB Verification
A J Correction Agmt.   A J Occ. Aff.   A J Sig./Name Aff.   A J Trust - Irr. / Living   A J Vehicle - O+VIN / TT
A J DOT / Mortgage   A J Own. Aff.   A J Survey Aff.   A J Will - LWT / Living   A J
A J Deed - G / QC / W   A J POA - L / D   A J   A J   A J C Other

---

5

Notarization Date and Time

Date on Document(s)   Reference #

Fees   Paid?
$

A J Compliance Agmt.   A J E & O   A J Proof of ID Aff.   A J Adv. Health. Dir.   A J SDB Verification
A J Correction Agmt.   A J Occ. Aff.   A J Sig./Name Aff.   A J Trust - Irr. / Living   A J Vehicle - O+VIN / TT
A J DOT / Mortgage   A J Own. Aff.   A J Survey Aff.   A J Will - LWT / Living   A J
A J Deed - G / QC / W   A J POA - L / D   A J   A J   A J C Other

---

6

Notarization Date and Time

Date on Document(s)   Reference #

Fees   Paid?
$

A J Compliance Agmt.   A J E & O   A J Proof of ID Aff.   A J Adv. Health. Dir.   A J SDB Verification
A J Correction Agmt.   A J Occ. Aff.   A J Sig./Name Aff.   A J Trust - Irr. / Living   A J Vehicle - O+VIN / TT
A J DOT / Mortgage   A J Own. Aff.   A J Survey Aff.   A J Will - LWT / Living   A J
A J Deed - G / QC / W   A J POA - L / D   A J   A J   A J C Other

---

7

Notarization Date and Time

Date on Document(s)   Reference #

Fees   Paid?
$

A J Compliance Agmt.   A J E & O   A J Proof of ID Aff.   A J Adv. Health. Dir.   A J SDB Verification
A J Correction Agmt.   A J Occ. Aff.   A J Sig./Name Aff.   A J Trust - Irr. / Living   A J Vehicle - O+VIN / TT
A J DOT / Mortgage   A J Own. Aff.   A J Survey Aff.   A J Will - LWT / Living   A J
A J Deed - G / QC / W   A J POA - L / D   A J   A J   A J C Other

---

8

Notarization Date and Time

Date on Document(s)   Reference #

Fees   Paid?
$

A J Compliance Agmt.   A J E & O   A J Proof of ID Aff.   A J Adv. Health. Dir.   A J SDB Verification
A J Correction Agmt.   A J Occ. Aff.   A J Sig./Name Aff.   A J Trust - Irr. / Living   A J Vehicle - O+VIN / TT
A J DOT / Mortgage   A J Own. Aff.   A J Survey Aff.   A J Will - LWT / Living   A J
A J Deed - G / QC / W   A J POA - L / D   A J   A J   A J C Other

1

☐ Driver's License ☐ Other ID #1 - describe ☐ Personally Known
☐ Passport ☐ Other ID #2 - describe ☐ Credible Witness(es)

Ref. #1

Ref. #2

Right Thumbprint

X _____ SIGN HERE _____

2

☐ Driver's License ☐ Other ID #1 - describe ☐ Personally Known
☐ Passport ☐ Other ID #2 - describe ☐ Credible Witness(es)

Ref. #1

Ref. #2

Right Thumbprint

X _____ SIGN HERE _____

3

☐ Driver's License ☐ Other ID #1 - describe ☐ Personally Known
☐ Passport ☐ Other ID #2 - describe ☐ Credible Witness(es)

Ref. #1

Ref. #2

Right Thumbprint

X _____ SIGN HERE _____

4

☐ Driver's License ☐ Other ID #1 - describe ☐ Personally Known
☐ Passport ☐ Other ID #2 - describe ☐ Credible Witness(es)

Ref. #1

Ref. #2

Right Thumbprint

X _____ SIGN HERE _____

5

☐ Driver's License ☐ Other ID #1 - describe ☐ Personally Known
☐ Passport ☐ Other ID #2 - describe ☐ Credible Witness(es)

Ref. #1

Ref. #2

Right Thumbprint

X _____ SIGN HERE _____

6

☐ Driver's License ☐ Other ID #1 - describe ☐ Personally Known
☐ Passport ☐ Other ID #2 - describe ☐ Credible Witness(es)

Ref. #1

Ref. #2

Right Thumbprint

X _____ SIGN HERE _____

7

☐ Driver's License ☐ Other ID #1 - describe ☐ Personally Known
☐ Passport ☐ Other ID #2 - describe ☐ Credible Witness(es)

Ref. #1

Ref. #2

Right Thumbprint

X _____ SIGN HERE _____

8

☐ Driver's License ☐ Other ID #1 - describe ☐ Personally Known
☐ Passport ☐ Other ID #2 - describe ☐ Credible Witness(es)

Ref. #1

Ref. #2

Right Thumbprint

X _____ SIGN HERE _____

1

Notarization Date and Time

Date on Document(s)   Reference #

Fees   Paid?
$

A J	Compliance Agmt.	A J	E & O	A J	Proof of ID Aff.	A J	Adv. Health. Dir.	A J	SDB Verification
A J	Correction Agmt.	A J	Occ. Aff.	A J	Sig./Name Aff.	A J	Trust - Irr. / Living	A J	Vehicle - O+VIN / TT
A J	DOT / Mortgage	A J	Own. Aff.	A J	Survey Aff.	A J	Will - LWT / Living	A J	
A J	Deed - G / QC / W	A J	POA - L / D	A J		A J		A J C	Other ▼

2

Notarization Date and Time

Date on Document(s)   Reference #

Fees   Paid?
$

A J	Compliance Agmt.	A J	E & O	A J	Proof of ID Aff.	A J	Adv. Health. Dir.	A J	SDB Verification
A J	Correction Agmt.	A J	Occ. Aff.	A J	Sig./Name Aff.	A J	Trust - Irr. / Living	A J	Vehicle - O+VIN / TT
A J	DOT / Mortgage	A J	Own. Aff.	A J	Survey Aff.	A J	Will - LWT / Living	A J	
A J	Deed - G / QC / W	A J	POA - L / D	A J		A J		A J C	Other ▼

3

Notarization Date and Time

Date on Document(s)   Reference #

Fees   Paid?
$

A J	Compliance Agmt.	A J	E & O	A J	Proof of ID Aff.	A J	Adv. Health. Dir.	A J	SDB Verification
A J	Correction Agmt.	A J	Occ. Aff.	A J	Sig./Name Aff.	A J	Trust - Irr. / Living	A J	Vehicle - O+VIN / TT
A J	DOT / Mortgage	A J	Own. Aff.	A J	Survey Aff.	A J	Will - LWT / Living	A J	
A J	Deed - G / QC / W	A J	POA - L / D	A J		A J		A J C	Other ▼

4

Notarization Date and Time

Date on Document(s)   Reference #

Fees   Paid?
$

A J	Compliance Agmt.	A J	E & O	A J	Proof of ID Aff.	A J	Adv. Health. Dir.	A J	SDB Verification
A J	Correction Agmt.	A J	Occ. Aff.	A J	Sig./Name Aff.	A J	Trust - Irr. / Living	A J	Vehicle - O+VIN / TT
A J	DOT / Mortgage	A J	Own. Aff.	A J	Survey Aff.	A J	Will - LWT / Living	A J	
A J	Deed - G / QC / W	A J	POA - L / D	A J		A J		A J C	Other ▼

5

Notarization Date and Time

Date on Document(s)   Reference #

Fees   Paid?
$

A J	Compliance Agmt.	A J	E & O	A J	Proof of ID Aff.	A J	Adv. Health. Dir.	A J	SDB Verification
A J	Correction Agmt.	A J	Occ. Aff.	A J	Sig./Name Aff.	A J	Trust - Irr. / Living	A J	Vehicle - O+VIN / TT
A J	DOT / Mortgage	A J	Own. Aff.	A J	Survey Aff.	A J	Will - LWT / Living	A J	
A J	Deed - G / QC / W	A J	POA - L / D	A J		A J		A J C	Other ▼

6

Notarization Date and Time

Date on Document(s)   Reference #

Fees   Paid?
$

A J	Compliance Agmt.	A J	E & O	A J	Proof of ID Aff.	A J	Adv. Health. Dir.	A J	SDB Verification
A J	Correction Agmt.	A J	Occ. Aff.	A J	Sig./Name Aff.	A J	Trust - Irr. / Living	A J	Vehicle - O+VIN / TT
A J	DOT / Mortgage	A J	Own. Aff.	A J	Survey Aff.	A J	Will - LWT / Living	A J	
A J	Deed - G / QC / W	A J	POA - L / D	A J		A J		A J C	Other ▼

7

Notarization Date and Time

Date on Document(s)   Reference #

Fees   Paid?
$

A J	Compliance Agmt.	A J	E & O	A J	Proof of ID Aff.	A J	Adv. Health. Dir.	A J	SDB Verification
A J	Correction Agmt.	A J	Occ. Aff.	A J	Sig./Name Aff.	A J	Trust - Irr. / Living	A J	Vehicle - O+VIN / TT
A J	DOT / Mortgage	A J	Own. Aff.	A J	Survey Aff.	A J	Will - LWT / Living	A J	
A J	Deed - G / QC / W	A J	POA - L / D	A J		A J		A J C	Other ▼

8

Notarization Date and Time

Date on Document(s)   Reference #

Fees   Paid?
$

A J	Compliance Agmt.	A J	E & O	A J	Proof of ID Aff.	A J	Adv. Health. Dir.	A J	SDB Verification
A J	Correction Agmt.	A J	Occ. Aff.	A J	Sig./Name Aff.	A J	Trust - Irr. / Living	A J	Vehicle - O+VIN / TT
A J	DOT / Mortgage	A J	Own. Aff.	A J	Survey Aff.	A J	Will - LWT / Living	A J	
A J	Deed - G / QC / W	A J	POA - L / D	A J		A J		A J C	Other ▼

Signer Name and Address	Method of Identification	Signature and Thumbprint	
	☐ Driver's License ☐ Other ID #1 - describe ☐ Personally Known ☐ Passport ☐ Other ID #2 - describe ☐ Credible Witness(es) Ref. #1 Ref. #2	X ___SIGN HERE___	Right Thumbprint 1
	☐ Driver's License ☐ Other ID #1 - describe ☐ Personally Known ☐ Passport ☐ Other ID #2 - describe ☐ Credible Witness(es) Ref. #1 Ref. #2	X ___SIGN HERE___	Right Thumbprint 2
	☐ Driver's License ☐ Other ID #1 - describe ☐ Personally Known ☐ Passport ☐ Other ID #2 - describe ☐ Credible Witness(es) Ref. #1 Ref. #2	X ___SIGN HERE___	Right Thumbprint 3
	☐ Driver's License ☐ Other ID #1 - describe ☐ Personally Known ☐ Passport ☐ Other ID #2 - describe ☐ Credible Witness(es) Ref. #1 Ref. #2	X ___SIGN HERE___	Right Thumbprint 4
	☐ Driver's License ☐ Other ID #1 - describe ☐ Personally Known ☐ Passport ☐ Other ID #2 - describe ☐ Credible Witness(es) Ref. #1 Ref. #2	X ___SIGN HERE___	Right Thumbprint 5
	☐ Driver's License ☐ Other ID #1 - describe ☐ Personally Known ☐ Passport ☐ Other ID #2 - describe ☐ Credible Witness(es) Ref. #1 Ref. #2	X ___SIGN HERE___	Right Thumbprint 6
	☐ Driver's License ☐ Other ID #1 - describe ☐ Personally Known ☐ Passport ☐ Other ID #2 - describe ☐ Credible Witness(es) Ref. #1 Ref. #2	X ___SIGN HERE___	Right Thumbprint 7
	☐ Driver's License ☐ Other ID #1 - describe ☐ Personally Known ☐ Passport ☐ Other ID #2 - describe ☐ Credible Witness(es) Ref. #1 Ref. #2	X ___SIGN HERE___	Right Thumbprint 8

1

Notarization Date and Time

Date on Document(s)   Reference #

Fees $
Paid? ☐

A J Compliance Agmt.	A J E & O	A J Proof of ID Aff.	A J Adv. Health. Dir.	A J SDB Verification
A J Correction Agmt.	A J Occ. Aff.	A J Sig./Name Aff.	A J Trust - Irr./ Living	A J Vehicle - O+VIN / TT
A J DOT / Mortgage	A J Own. Aff.	A J Survey Aff.	A J Will - LWT / Living	A J
A J Deed - G / QC / W	A J POA - L / D	A J	A J	A J C ☐ Other ▼

2

Notarization Date and Time

Date on Document(s)   Reference #

Fees $
Paid? ☐

A J Compliance Agmt.	A J E & O	A J Proof of ID Aff.	A J Adv. Health. Dir.	A J SDB Verification
A J Correction Agmt.	A J Occ. Aff.	A J Sig./Name Aff.	A J Trust - Irr./ Living	A J Vehicle - O+VIN / TT
A J DOT / Mortgage	A J Own. Aff.	A J Survey Aff.	A J Will - LWT / Living	A J
A J Deed - G / QC / W	A J POA - L / D	A J	A J	A J C ☐ Other ▼

3

Notarization Date and Time

Date on Document(s)   Reference #

Fees $
Paid? ☐

A J Compliance Agmt.	A J E & O	A J Proof of ID Aff.	A J Adv. Health. Dir.	A J SDB Verification
A J Correction Agmt.	A J Occ. Aff.	A J Sig./Name Aff.	A J Trust - Irr./ Living	A J Vehicle - O+VIN / TT
A J DOT / Mortgage	A J Own. Aff.	A J Survey Aff.	A J Will - LWT / Living	A J
A J Deed - G / QC / W	A J POA - L / D	A J	A J	A J C ☐ Other ▼

4

Notarization Date and Time

Date on Document(s)   Reference #

Fees $
Paid? ☐

A J Compliance Agmt.	A J E & O	A J Proof of ID Aff.	A J Adv. Health. Dir.	A J SDB Verification
A J Correction Agmt.	A J Occ. Aff.	A J Sig./Name Aff.	A J Trust - Irr./ Living	A J Vehicle - O+VIN / TT
A J DOT / Mortgage	A J Own. Aff.	A J Survey Aff.	A J Will - LWT / Living	A J
A J Deed - G / QC / W	A J POA - L / D	A J	A J	A J C ☐ Other ▼

5

Notarization Date and Time

Date on Document(s)   Reference #

Fees $
Paid? ☐

A J Compliance Agmt.	A J E & O	A J Proof of ID Aff.	A J Adv. Health. Dir.	A J SDB Verification
A J Correction Agmt.	A J Occ. Aff.	A J Sig./Name Aff.	A J Trust - Irr./ Living	A J Vehicle - O+VIN / TT
A J DOT / Mortgage	A J Own. Aff.	A J Survey Aff.	A J Will - LWT / Living	A J
A J Deed - G / QC / W	A J POA - L / D	A J	A J	A J C ☐ Other ▼

6

Notarization Date and Time

Date on Document(s)   Reference #

Fees $
Paid? ☐

A J Compliance Agmt.	A J E & O	A J Proof of ID Aff.	A J Adv. Health. Dir.	A J SDB Verification
A J Correction Agmt.	A J Occ. Aff.	A J Sig./Name Aff.	A J Trust - Irr./ Living	A J Vehicle - O+VIN / TT
A J DOT / Mortgage	A J Own. Aff.	A J Survey Aff.	A J Will - LWT / Living	A J
A J Deed - G / QC / W	A J POA - L / D	A J	A J	A J C ☐ Other ▼

7

Notarization Date and Time

Date on Document(s)   Reference #

Fees $
Paid? ☐

A J Compliance Agmt.	A J E & O	A J Proof of ID Aff.	A J Adv. Health. Dir.	A J SDB Verification
A J Correction Agmt.	A J Occ. Aff.	A J Sig./Name Aff.	A J Trust - Irr./ Living	A J Vehicle - O+VIN / TT
A J DOT / Mortgage	A J Own. Aff.	A J Survey Aff.	A J Will - LWT / Living	A J
A J Deed - G / QC / W	A J POA - L / D	A J	A J	A J C ☐ Other ▼

8

Notarization Date and Time

Date on Document(s)   Reference #

Fees $
Paid? ☐

A J Compliance Agmt.	A J E & O	A J Proof of ID Aff.	A J Adv. Health. Dir.	A J SDB Verification
A J Correction Agmt.	A J Occ. Aff.	A J Sig./Name Aff.	A J Trust - Irr./ Living	A J Vehicle - O+VIN / TT
A J DOT / Mortgage	A J Own. Aff.	A J Survey Aff.	A J Will - LWT / Living	A J
A J Deed - G / QC / W	A J POA - L / D	A J	A J	A J C ☐ Other ▼

Signer Name and Address	Method of Identification	Signature and Thumbprint	
	☐ Driver's License ☐ Other ID #1 - describe ☐ Personally Known ☐ Passport ☐ Other ID #2 - describe ☐ Credible Witness(es) Ref. #1 Ref. #2	**X** SIGN HERE	Right Thumbprint **1**
	☐ Driver's License ☐ Other ID #1 - describe ☐ Personally Known ☐ Passport ☐ Other ID #2 - describe ☐ Credible Witness(es) Ref. #1 Ref. #2	**X** SIGN HERE	Right Thumbprint **2**
	☐ Driver's License ☐ Other ID #1 - describe ☐ Personally Known ☐ Passport ☐ Other ID #2 - describe ☐ Credible Witness(es) Ref. #1 Ref. #2	**X** SIGN HERE	Right Thumbprint **3**
	☐ Driver's License ☐ Other ID #1 - describe ☐ Personally Known ☐ Passport ☐ Other ID #2 - describe ☐ Credible Witness(es) Ref. #1 Ref. #2	**X** SIGN HERE	Right Thumbprint **4**
	☐ Driver's License ☐ Other ID #1 - describe ☐ Personally Known ☐ Passport ☐ Other ID #2 - describe ☐ Credible Witness(es) Ref. #1 Ref. #2	**X** SIGN HERE	Right Thumbprint **5**
	☐ Driver's License ☐ Other ID #1 - describe ☐ Personally Known ☐ Passport ☐ Other ID #2 - describe ☐ Credible Witness(es) Ref. #1 Ref. #2	**X** SIGN HERE	Right Thumbprint **6**
	☐ Driver's License ☐ Other ID #1 - describe ☐ Personally Known ☐ Passport ☐ Other ID #2 - describe ☐ Credible Witness(es) Ref. #1 Ref. #2	**X** SIGN HERE	Right Thumbprint **7**
	☐ Driver's License ☐ Other ID #1 - describe ☐ Personally Known ☐ Passport ☐ Other ID #2 - describe ☐ Credible Witness(es) Ref. #1 Ref. #2	**X** SIGN HERE	Right Thumbprint **8**

Concluding Instructions ▼

Thank you for using the *Modern Journal of Notarial Events*. If you have completed the last entry on pages 121 - 122, you may record the date of that entry on *page iii* in the box labeled *Date of Last Event*. The box labeled *Date of First Event* should contain the date of entry 1-1 (Page 1, Row 1). If state law requires that this journal be deposited with a state authority, you may do so now. Otherwise, please store your *Journal* in a safe and secure location. It is recommended you keep it for 8 years from the date of last entry or for as long as required by state law where applicable.

In the event of your death or incapacitation, state law may require that this journal be delivered to a county recorder or other authority. Please provide instructions pertaining to the disposition of this journal to the person(s) responsible for your estate or personal affairs in the following box. It is recommended you notify them in advance of such requirements.

Special Instructions to be Followed in the Event of Notary Death

Notes ▼

About the Author ▼

Notary Rotary and its affiliates are dedicated to the service and fair treatment of notaries public. Our website features include a highly searchable nationwide directory of mobile notaries, discussion forums, a listing of companies interested in the services of mobile notaries, workflow tools, company ratings and, of course, quality products. You may visit us on the Internet at http://www.notaryrotary.com or http://www.thenotaryshop.com for an exceptional shopping experience.

www.notaryrotary.com